QUANTUM COMPUTING
Progress and Prospects

Emily Grumbling and Mark Horowitz, Editors

Committee on Technical Assessment of the
Feasibility and Implications of Quantum Computing

Computer Science and Telecommunications Board

Intelligence Community Studies Board

Division on Engineering and Physical Sciences

A Consensus Study Report of

The National Academies of
SCIENCES • ENGINEERING • MEDICINE

THE NATIONAL ACADEMIES PRESS
Washington, DC
www.nap.edu

THE NATIONAL ACADEMIES PRESS 500 Fifth Street, NW Washington, DC 20001

This activity was supported by the Office of the Director of National Intelligence. Any opinions, findings, conclusions, or recommendations expressed in this publication are those of the authors and do not necessarily reflect the views of any organization or agency that provided support for the project.

International Standard Book Number-13: 978-0-309-47969-1
International Standard Book Number-10: 0-309-47969-X
Digital Object Identifier: https://doi.org/10.17226/25196

Additional copies of this publication are available for sale from the National Academies Press, 500 Fifth Street, NW, Keck 360, Washington, DC 20001; (800) 624-6242 or (202) 334-3313; http://www.nap.edu.

Copyright 2019 by the National Academy of Sciences. All rights reserved.

Printed in the United States of America

Suggested citation: National Academies of Sciences, Engineering, and Medicine. 2019. *Quantum Computing: Progress and Prospects*. The National Academies Press, Washington, DC. doi: https://doi.org/10.17226/25196.

The National Academies of
SCIENCES · ENGINEERING · MEDICINE

The **National Academy of Sciences** was established in 1863 by an Act of Congress, signed by President Lincoln, as a private, nongovernmental institution to advise the nation on issues related to science and technology. Members are elected by their peers for outstanding contributions to research. Dr. Marcia McNutt is president.

The **National Academy of Engineering** was established in 1964 under the charter of the National Academy of Sciences to bring the practices of engineering to advising the nation. Members are elected by their peers for extraordinary contributions to engineering. Dr. C. D. Mote, Jr., is president.

The **National Academy of Medicine** (formerly the Institute of Medicine) was established in 1970 under the charter of the National Academy of Sciences to advise the nation on medical and health issues. Members are elected by their peers for distinguished contributions to medicine and health. Dr. Victor J. Dzau is president.

The three Academies work together as the **National Academies of Sciences, Engineering, and Medicine** to provide independent, objective analysis and advice to the nation and conduct other activities to solve complex problems and inform public policy decisions. The National Academies also encourage education and research, recognize outstanding contributions to knowledge, and increase public understanding in matters of science, engineering, and medicine.

Learn more about the National Academies of Sciences, Engineering, and Medicine at **www.nationalacademies.org**.

The National Academies of
SCIENCES • ENGINEERING • MEDICINE

Consensus Study Reports published by the National Academies of Sciences, Engineering, and Medicine document the evidence-based consensus on the study's statement of task by an authoring committee of experts. Reports typically include findings, conclusions, and recommendations based on information gathered by the committee and the committee's deliberations. Each report has been subjected to a rigorous and independent peer-review process and it represents the position of the National Academies on the statement of task.

Proceedings published by the National Academies of Sciences, Engineering, and Medicine chronicle the presentations and discussions at a workshop, symposium, or other event convened by the National Academies. The statements and opinions contained in proceedings are those of the participants and are not endorsed by other participants, the planning committee, or the National Academies.

For information about other products and activities of the National Academies, please visit www.nationalacademies.org/about/whatwedo.

COMMITTEE ON TECHNICAL ASSESSMENT OF THE FEASIBILITY AND IMPLICATIONS OF QUANTUM COMPUTING

MARK A. HOROWITZ, NAE,[1] Stanford University, *Chair*
ALÁN ASPURU-GUZIK, University of Toronto
DAVID D. AWSCHALOM, NAS[2]/NAE, University of Chicago
BOB BLAKLEY, Citigroup
DAN BONEH, NAE, Stanford University
SUSAN N. COPPERSMITH, NAS, University of Wisconsin, Madison
JUNGSANG KIM, Duke University
JOHN M. MARTINIS, Google, Inc.
MARGARET MARTONOSI, Princeton University
MICHELE MOSCA, University of Waterloo
WILLIAM D. OLIVER, Massachusetts Institute of Technology
KRYSTA SVORE, Microsoft Research
UMESH V. VAZIRANI, NAS, University of California, Berkeley

Staff

EMILY GRUMBLING, Study Director, Computer Science and Telecommunications Board (CSTB)
SHENAE BRADLEY, Administrative Assistant, CSTB
JON EISENBERG, Senior Director, CSTB
KATIRIA ORTIZ, Associate Program Officer, CSTB
JANKI PATEL, Senior Program Assistant, CSTB

---

[1] Member, National Academy of Engineering.
[2] Member, National Academy of Sciences.

COMPUTER SCIENCE AND TELECOMMUNICATIONS BOARD

FARNAM JAHANIAN, Carnegie Mellon University, *Chair*
LUIZ BARROSO, Google, Inc.
STEVE M. BELLOVIN, NAE,[1] Columbia University
ROBERT F. BRAMMER, Brammer Technology, LLC
DAVID CULLER, NAE, University of California, Berkeley
EDWARD FRANK, Cloud Parity, Inc.
LAURA HAAS, NAE, University of Massachusetts, Amherst
MARK HOROWITZ, NAE, Stanford University
ERIC HORVITZ, NAE, Microsoft Corporation
VIJAY KUMAR, NAE, University of Pennsylvania
BETH MYNATT, Georgia Institute of Technology
CRAIG PARTRIDGE, Colorado State University
DANIELA RUS, NAE, Massachusetts Institute of Technology
FRED B. SCHNEIDER, NAE, Cornell University
MARGO SELTZER, University of British Columbia
MOSHE VARDI, NAS[2]/NAE, Rice University

Staff

JON EISENBERG, Senior Director
LYNETTE I. MILLETT, Associate Director
SHENAE BRADLEY, Administrative Assistant
EMILY GRUMBLING, Program Officer
RENEE HAWKINS, Financial and Administrative Manager
KATIRIA ORTIZ, Associate Program Officer
JANKI PATEL, Senior Program Assistant

For more information on the CSTB, see its website at http://www.cstb.org, write to CSTB, National Academies of Sciences, Engineering, and Medicine, 500 Fifth Street, NW, Washington, DC 20001, call (202) 334-2605, or e-mail the CSTB at cstb@nas.edu.

---

[1] Member, National Academy of Engineering.
[2] Member, National Academy of Sciences.

INTELLIGENCE COMMUNITY STUDIES BOARD

FREDERICK CHANG, NAE,[1] Southern Methodist University, *Co-Chair*
ROBERT C. DYNES, NAS,[2] University of California, San Diego, *Co-Chair*
JULIE BRILL, Microsoft Corporation
TOMÁS DÍAZ DE LA RUBIA, Purdue University Discovery Park
ROBERT FEIN, McLean Hospital/Harvard Medical School
MIRIAM JOHN, Independent Consultant
ANITA JONES, NAE, University of Virginia
DONALD M. KERR, Independent Consultant
ROBERT H. LATIFF, R. Latiff Associates
MARK LOWENTHAL, Intelligence & Security Academy, LLC
MICHAEL MARLETTA, NAS/NAM,[3] University of California, Berkeley
L. ROGER MASON, JR., Peraton
ELIZABETH RINDSKOPF PARKER, Retired, State Bar of California
WILLIAM H. PRESS, NAS, University of Texas, Austin
DAVID A. RELMAN, NAM, Stanford University
SAMUEL VISNER, The MITRE Corporation

Staff

ALAN SHAW, Director
CARYN LESLIE, Senior Program Officer
CHRIS JONES, Financial Manager
MARGUERITE SCHNEIDER, Administrative Coordinator
DIONNA ALI, Research Associate
ADRIANNA HARGROVE, Financial Assistant
NATHANIEL DEBEVOISE, Senior Program Assistant

---

[1] Member, National Academy of Engineering.
[2] Member, National Academy of Sciences.
[3] Member, National Academy of Medicine.

Acknowledgment of Reviewers

This Consensus Study Report was reviewed in draft form by individuals chosen for their diverse perspectives and technical expertise. The purpose of this independent review is to provide candid and critical comments that will assist the National Academies of Sciences, Engineering, and Medicine in making each published report as sound as possible and to ensure that it meets the institutional standards for quality, objectivity, evidence, and responsiveness to the study charge. The review comments and draft manuscript remain confidential to protect the integrity of the deliberative process.

We thank the following individuals for their review of this report:

Scott Aaronson, University of Texas at Austin,
Kenneth R. Brown, Duke University,
Jerry M. Chow, IBM Thomas J. Watson Research Center,
William J. Dally, NAE,[1] NVIDIA Corporation,
Sean Hallgren, Pennsylvania State University,
John P. Hayes, University of Michigan,
Daniel Lidar, University of Southern California,
John Manferdelli, Northeastern University,
Anne Matsuura, Intel Labs,
William H. Press, NAS,[2] University of Texas at Austin, and
Steven J. Wallach, NAE, Micron Technology.

---

[1] Member, National Academy of Engineering.
[2] Member, National Academy of Sciences.

Although the reviewers listed above provided many constructive comments and suggestions, they were not asked to endorse the conclusions or recommendations of this report nor did they see the final draft before its release. The review of this report was overseen by Samuel H. Fuller, NAE, Analog Devices, Inc. He was responsible for making certain that an independent examination of this report was carried out in accordance with the standards of the National Academies and that all review comments were carefully considered. Responsibility for the final content rests entirely with the authoring committee and the National Academies.

Preface

Quantum computing, a topic unknown to most of the population a decade ago, has burst into the public's imagination over the past few years. Part of this interest can be attributed to concerns about the slowing of technology scaling, also known as Moore's law, which has driven computing performance for over half a century, increasing interest in alternative computing technology. But most of the excitement comes from the unique computational power of a quantum computer and recent progress in creating the underlying hardware, software, and algorithms necessary to make it work.

Before quantum computers, all known realistic computing devices satisfied the extended Church-Turing thesis,[1,2] which said that the power of any computing device built could be only polynomially faster than a regular "universal" computer—that is, any relative speedup would scale only according to a power law. Designers of these "classical"[3] computing devices increased computing performance by many orders of magnitude by making the operations faster (increasing the clock frequency) and increasing the number of operations completed during each clock cycle.

---

[1] M.A. Nielsen and I. Chuang, 2016, *Quantum Computation and Quantum Information*, Cambridge University Press, U.K.

[2] P. Kaye, R. Laflamme, and M. Mosca, 2007, *An Introduction to Quantum Computing*, Oxford University Press, Oxford, UK.

[3] In the field of quantum computing, and throughout this report, computers that process information according to classical laws of physics are referred to as "classical computers," in order to distinguish them from "quantum computers," which rely upon quantum effects in the processing of information.

While these changes have increased computing performance by many orders of magnitude, the result is just a (large) constant factor faster than the universal computing device. Bernstein et al. showed in 1993 that quantum computers could violate the extended Church-Turing thesis,[4] and in 1994 Peter Shor showed a practical example of this power in factoring a large number: a quantum computer could solve this problem exponentially faster than a classical computer. While this result was exciting, at that time no one knew how to build even the most basic element of a quantum computer, a quantum bit, or "qubit," let alone a full quantum computer. But that situation has recently changed.

Two technologies, one using trapped ionized atoms (trapped ions) and the other using miniature superconducting circuits, have advanced to the point where research groups are able to build small demonstration quantum computing systems, and some groups are making these available to the research community. These recent advances have led to an explosion of interest in quantum computing worldwide; however, with this interest also comes hype and confusion about both the potential of quantum computing and its current status. It is not uncommon to read articles about how quantum computing will enable continued computer performance scaling (it will not) or change the computer industry (its short-term effects will be small, and its long-term effects are unknown).

The Committee on Technical Assessment of the Feasibility and Implications of Quantum Computing was assembled to explore this area to help bring clarity about the current state of the art, likely progress toward, and ramifications of, a general-purpose quantum computer. In responding to its charge, the committee also saw an opportunity to clarify the theoretical characteristics and limitations of quantum computing and to correct some common public misperceptions about the field.

The committee conducted its work through three in-person meetings, a series of teleconferences, and remote collaboration. In order to respond to its charge, the committee focused on understanding the current state of quantum computing hardware, software, and algorithms, and what advances would be needed to create a scalable, gate-based quantum computer capable of deploying Shor's algorithm. Early in this process, it became clear that the current engineering approaches could not directly scale to the size needed to create this scalable, fully error corrected quantum computer. As a result, the group focused on finding intermediate milestones and metrics to track the progress toward this goal. Throughout this work, the committee endeavored to integrate multiple disciplinary

---

[4] E. Bernstein and U. Vazirani, 1993, "Quantum Complexity Theory," in *Proceedings of the Twenty-Fifth Annual ACM Symposium on Theory of Computing* (STOC '93), ACM, New York, 11-20, http://dx.doi.org.stanford.idm.oclc.org/10.1145/167088.167097.

perspectives and to think about progress toward building a practical quantum computer from a systems perspective, rather than in terms of a single component or a single discipline.

This work was conducted in its entirety on an unclassified basis. As a result, the committee's assessments of progress, feasibility, and implications of quantum computing were made using only committee members' expertise and experience, data gathered in open meetings, one-on-one conversations with outside experts, and information broadly available in the public sphere. No information regarding any nation-state's classified activities was made available to the committee. As a result, while the committee believes its assessment to be accurate, it recognizes that the assessment is necessarily based upon incomplete information, and it does not preclude the possibility that knowledge of research outside the arena of open science (either privately held or classified by a nation-state) might have altered its assessment.

READING THIS REPORT

This report presents the results of the committee's study. The reader is encouraged to start with the Summary to get a quick sense of the main findings of this report. The Summary also provides pointers to the sections in the report that describe each of these topics in more detail, to enable the reader to dive into the details of specific topics of interest.

A brief description of each chapter is given below:

- Chapter 1 provides background and context on the field of computing, introducing the computational advantage of a quantum computer. It takes a careful look at why and how classical computing technologies scaled in performance for over half a century. This scaling was mostly the result of a virtuous cycle, where products using new technology allowed the industry to make more money, which it then used to create newer technology. For quantum computing to be similarly successful, it must either create a virtuous cycle to fund the development of increasingly useful quantum computers (with government funding required to support this effort until this stage is reached) or be pursued by an organization committed to providing the necessary investment in order to achieve a practically useful machine even in the absence of intermediate returns or utility (although the total investment is likely to be prohibitively large).
- Chapter 2 introduces the principles of quantum mechanics that make quantum computing different, exciting, and challenging to implement, and compares them with operations of the computers

deployed today, which process information according to classical laws of physics—known in the quantum computing community as "classical computers." This chapter explains why adding one additional qubit to a quantum computer doubles the size of the problem the quantum computer can represent. This increased computational ability comes with the limitations of noisy gates (qubit gate operations have significant error rates), a general inability to read in data efficiently, and limited ability to measure the system, which makes creating effective quantum algorithms difficult. It introduces the three different types of quantum computing studied in this report: analog quantum, digital noisy intermediate-scale quantum (digital NISQ), and fully error corrected quantum computers.

- Recognizing the difficulty of harnessing the power of quantum computing, Chapter 3 looks at quantum algorithms in more depth. The chapter starts with known foundational algorithms for fully error corrected machines but then shows that the overhead for error correction is quite large—that is, it takes many physical qubits and physical gate operations to emulate an error-free, so-called logical qubit that can be used in complex algorithms. Such machines are therefore unlikely to exist for a number of years. It then examines potential algorithms for both analog and digital NISQ computers that would enable practical utility and shows that more work is needed in this area.
- Because Shor's algorithm breaks currently deployed asymmetric ciphers—that is, it would enable them to be decrypted without a priori knowledge of the secret key—Chapter 4 discusses the classical cryptographic ciphers currently used to protect electronic data and communications, how a large quantum computer could defeat these systems, and what the cryptography community should do now (and has begun to do) to address these vulnerabilities.
- Chapters 5 and 6 discuss general architectures and progress to date in building the necessary hardware and software components, respectively, required for quantum computing.
- Chapter 7 provides the committee's assessment of the technical progress and other factors required to make significant progress in quantum computing, tools for assessing and reassessing the possible time frames and implications of such developments, and an outlook for the future of the field.

While the committee has tried to make the report accessible to non-experts, a few of the chapters do become a little (or more than a little) technical in order to describe some of the issues at play more precisely. Feel free to skip over these sections when you find them—the key points of these sections are either highlighted as chapter-level findings or are summarized either at the end of the section or chapter.

ACKNOWLEDGMENTS

This work would not have been possible without the contributions of a host of individuals to whom the committee and the National Academies extend our sincere thanks. Jake Farinholt at the U.S. Dahlgren Naval Surface Warfare Research Center provided a bibliometric analysis of research in quantum computing and related areas, which provided a helpful illustration of global engagement in these fields. Dr. Mary Kavanagh, minister counsellor at the European Commission's Delegation to the United States, and Mr. Anthony Murfett, minister counsellor at the Australian Embassy in Washington, D.C., helpfully provided information about EU and Australian research efforts in quantum science and technology.

In addition to all of the speakers who presented technical input at committee meetings, the committee would also like to acknowledge Mark Saffman, Jonathan Dowling, Pete Shadbolt, Jelena Vuckovic, Helmut Katzgraber, Robert Colwell, and Eddie Farhi for helpful conversations or correspondence with individual committee members over the course of this activity that helped to clarify technical issues of relevance to this report.

We would also like to thank the sponsor of this research, the Office of the Director of National Intelligence of the United States of America, for financial support of this study, and Jon Eisenberg, senior director of the Computer Science and Telecommunications Board, for his guidance.

I am deeply grateful to the members of the committee who generously spent their valuable time creating this report and educating a chair who was not an expert in quantum computing. I would especially like to thank Emily Grumbling, study director, who put in long hours to create the report in front of you. It would not exist without her help. While it might not be rare for a committee chair to say that he enjoyed chairing the study group, in this case it actually is true. I had a wonderful time learning about the power, progress, and problems of quantum computing. I hope that this report is helpful in your exploration of the subject as well.

Mark Horowitz, *Chair*
Committee on Technical Assessment of the
Feasibility and Implications of Quantum Computing

Contents

SUMMARY		1
1	PROGRESS IN COMPUTING	12

    1.1 Origins of Contemporary Computing, 12
    1.2 Quantum Computing, 14
    1.3 Historical Progress in Computing: Moore's Law, 16
    1.4 Converting Transistors to Cheap Computers, 19
    1.5 A Slowdown in Scaling, 20
    1.6 Quantum: A New Approach to Computing, 21
    1.7 Notes, 22

2   QUANTUM COMPUTING: A NEW PARADIGM   24

    2.1 The Nonintuitive Physics of the Quantum World, 25
    2.2 The Landscape of Quantum Technology, 27
    2.3 Bits and Qubits, 30
    2.4 Computing with Qubits, 38
    2.5 Quantum Computer Design Constraints, 46
    2.6 The Potential for Functional Quantum Computers, 51
    2.7 Notes, 55

3   QUANTUM ALGORITHMS AND APPLICATIONS   57

    3.1 Quantum Algorithms for an Ideal Gate-Based Quantum Computer, 60
    3.2 Quantum Error Correction and Mitigation, 71
    3.3 Quantum Approximation Algorithms, 79

3.4 Applications of a Quantum Computer, 82
3.5 The Potential Role of Quantum Computers in the Computing Ecosystem, 86
3.6 Notes, 87

4 QUANTUM COMPUTING'S IMPLICATIONS FOR CRYPTOGRAPHY   95
4.1 Cryptographic Algorithms in Current Use, 96
4.2 Sizing Estimates, 104
4.3 Post-Quantum Cryptography, 105
4.4 Practical Deployment Challenges, 108
4.5 Notes, 112

5 ESSENTIAL HARDWARE COMPONENTS OF A QUANTUM COMPUTER   113
5.1 Hardware Structure of a Quantum Computer, 114
5.2 Trapped Ion Qubits, 119
5.3 Superconducting Qubits, 122
5.4 Other Technologies, 127
5.5 Future Outlook, 129
5.6 Notes, 130

6 ESSENTIAL SOFTWARE COMPONENTS OF A SCALABLE QUANTUM COMPUTER   135
6.1 Challenges and Opportunities, 136
6.2 Quantum Programming Languages, 137
6.3 Simulation, 145
6.4 Specification, Verification, and Debugging, 146
6.5 Compiling from a High-Level Program to Hardware, 149
6.6 Summary, 152
6.7 Notes, 153

7 FEASIBILITY AND TIME FRAMES OF QUANTUM COMPUTING   156
7.1 The Current State of Progress, 156
7.2 A Framework for Assessing Progress in Quantum Computing, 161
7.3 Milestones and Time Estimates, 169
7.4 Quantum Computing R&D, 179
7.5 Targeting a Successful Future, 187
7.6 Notes, 189

APPENDIXES

A	Statement of Task	195
B	Trapped Ion Quantum Computers	196
C	Superconducting Quantum Computers	205
D	Other Approaches to Building Qubits	212
E	Global R&D Investment	226
F	Committee and Staff Biographical Information	230
G	Briefers to the Committee	239
H	Acronyms and Abbreviations	241
I	Glossary	244

Summary

Quantum mechanics, the subfield of physics that describes the behavior of very small particles, provides the basis for a new paradigm of computing. Quantum computing (QC) was first proposed in the 1980s as a way to improve computational modeling of the behavior of very small ("quantum") physical systems. Interest in the field grew in the 1990s with the introduction of Shor's algorithm, which, if implemented on a quantum computer, would exponentially speed up an important class of cryptanalysis and potentially threaten some of the cryptographic methods used to protect government and civilian communications and stored data. In fact, quantum computers are the only known model for computing that could offer exponential speedup over today's computers.[1]

While these results were very exciting in the 1990s, they were only of theoretical interest: no one knew of a method to build a computer out of quantum systems. Today, nearly 25 years later, progress in creating and controlling bits of quantum information, or "qubits," has advanced to the point that a number of research groups have demonstrated small

---

[1] These early theoretical results demonstrated the unique potential power of quantum computers. The performance of all other known computing devices can be only polynomially faster than a very simple "universal" computer, a probabilistic Turing machine, according to the extended Church-Turing thesis. Quantum computers are the only known computing technology that violates this thesis. Nielsen, Michael A., and Isaac Chuang. "Quantum computation and quantum information." (2002): 558-559. Kaye, Phillip, Raymond Laflamme, and Michele Mosca. An introduction to quantum computing. Oxford University Press, 2007.

proof-of-principle quantum computers. This work has reinvigorated the field and led to significant private sector investment.

WHY BUILDING AND USING A QUANTUM COMPUTER IS CHALLENGING

A classical computer uses bits to represent the values it is operating on; a quantum computer uses quantum bits, or qubits. A bit can either be 0 or 1, while a qubit can represent the values 0 or 1, or some combination of both at the same time (known as a "superposition"). While the state of a classical computer is determined by the binary values of a collection of bits, at any single point in time the state of a quantum computer with the same number of quantum bits can span all possible states of the corresponding classical computer, and thus works in an exponentially larger problem space. However, the ability to make use of this space requires that all of the qubits be intrinsically interconnected ("entangled"), well-isolated from the outside environment, and very precisely controlled.

Many innovations over the past 25 years have enabled researchers to build physical systems that are starting to provide the needed isolation and control for quantum computing. In 2018, two technologies are used in most quantum computers (trapped ions and artificial "atoms" generated by superconducting circuits), but many different technologies are currently being explored for the basic physical implementation of qubits, or "physical qubits." Given the rapid progress in the field, and the large improvements still needed, it is too early to "bet" on one technology for quantum computing (see Chapter 5).

Even if one is able to make very high quality qubits, creating and making use of these quantum computers (QCs) brings a new set of challenges. They use a different set of operations than those of classical computers, requiring new algorithms, software, control technologies, and hardware abstractions.

Technical Risks

Qubits Cannot Intrinsically Reject Noise

One of the major differences between a classical computer and a quantum computer is in how it handles small unwanted variations, or noise, in the system. Since a classical bit is either one or zero, even if the value is slightly off (some noise in the system) it is easy for the operations on that signal to remove that noise. In fact, today's classical gates, which operate on bits and are used to create computers, have very large noise margins—they can reject large variations in their inputs and still produce clean, noise-free outputs. Because a qubit can be any combination of one and zero, qubits and quantum gates cannot readily reject small errors (noise) that occur in physical circuits. As a result, small errors in creating the desired quantum operations, or any stray signals that couple into the physical system, can eventually lead to wrong outputs appearing in the computation. Thus, one of the most important design parameters for systems that operate on physical qubits is their error rate. Low error rates have been difficult to achieve; even in mid-2018, the error rates for 2-qubit operations on systems with 5 or more qubits are more than a few percent. Better error rates have been demonstrated in smaller systems, and this improved operation fidelity needs to move to larger qubit systems for quantum computing to be successful (see Section 2.3).

Error-Free QC Requires Quantum Error Correction

Although the physical qubit operations are sensitive to noise, it is possible to run a quantum error correction (QEC) algorithm on a physical quantum computer to emulate a noise-free, or "fully error corrected," quantum computer. Without QEC, it is unlikely that a complex quantum program, such as one that implements Shor's algorithm, would ever run correctly on a quantum computer. However, QEC incurs significant overheads in terms of both the number of physical qubits required to emulate a more robust and stable qubit, called a "logical qubit," and the number of primitive qubit operations that must be performed on physical qubits to emulate a quantum operation on this logical qubit. While QECs will be essential to create error-free quantum computers in the future, they are too resource intensive to be used in the short term: quantum computers in the near term are likely to have errors. This class of machines is referred to as noisy intermediate-scale quantum (NISQ) computers (see Section 3.2).

Large Data Inputs Cannot Be Loaded into a QC Efficiently

While a quantum computer can use a small number of qubits to represent an exponentially larger amount of data, there is not currently a method to rapidly convert a large amount of classical data to a quantum state[2] (this does not apply if the data can be generated algorithmically). For problems that require large inputs, the amount of time needed to create the input quantum state would typically dominate the computation time, and greatly reduce the quantum advantage.

---

[2] While there are proposals for quantum random access memory (QRAM) that can perform this function, at the time of this report, there aren't any practical implementation technologies.

Quantum Algorithm Design Is Challenging

Measuring the state of a quantum computer "collapses" the large quantum state to a single classical result. This means that one can extract only the same amount of data from a quantum computer that one could from a classical computer of the same size. To reap the benefit of a quantum computer, quantum algorithms must leverage uniquely quantum features such as interference and entanglement to arrive at the final classical result. Thus, achieving quantum speedup requires totally new kinds of algorithm design principles and very clever algorithm design. Quantum algorithm development is a critical aspect of the field (see Chapter 3).

Quantum Computers Will Need a New Software Stack

As with all computers, building a useful device is much more complex than just creating the hardware—tools are needed to create and debug QC-specific software. Since quantum programs are different from programs for classical computers, research and development is needed to further develop the software tool stack. Because these software tools drive the hardware, contemporaneous development of the hardware and software tool chain will shorten the development time for a useful quantum computer. In fact, using early tools to complete the end-to-end design (application design to final results) helps elucidate hidden issues and drives toward designs with the best chance for overall success, an approach used in classical computer design (see Section 6.1).

The Intermediate State of a Quantum Computer Cannot Be Measured Directly

Methods to debug quantum hardware and software are of critical importance. Current debugging methods for classical computers rely on memory, and the reading of intermediate machine states. Neither is possible in a quantum computer. A quantum state cannot simply be copied (per the so-called no-cloning theorem) for later examination, and any measurement of a quantum state collapses it to a set of classical bits, bringing computation to a halt. New approaches to debugging are essential for the development of large-scale quantum computers (see Section 6.4).

TIME FRAMES FOR ACHIEVING QUANTUM COMPUTING

Predicting the future is always risky, but it can be attempted when the product of interest is an extrapolation of current devices that does not span too many orders of magnitude. However, to create a quantum computer that can run Shor's algorithm to find the private key in a 1024-bit

RSA encrypted message requires building a machine that is more than five orders of magnitude larger and has error rates that are about two orders of magnitude better than current machines, as well as developing the software development environment to support this machine.

The progress required to bridge this gap makes it impossible to project the time frame for a large error-corrected quantum computer, and while significant progress in these areas continues, there is no guarantee that all of these challenges will be overcome. The process of bridging this gap might expose unanticipated challenges, require techniques that are not yet invented, or shift owing to new results of foundational scientific research that change our understanding of the quantum world. Rather than speculating on a specific time frame, the committee identified factors that will affect the rate of technology innovation and proposed two metrics and several milestones for monitoring progress in the field moving forward (see Section 7.2).

Given the unique characteristics and challenges of quantum computers, they are unlikely to be useful as a direct replacement for classical computers. In fact, they require a number of classical computers to control their operations and carry out computations needed to implement quantum error correction. Thus, they are currently being designed as special-purpose devices operating in a complementary fashion with classical processors, analogous to a co-processor or an accelerator (see Section 5.1).

In rapidly advancing fields, where there are many unknowns and hard problems, the rate of overall development is set by the ability of the whole community to take advantage of new approaches and insights. Fields where research results are kept secret or proprietary progress much more slowly. Fortunately, many quantum computing researchers have been open about sharing advances to date, and the field will benefit greatly by continuing with this philosophy (see Section 7.4.3).

Key Finding 9: An open ecosystem that enables cross-pollination of ideas and groups will accelerate rapid technology advancement. (Chapter 7)

It is also clear that a technology's progress depends on the resources, both human and capital, devoted to it. Although many people think that there will be a Moore's law-type scaling for the number of qubits in a system, it is important to remember that Moore's law resulted from a virtuous cycle, where improved technology generated exponentially increasing revenue, enabling reinvestment in research and development (R&D) and attracting new talent and industries to help innovate and scale the technology to the next level. As with silicon technology, a Moore's law-type of sustained exponential growth for qubits requires an exponentially growing investment, sustaining this investment will likely require a similar virtuous cycle for quantum computers, where smaller machines are commercially successful enough to grow investment in the overall area. In the absence of intermediate successes yielding commercial revenue, progress will depend on governmental agencies continuing to increase funding of this effort. Even in this scenario, successful completion of intermediate milestones is likely to be essential (see Section 1.3).

Given the overhead of QEC, near-term machines will almost certainly be noisy intermediate-scale quantum (NISQ) computers. While many interesting applications exist for large error-corrected quantum computers, practical applications for NISQ computers do not currently exist. Creating practical applications for NISQ computers is a relatively new area of research and will require work on new types of quantum algorithms. Developing commercial NISQ computer applications by the early 2020s will be essential to starting this virtuous cycle of investment (see Section 3.4.1).

Key Finding 3: Research and development into practical commercial applications of noisy intermediate-scale quantum (NISQ) computers is an issue of immediate urgency for the field. The results of this work will have a profound impact on the rate of development of large-scale quantum computers and on the size and robustness of a commercial market for quantum computers. (Chapter 7)

Quantum computers can be divided into three general categories or types. "Analog quantum computers" directly manipulate the interactions between qubits without breaking these actions into primitive gate operations. Examples of analog machines include quantum annealers, adiabatic quantum computers, and direct quantum simulators. "Digital NISQ computers" operate by carrying out an algorithm of interest using primitive gate operations on physical qubits. Noise is present in both of these types of machine, which means that the quality (measured by error rates and qubit coherence times) will limit the complexity of the problems that these machines can solve. "Fully error-corrected quantum computers" are a version of gate-based QCs made more robust through deployment of quantum error correction (QEC), which enables noisy physical qubits to emulate stable logical qubits so that the computer behaves reliably for any computation (see Section 2.6).

Milestones

The first milestones of progress in QC were the demonstration of simple proof-of-principle analog and digital systems. Small digital NISQ computers became available in 2017, with tens of qubits with errors too high to be corrected. Work in quantum annealing began approximately a decade earlier using qubits built with a technology that had lower coherence times but that allowed them to scale more rapidly. Thus, by 2017 experimental quantum annealers had grown to machines with around 2,000 qubits. From this starting point, progress can be identified with the achievement of one of several possible milestones. Demonstration of "quantum supremacy"—that is, completing a task that is intractable on a classical computer, whether or not the task has practical utility—is one. While several teams have been focused on this goal, it has not yet been demonstrated (as of mid-2018). Another major milestone is creating a commercially useful quantum computer, which would require a QC that carries out at least one practical task more efficiently than any classical computer. While this milestone is in theory harder than achieving quantum supremacy—since the application in question must be better and more useful than available classical approaches—*proving* quantum supremacy could be difficult, especially for analog QC. Thus, it is possible that a useful application could arise before quantum supremacy is demonstrated. Deployment of QEC on a QC to create a logical qubit with a significant reduction in error rate is another major milestone and is the first step to creating fully error-corrected machines (see Section 7.3).

Metrics

Progress in gate-based quantum computing can be monitored by tracking the key properties that define the quality of a quantum processor: the effective error rates of the single-qubit and two-qubit operations, the interqubit connectivity, and the number of qubits contained within a single hardware module.

Key Finding 4: Given the information available to the committee, it is still too early to be able to predict the time horizon for a scalable quantum computer. Instead, progress can be tracked in the near term by monitoring the scaling rate of physical qubits at *constant average gate error rate*, as evaluated using randomized benchmarking, and in the long term by monitoring the effective number of logical (error-corrected) qubits that a system represents. (Chapter 7)

Tracking the size and scaling rate for logical qubits will provide a better estimate on the timing of future milestones.

Key Finding 5: The state of the field would be much easier to monitor if the research community adopted clear reporting conventions to enable comparison between devices and translation into metrics such as those proposed in this report. A set of benchmarking applications that enable comparison between different machines would help drive improvements in the efficiency of quantum software and the architecture of the underlying quantum hardware. (Chapter 7)

Players Working to Build and Use a Quantum Computer

It is clear that efforts to develop quantum computers and other quantum technologies are under way around the world. It is expected that large, concerted research efforts entailing both foundational scientific advances and new strategies in engineering—spanning multiple traditional disciplines—will be required to build a successful QC.

Key Finding 8: While the United States has historically played a leading role in developing quantum technologies, quantum information science and technology is now a global field. Given the large resource commitment several non-U.S. nations have recently made, continued U.S. support is critical if the United States wants to maintain its leadership position. (Chapter 7)

Furthermore, the private sector currently plays a large role in the U.S. quantum computing R&D ecosystem.

Key Finding 2: If near-term quantum computers are not commercially successful, government funding may be essential to prevent a significant decline in quantum computing research and development. (Chapter 7)

QUANTUM COMPUTERS AND CRYPTOGRAPHY

Quantum computing will have a major impact on cryptography, which relies upon hard-to-compute problems to protect data. Shor's algorithm running on a large quantum computer will greatly reduce the required computation (the workfactor) to extract the private key from the asymmetric ciphers used to protect almost all Internet traffic and stored encrypted data. There is strong commercial interest in deploying post-quantum cryptography well before such a quantum computer has been built. Companies and governments cannot afford to have their now-private communications decrypted in the future, even if that future is 30 years away. For this reason, there is a need to begin the transition to post-quantum cryptography as soon as possible, especially since it takes over a decade to make existing Web standards obsolete (see Section 4.4).

Key Finding 1: Given the current state of quantum computing and recent rates of progress, it is highly unexpected that a quantum computer that can compromise RSA 2048 or comparable discrete logarithm-based public key cryptosystems will be built within the next decade. (Chapter 7)

Key Finding 10: Even if a quantum computer that can decrypt current cryptographic ciphers is more than a decade off, the hazard of such a machine is high enough—and the time frame for transitioning to a new security protocol is sufficiently long and uncertain—that prioritization of the development, standardization, and deployment of post-quantum cryptography is critical for minimizing the chance of a potential security and privacy disaster. (Chapter 7)

Given the large risk a quantum computer poses to current protocols, there is an active effort to develop post-quantum cryptography, asymmetric ciphers that a quantum computer cannot defeat. These are likely to be standardized in the 2020s. While the potential utility of Shor's algorithm for cracking deployed cryptography was a major driver of early enthusiasm in quantum computing research, the existence of cryptographic algorithms that are believed to be quantum-resistant will reduce the usefulness of a quantum computer for cryptanalysis and thus will reduce the extent to which this application will drive quantum computing R&D in the long term (see Section 4.3).

RISKS AND BENEFITS OF PURSUING QUANTUM COMPUTING

Significant technical barriers remain before a practical QC can be achieved, and there is no guarantee that they will be overcome. Building and using QCs will require not only device engineering but also fundamental progress at the convergence of a host of scientific disciplines—from computer science and mathematics to physics, chemistry, and materials science. Yet these efforts also offer potential benefits. For example, results from QC R&D have already helped to advance progress in physics—for example, in the area of quantum gravity—and in classical computer science by motivating or informing improvements in classical algorithms.

Key Finding 6: Quantum computing is valuable for driving foundational research that will help advance humanity's understanding of the universe. As with all foundational scientific research, discoveries from this field could lead to transformative new knowledge and applications. (Chapter 7)

The challenges to creating a large, error-corrected quantum computer are significant. Successful quantum computation will require unprecedented control of quantum coherence, pushing the boundaries of what is possible by refining existing tools and techniques—or perhaps even by developing new ones. Related technologies, such as quantum sensing and quantum communication, that also rely upon quantum coherence control may also leverage these advances (see Section 2.2).

Key Finding 7: Although the feasibility of a large-scale quantum computer is not yet certain, the benefits of the effort to develop a practical QC are likely to be large, and they may continue to spill over to other nearer-term applications of quantum information technology, such as qubit-based sensing. (Chapter 7)

In addition to the intellectual and potential societal benefits of quantum computing, this field has implications for national security. Any entity in possession of a large-scale, practical quantum computer could break today's asymmetric cryptosystems—a significant signals intelligence advantage. Awareness of this risk has launched efforts to create and deploy cryptographic-systems that are robust to quantum cryptanalysis, for which there are several candidates currently believed to be quantum safe. However, while deploying post-quantum cryptography in government and civilian systems may protect subsequent communications, it will not remove the security risk to prequantum encrypted data that has already been intercepted by an adversary, although the magnitude of this risk decreases as the arrival time of a QC capable of deploying Shor's algorithm increases and the data becomes less relevant. Furthermore, new quantum algorithms or implementations could lead to new quantum cryptanalytic techniques; as with cybersecurity in general, post-quantum resilience will require ongoing security research.

But the national security issues transcend cryptography. The larger strategic question is about future economic and technological leadership. Historically, classical computing has had a transformative impact across society. While the potential for applying quantum algorithms to industrial and research applications has only begun to be explored, it is clear that quantum computing has the potential to transcend current computational boundaries. The potential to improve efficiency in many areas of computation suggests that supporting a robust QC research community in the United States is of strategic value.

CONCLUSION

Based on evaluation of publicly available information regarding progress to date in the field of quantum computing, the committee saw no fundamental reason why a large, fault-tolerant quantum computer could not be built in principle. However, significant technical challenges remain on the path to building such a system, and to deploying it to practical advantage for a valuable task. Furthermore, future decisions on funding levels, likely dependent on near-term successes and commercial applications, as well as the strength and openness of the research community both in the United States and abroad, will influence the timeline for achieving a practical computer in the public domain. Progress in the field can be tracked using the metrics proposed in Key Finding 3. Regardless of when—or whether—a large, error-corrected quantum computer is built, continued R&D in quantum computing and quantum technologies will expand the boundaries of humanity's scientific knowledge, and the results yet to be gleaned could transform our understanding of the universe.

1

Progress in Computing

Recently, stories about the development of small-scale quantum computers and their potential capabilities have regularly appeared in the popular press, driven largely by the rapid advance of ongoing public research in the field, the beginning of corporate investment, and concern about the future of performance scaling of traditional computers [1]. While progress in the field of quantum computing has been impressive, many open questions exist about the potential applications of such a system, how these types of computers could be built, and when—or whether—this technology will disrupt today's computing paradigm.

The goal of this report is to assess the feasibility, time frame, and implications of building a general-purpose quantum computer. Before examining the capabilities of this emerging technology, it is instructive to review the origin and capabilities of current commercial computing technologies, the economic forces that drove their development, and the limitations that are beginning to confront them. This information will provide context for understanding the unique potential of quantum computing along with potential challenges to development of any new and competitive computing technology and will serve as a comparative framework for understanding progress toward a practical quantum computer.

1.1 ORIGINS OF CONTEMPORARY COMPUTING

Progress in one area of science and engineering often catalyzes or accelerates discovery in another, creating new pathways forward for both new science and the design and deployment of new technologies. Such interconnections are particularly visible in the development of computing technologies, which emerged from millennia of progress in mathematical and physical sciences to launch a transformative industry in the mid-20th century. In less than one hundred years, research, development, and deployment of practical computing technologies have transformed science, engineering, and society at large.

Before the mid-20th century, practical "computers" were not machines, but people who performed mathematical computations with the aid of simple tools, such as the abacus or the slide rule. Today, we generally define a computer as a complex machine that can solve many problems more rapidly, precisely, or accurately than a human, by manipulating abstract representations of data embodied within some physical system using a set of well-defined rules. Given the appropriate input and the right set of instructions, a computer can output the answers to a host of problems. In the early 1800s, Charles Babbage designed a mechanical computer, the "difference engine," to print astronomical tables, and later proposed a more complex mechanical computing machine, the "analytical engine." Due to the absence of practical manufacturing technologies, neither was built at that time, but this engine was the first conception of a general-purpose programmable computer. The contemporary concept of a computer further coalesced in the 1930s with the work of Alan Turing. His abstract, mathematical model of a simple computer capable of simulating any other computing device, "the Turing machine," described the foundational capabilities of all digital computers.

While computing is predicated by millennia of exploration of mathematical principles, practical devices require a concrete, physical implementation of abstract and theoretical ideas. The first successful realizations of such devices emerged during World War II. Alan Turing built a special-purpose electromechanical computer for cryptanalysis, the "Bombe," and developed a detailed specification for an "automatic computing engine," a real general-purpose stored-program computer. In Germany, in a separate development, Konrad Zuse created the Z1, the first programmable computer, using electromechanical relays. Subsequent to the war, the so-called von Neumann architecture[1] — a reformulation of the universal Turing machine in terms of the stored program model of computing—became the dominant architecture for most computer systems.

In subsequent decades, driven mostly by military funding, computers continued to improve in performance and capabilities. The physical components used to create computers also improved with time. Since the nascent computer industry was too small to drive technology

---

[1] So-named for John von Neumann, the first to propose the stored-program model.

development, its designers leveraged the technology (vacuum tubes, then transistors, and finally integrated circuits) that was developed to support radio, television, and telephony, which were the driving commercial applications of the day. Over time, the computing industry grew much larger than the military sector that started it, and large enough to support customized technology development. Today, computing is one of the largest commercial drivers of integrated circuit development, and many other areas leverage integrated circuits designed for the computing industry for their needs. As a result, today's electronic computers—from mobile devices and laptops to supercomputers—are the fruits of tremendous progress in human understanding of and control over physical materials and systems.

1.2 QUANTUM COMPUTING

While today's computing machines leverage exquisite control over nature to create designs of immense complexity, the representation and logical processing of information in these machines can be explained using the laws of classical physics.[2] These classical descriptions of electromagnetism and Newtonian physics provide an intuitive and deterministic explanation of the physical universe, but they fail to predict all observable phenomena. This realization, made around the turn of the 20th century, led to the most important transformation in physics: the discovery of the principles of quantum mechanics. Quantum mechanics (or quantum physics) is a theory of the physical world that is not deterministic, but probabilistic, with inherent uncertainty. While the dynamics it describes at a small scale are exotic and counterintuitive, it accurately predicts a wide range of observable phenomena that classical physics could not, and replicates correct classical results for larger systems. The development of this field has transformed the way scientists understand nature. Very small systems whose behavior cannot be adequately approximated by the equations of classical physics are often referred to as "quantum systems."

While classical physics is often a good approximation for observable phenomena, all matter is fundamentally quantum mechanical—including the materials from which today's computers are built. However, even as the design of their hardware components is increasingly informed by the quantum properties of materials, and as the ever-shrinking size of these components means that quantum phenomena introduce more constraints

---

[2] While the laws of quantum mechanics must be invoked to design or explain the operation of semiconductor materials whose bandgaps enable the implementation of today's widely deployed conventional computer logic gates, the nature of the logical information processing itself is based upon the flow of a classical model of a charged particle.

on their design, the principles and operations that these computers implement have remained classical.

Despite the extraordinary power of today's computers, there are applications that are difficult for them to compute but seem to be easily "computed" by the quantum world: estimating the properties and behavior of quantum systems. While today's classical computers can simulate simple quantum systems, and often find useful approximate solutions for more complicated ones, for many such problems the amount of memory needed for the simulation grows exponentially with the size of the system simulated.

In 1982, physicist Richard Feynman suggested that quantum mechanical phenomena could themselves be used to simulate a quantum system more efficiently than a naïve simulation on a classical computer [2,3]. In 1993, Bernstein and Vazirani showed [4] that quantum computers could violate the extended Church-Turing thesis—a foundational principle of computer science that said that the performance of all computers was only polynomially faster than a probabilistic Turing machine [5,6]. Their quantum algorithm offered an exponential speedup over any classical algorithm for a certain computational task called recursive Fourier sampling. Another example of a quantum algorithm demonstrating exponential speedup for a different computational problem was provided in 1994 by Dan Simon [7]. Quantum computation is the only model of computation to date to violate the extended Church-Turing thesis, and therefore only quantum computers are capable of exponential speedups over classical computers.

In 1994, Peter Shor showed that several important computational problems could, in principle, be solved significantly more efficiently using a quantum computer—if such a machine could be built. Specifically, he derived algorithms for factoring large integers and solving discrete logarithms rapidly—problems that could take even the largest computer today thousands or millions of years—or even the lifetime of the universe—to compute. This was a striking discovery because it also suggested that anyone with a real-world quantum computer could break the cryptographic codes that make use of these problems, compromising the security of encrypted communications and encrypted stored data, and potentially uncovering protected secrets or private information. These results catalyzed interest among researchers in developing other quantum algorithms with exponentially better performance than classical algorithms, and trying to create the basic quantum building blocks from which a quantum computer could be built.

During the past few decades, this research has progressed to the point where very simple quantum computers have been built, and a positive outlook is emerging based upon the assumption that the complexity of these machines will grow exponentially with time, analogous to the growth that has been achieved in performance of classical computers. Given the importance of this scaling assumption to the future of quantum computing, understanding the factors that drive scaling is critical.

1.3 HISTORICAL PROGRESS IN COMPUTING: MOORE'S LAW

While the early computers were huge, expensive, and power-hungry devices often funded by the government, today's computers are dramatically smaller, cheaper, more efficient, and more powerful as a result of improvements in hardware, software, and architecture. Today's smartphones, computers that fit in one's pocket, have as much computational power as the fastest supercomputers of 20 years ago. The low cost of computer hardware has led to the permeation of computers throughout various environments and has enabled the aggregation of tens to hundreds of thousands of computers that provide the Web computing services that many have come to depend on. Computers are now commonly embedded in increasing numbers of manufactured goods, from washing machines to singing greeting cards. This section describes how this happened, which reveals a number of lessons and challenges for any new computing technology.

The process used to create integrated circuits, the key components of today's computers, emerged as an unplanned advance amid efforts in the 1960s to improve the industrial manufacturing process for transistors. Transistors are small electrical devices that can be used as electronic switches or amplifiers, and were used at the time in a variety of electronic devices, including radios, TVs, audio amplifiers, and early computers. Efforts to increase transistor quality and manufacturing yield (which lower costs) led to several inventions at Fairchild Semiconductor, a transistor startup company. The first was a method of fabricating transistors called the "planar process," which enabled transistors to operate after being fabricated on the surface of a flat piece of silicon. Previously, the material outside of the transistor needed to be etched away, creating a silicon transistor "mesa." The planar processes enabled the fabrication of many transistors on a given piece of silicon, which could then be cut to separate them. The second invention was a means for connecting a few of these transistors together via a metal layer on the silicon surface to create a complete circuit. Since this transistor circuit was integrated on one piece of silicon, the result was called an "integrated circuit," or IC. This concept of connecting multiple devices on one substrate had been demonstrated a year earlier in a crude germanium prototype by Jack Kilby at Texas Instruments, also with the intent of lowering the cost and improving the reliability of transistor circuits.

The manufacturing process for creating an integrated circuit, which has become increasingly complex over time, can be viewed as a type of layered printing process. A transistor can be created by successive "printing" of different shapes in a series of layers. For an integrated circuit, the shapes for all of the circuit's transistors are "printed" at the same time, layer by layer, onto a piece of silicon. The process takes the same amount of time regardless of the number of transistors in the circuit; further reduction of costs can be achieved by making multiple copies of the circuit at the same time on a large piece of silicon, called a wafer. As a result, an IC's production cost is set by the size of the silicon that it occupies (which determines how many circuits can be manufactured in the processing of a single wafer), rather than the number of transistors in the circuit.

In 1964, Gordon Moore, also at Fairchild, examined the costs of creating integrated circuits. He noticed that, as a result of design and processing improvements, the number of transistors that could be economically printed on each circuit had been increasing exponentially over time—doubling roughly every year. Moore conjectured that IC fabrication technology would continue to improve with exponential growth in number of transistors per integrated circuit, and he pondered in a 1964 paper how the world would use all of these devices. In the many decades that followed, his conjecture of exponential growth has borne out as an accurate one, and is now commonly referred to as "Moore's law."

Moore's law is not a physical law; it is simply the empirical production trend for the integrated circuit industry as a result of its business cycle. While the exponential growth in the capability of integrated circuits is commonly touted, the costs that support this growth are often overlooked. During the past 50 years, the revenue of the computer hardware industry also grew exponentially, increasing by more than one thousand-fold, to just under half a trillion U.S. dollars annually today. Over this same period, the share of this revenue reinvested into the industry's research and development (R&D) operations remained roughly constant, meaning that the financial cost of the technology improvements underlying Moore's law also increased exponentially. Interestingly, in addition to this exponential growth, both the cost of building an IC manufacturing plant and the cost of creating a design to be manufactured also displayed exponential growth.

This illustrates a critical point: Moore's law is the result of a virtuous cycle, where improvements in integrated circuit manufacturing allow the manufacturer to reduce the price of their product, which in turn causes them to sell more products and increase their sales and profits. This increased revenue then enables them to improve the manufacturing process again, which is harder this time, since the easier changes have already been made.[3] The key to this cycle is to create a growing market for one's product. For integrated circuits, the new affordability causes designers of many general products to replace some existing mechanism with an IC because it makes the product better or cheaper (e.g., changing a key lock to an electronic lock), which grows the market for ICs, creating the growing revenue needed to continue scaling their complexity.

It is hard to achieve this type of exponential scaling without such a virtuous cycle. This is apparent from the historical example of efforts to make transistors out of a material other than silicon. Because transistors made from gallium arsenide (GaAs) are capable of higher performance than silicon transistors, researchers believed that computers built from GaAs ICs would have higher performance than those built using silicon ICs. Given this promise, by the mid-1970s many research groups—and, later, companies—worked toward making ICs using GaAs transistors. However, by the time this effort started, the silicon IC industry was large, and companies had already begun reinvesting part of their revenue in improvements to their manufacturing process. The manufacturing process for GaAs was sufficiently different from silicon that developers needed to develop new GaAs-specific fabrication steps. This development put GaAs manufacturers in a Catch-22 situation: to fund their manufacturing R&D, they needed robust sales; to get robust sales, they needed state-of-the-art manufacturing techniques to compete against the silicon alternatives, which were constantly improving. The industry was never able to break this cycle, and the efforts to build commercially successful GaAs ICs ultimately failed; general-purpose digital GaAs ICs never became competitive.

The virtuous cycle underlying Moore's law is not just financial. It also depends on the existence of a vibrant ecosystem to support the growth of the market. In many ways, the integrated circuit industry created—and then grew to depend upon—Silicon Valley, which later globalized to its position today. The growing capabilities of, and market for, computer hardware attracted venture funding, support industries, and, most importantly, talent into the field. This growing community was then able to solve previously unsolvable problems, further contributing to advances and growth in the industry, which in turn brought even more people to the area. The result of this virtuous cycle is amazing. In today's technologies, a digital gate, the simple building block of a computer, costs around a few millionths of a penny (100,000,000 gates per dollar), and each gate can compute its result in under 10 picoseconds (that is, one hundredth of a billionth of a second) at low-enough power levels to work in a cell phone.

---

[3] This is one of the reasons behind the so-called Rock's law, which states that the cost of building a new semiconductor fabrication facility doubles every 4 years.

Finding: Moore's law for integrated circuits resulted from a virtuous cycle, where improved technology generated exponentially increasing revenue, enabling reinvestment in R&D and attracting new talent and industries to help innovate and scale the technology to the next level.

1.4 CONVERTING TRANSISTORS TO CHEAP COMPUTERS

Moore's law of technology scaling has roughly halved the cost of building a transistor every two years. Over the past half-century, this has translated to a cost decrease by a factor of more than 30 million. While this decrease in transistor cost made it cost effective to manufacture ICs with increasing transistor complexity, designing these complex ICs becomes increasingly difficult. Designing a circuit with 8 transistors is not hard; designing a circuit with 100 million transistors is a different story. To deal with this increasing complexity, designers of computing hardware created new ways of thinking about transistor circuits that allowed them to reason about a smaller number of objects. While initially they thought in terms of connecting individual transistors, soon they began thinking in terms of "logic gates"—collections of transistors that could be represented and modeled using Boolean logic (rules that combine signals that can be either false [represented as 0] or true [represented as 1], via operations that yield defined outputs). As complexity continued to increase, logic gates were grouped into a larger circuit such as an adder or a memory block, again reducing the complexity that the designer needed to work with. These different levels of thinking about design, which allow people to build systems without thinking about every detail all at once, are called "abstractions." Abstractions enable the essential components of a computer to be grouped conceptually by form or function.

A computer is another design abstraction. It represents a transistor circuit whose function is controlled by a set of instructions read from an attached memory. Once it became possible to build complex integrated circuits, it became possible to integrate a small computer onto a single IC, creating a "micro-computer," or "microprocessor." This design made it much easier to leverage cheap transistors; new applications no longer required the design and fabrication of an application-specific IC but could instead be implemented by changing the instructions provided to an existing microprocessor to create the desired solution. The ease of developing and deploying computer-based solutions, coupled with the decreasing cost of computing, greatly increased the demand for this type of device. Thus, the ubiquity of computing is both enabled by (via cheaper computing) and enabling to (via higher revenue) Moore's law. Computing is one way that the industry creates products people want to buy out of increasingly cheap transistors.

Continued benefits from the exponentially falling cost of transistors required the creation of many abstraction layers like those described above, and new software (computer programs) and design frameworks. While these software and design frameworks were expensive to develop, their cost was supported by the revenue streams of previous products, and the projected revenue of the future products that they would enable. Yet, even with this additional support, design of a state-of-the-art chip is still expensive, costing over $100 million. Since the cost of each device is the manufacturing cost plus the amortized design cost, IC-based computing is cheap only if it is sold in high enough volume (typically 10 million units or more), ensuring that the amortized design cost does not dominate the manufacturing cost. It is the amortization of design costs that makes commodity computing devices so much cheaper than specialized computers.

New computing approaches, such as quantum computing, that change the fundamental building blocks of a computer will require creation of not only a new type of hardware building blocks but also new abstraction layers, software, and design frameworks to enable designers to build and use these systems if their complexity will need to scale over time. The costs of creating these new hardware and software tools are important for new technologies, since the price of early machines will need to be high enough to start recovering some of the costs. This premium always penalizes new approaches when competing against an established player.

1.5 A SLOWDOWN IN SCALING

Although Moore's law reflects great progress in classical computing over several decades, it is clear that the exponential trend cannot be sustained indefinitely, due to both physical limitations and the finite size of the world market. While there is much debate over when exactly this scaling will cease, signs of the end of scaling have come into clearer view over the past decade. Since Moore's law is really about transistor cost, one indication of scaling issues is the fact that transistor costs are not dropping at their historical rate in the most advanced technologies. It is also interesting to note that the International Technology Roadmap for Semiconductors, an international consortium that was formed to help keep technology scaling in line with Moore's law and address possible roadblocks to doing so, decided to stop its scaling projections with the 5-7 nanometer feature sizes expected around 2021.

Decreased growth is also apparent in net revenue trends for the integrated circuit industry, illustrated in Figure 1.1. This semi-log plot of revenue over time shows a straight line when revenue growth is exponential. The data shows a strong exponential growth in revenue through 2000,

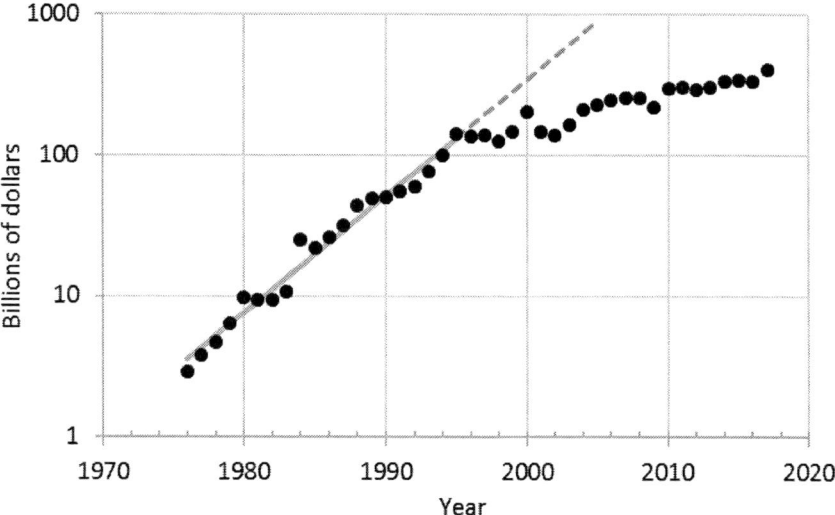

FIGURE 1.1 Total global semiconductor sales annually, in billions of dollars, shown on a semi-log plot with trend line. This plot shows nearly exponential growth in sales through roughly 1995 (the gray trend line corresponds to exponential growth with an annual growth rate of 21 percent), followed by more modest growth. SOURCE: Data from "Industry Statistics," Semiconductor Industry Association, last modified February 6, 2018, http://www.semiconductors.org/index.php?src= directory&view=IndustryStatistics&srctype=billing_reports&submenu=Statistics.

followed by a decrease in growth rate. This plot indicates that the virtuous cycle, where each improvement in technology brought more money to the industry, has begun to slow down. This slowdown in revenue growth is likely to affect technology development cycles, which will affect technology scaling. The slowing of growth is not surprising: at $300-$400 billion in revenue, this industry represents a few percent of the manufacturing sector's contribution to the world's entire GDP. It cannot continue to increase forever at a rate faster than the world's GDP.

1.6 QUANTUM: A NEW APPROACH TO COMPUTING

It is against this backdrop that the theory and prototypes for quantum computing have emerged. As noted in Section 1.2, quantum computing uses a very different approach to computation by leveraging some of the unusual properties of the quantum world. When the idea was formally proposed in the 1980s, and new algorithms were discovered in the 1990s, no one knew how to actually build this type of machine. Over the past two decades, efforts to create a working quantum computer have made noteworthy progress, reviving interest in the potential of this technology. It remains to be seen whether practical quantum computers can or will be developed in a way that will sustain Moore's law-type growth in computational capabilities. The failed GaAs IC experiment illustrates the difficulty of trying to enter an established market with an existing dominant player. Nonetheless, quantum computing is the only truly new model of computing that has been proposed, in the sense that it is not bound by the extended Church-Turing thesis. As a more general model of computing—in much the same way in which quantum mechanics is a more general model of physics than classical mechanics—quantum computing has the theoretical potential to solve some problems that no classical computer could realistically attack. This "quantum advantage," which could manifest as a disruptive rather than an incremental innovation, is what makes quantum computing so interesting, and motivates both the commercial interest in quantum computing and the rest of this report.

The next chapter describes the physical phenomena that underlie quantum computing, comparing the associated operation principles to those of conventional computers. Subsequent chapters then describe tasks at which quantum computers could potentially outperform classical computers, their implications for cryptography, the hardware and software needed to create a working quantum computer, and the strengths and weaknesses of the underlying physical technologies for creating quantum computers. The report closes by assessing the feasibility of implementing a practical quantum computer, the associated timelines and resources required, and milestones and metrics that can be used to track future progress.

1.7 NOTES

[1] See, for example, J. Dongarra, 2018, "The U.S. Once Again Has the World's Fastest Supercomputer. Keep Up the Hustle," *The Washington Post*, June 25, https://www.washingtonpost.com/opinions/united-states-wins-top-honors-in-supercomputer-race/2018/06/25/82798c2c-78b1-11e8-aeee-4d04c8ac6158_story.html;

J. Nicas, 2017, "How Google's Quantum Computer Could Change the World," *Wall Street Journal*, October 16, https://www.wsj.com/articles/how-googles-quantum-computer-could-change-the-world-1508158847;

J. Asmundsson, 2017, "Quantum Computing Might Be Here Sooner than You Think," *Bloomberg*, June 14, https://www.bloomberg.com/news/features/2017-06-14/the-machine-of-tomorrow-today-quantum-computing-on-the-verge;

D. Castevecchi, 2017, Quantum computers ready to leap out of the lab in 2017, *Nature* 541(7635):9-10.

[2] R.P. Feynman, 1982, Simulating physics with computers, *International Journal of Theoretical Physics* 21(6-7):467-488.

[3] S. Lloyd, 1996, Universal quantum simulators, *Science* 273(5278):1073-1078.

[4] E. Bernstein and U. Vazirani, 1993, "Quantum Complexity Theory," pp. 11-20 in *Proceedings of the Twenty-Fifth Annual ACM Symposium on Theory of Computing (STOC '93)*, Association of Computing Machinery, New York, https://dl.acm.org/citation.cfm?id=167097.
[5] P. Kaye, R. Laflamme, and M. Mosca, 2007, *An Introduction to Quantum Computing*, Oxford University Press, Oxford, U.K.
[6] M.A. Nielsen and I. Chuang, 2002, *Quantum Computation and Quantum Information*, Cambridge University Press, Cambridge, U.K.
[7] D. Simon, 1997, On the power of quantum computation, *SIAM Journal on Computing* 26(5):1474-1483.

2

Quantum Computing: A New Paradigm

Computers today work by converting information to a series of binary digits, or bits, and operating on these bits using integrated circuits (ICs) containing billions of transistors. Each bit has only two possible values, 0 or 1. Through manipulations of these so-called binary representations, computers process text documents and spreadsheets, create amazing visual worlds in games and movies, and provide the Web-based services on which many have come to depend.

A quantum computer also represents information as a series of bits, called quantum bits, or qubits. Like a normal bit, a qubit can be either 0 or 1, but unlike a normal bit, which can only be 0 or 1, a qubit can also be in a state where it is both at the same time. When extended to systems of many qubits, this ability to be in all possible binary states at the same time gives rise to the potential computational power of quantum computing. However, the rules that govern quantum systems also make it difficult to take advantage of this power. How best to make use of quantum properties—and the nature of the improvements these properties make possible—is neither trivial nor obvious.

This chapter provides an introduction to some of the unique properties of the quantum world, showing how some provide computational advantages while others constrain the ability to use these advantages. The mechanisms for manipulating classical and quantum bits are compared and contrasted to illustrate the unique challenges and benefits of quantum computing. The chapter concludes by describing the types of quantum computers currently being pursued by researchers, providing a first look at the progress that will be assessed in the chapters to follow.

2.1 THE NONINTUITIVE PHYSICS OF THE QUANTUM WORLD

Originally introduced in the early 20th century, quantum mechanics is one of the most well-tested models for explaining the physical world. The theory—that is, the underlying abstract rules and their mathematical representations—describes the behavior of particles at very small distances and energy scales. These properties are the basis for understanding the physical and chemical properties of all matter. Quantum mechanics provides the same observable and intuitive results we expect for large objects, but its descriptions of the small-scale behavior of subatomic particles, although accurate, are exotic and nonintuitive.[1]

According to the theory, a quantum object does not generally exist in a completely determined and knowable state. In fact, each time one observes a quantum object it looks like a particle, but when it is not being observed it behaves like a wave. This so-called wave-particle duality leads to many interesting physical phenomena.

For example, quantum objects can exist in multiple states all at once, with each of the states adding together and interfering like waves to define the overall quantum state. In general, the state of any quantum system is described in terms of "wave functions." In many cases, the state of a system can be expressed mathematically as a sum of the possible contributing states,[2] each scaled by a complex number[3] coefficient that reflects the relative weight of the state. Such states are said to be "coherent," because the contributing states can interfere with each other constructively and destructively, much like wavefronts.[4]

However, when one attempts to observe a quantum system, only one of its components is observed, with a probability proportional to the square of the absolute value of its coefficient. To an observer, the system

---

[1] This simple overview of quantum phenomena is intended to provide context for discussion of quantum computing. The foundational theory and scientific history of the field are fascinating and extensive, and beyond the ability of this report to fully convey. The committee refers the interested reader to the following reference for additional explanation and discussion of quantum mechanical phenomena: N.D. Mermin, 1981, "Quantum Mysteries for Anyone," *Journal of Philosophy* 78(7):397-408.

[2] Strictly speaking, each of the contributing states is also called a "wave function"; the state of any coherent quantum system is defined by a wave function.

[3] The wave-like nature of the wave function means that the coefficients can describe both the amplitude and phase of this state. In this usage, "complex" means a number that is represented by two real numbers, one defining the amplitude, and the other the phase. This is often represented as $Ae^{i\theta}$, where A is the amplitude, and θ is the phase shift. A phase shift of $\pi/2$ or 90 degrees is written as i and a phase shift of π or 180 degrees is -1.

[4] Quantum systems that are not fully coherent must be represented using a "density matrix," which defines the classical probability that a system is in any particular quantum state—in this case, the possible contributing states do not interfere with each other.

will always look classical when measured. Observation of a quantum object (or quantum system—that is, a system of quantum objects), formally called "measurement," occurs when the object interacts with some larger physical system that extracts information from it. Measurement fundamentally disrupts a quantum state: it "collapses" the aspect of wave function that was measured into a single observable state, resulting in a loss of information. After the measurement, the quantum object's wave function is that of the state that was detected, rather than that of its pre-measurement state.

To visualize this, consider an ordinary coin on a table-top. In the classical world that we experience daily, its state is either heads-up (U) or heads-down (D). A quantum version of a coin would exist in a combination, or "superposition," of both states at the same time. The wave function of a quantum coin could be written as a weighted sum of both states, scaled by coefficients C_U and C_D. However, an attempt to observe the state of a quantum coin will result in finding it to be only heads up or heads down—upon measurement, it will be in only one of the two states, with a probability proportional to the square of the corresponding coefficient.

Because a pair of conventional coins has four possible states (UU, UD, DU, and DD), a pair of quantum coins could exist as a superposition of these four conventional states, each weighted by its own coefficient, C_{UU}, C_{UD}, C_{DU}, C_{DD}—and so on for larger collections of quantum coins.

Upon measurement, a pair of quantum coins will appear like a pair of classical coins—in only one of the four possible configurations on the table-top. Similarly, a system of n quantum coins will only ever be observed to be in one of its 2^n possible states.

Under some circumstances, two or more quantum objects in a system can be intrinsically linked such that measurement of one dictates the possible measurement outcomes for another, regardless of how far apart the two objects are. The property underlying this phenomenon, known as "entanglement," is key to the potential power of quantum computing.

The evolution of any quantum system is governed by the Schrödinger equation, which relates how the wave function of the system changes given the energy environment that it experiences. This environment is defined by the so-called Hamiltonian of the system, a mathematical representation of the energies resulting from all forces felt by all elements of the system.[5] In order to control a quantum system, one must therefore carefully control its energy environment, both by isolating the system from

---

[5] Strictly speaking, the Hamiltonian is the mathematical description of the environment, which, for a quantum-mechanical system, takes the form of an operator. However, the term is often also used to refer to the environment itself; this convention may also be used in this report.

the rest of the universe (which contains forces not easily controlled), and by deliberately applying energy fields within the isolation region to elicit a desired behavior. In practice, complete isolation is impossible, although interactions with the environment can be minimized; the quantum system will ultimately exchange some energy and information with the broader environment over time, a process known as "decoherence." This can be thought of as the environment continually making small random measurements on the system, each of which causes a partial collapse of the wave function.

The unique properties described above, and summarized in Box 2.1, were revealed through foundational scientific discovery. When carefully controlled, these intrinsic characteristics of matter also present new potential paradigms for engineering—in particular, for encoding, manipulating, and transferring information.

2.2 THE LANDSCAPE OF QUANTUM TECHNOLOGY

Over the past several decades, significant progress has been made in R&D for controlling and harnessing the power of quantum systems, revealing the potential for transformative quantum technologies. While the field of quantum computing has been perhaps most visible in the public eye, it is important to recognize that the range of applications of quantum phenomena is broader than quantum computing alone. Under the general heading of quantum information science, the fields of quantum communication and networking, and quantum sensing and metrology are also thriving areas of foundational scientific research with distinct technological objectives. While these fields are at differing levels of technological maturity, the boundaries between them are not always easily defined, because all of the fields are based upon the same underlying phenomena and face many of the same challenges [1]. They all make use of the unique properties of quantum systems, are based upon the same underlying physical theory, and share many common hardware and laboratory techniques. As a result, their progress is mutually dependent. For a rough sense of research output in each of these areas, one may examine the number of published research papers produced over time. Research trends for quantum computing and algorithms, quantum communications, and quantum sensing and metrology are illustrated in Figure 2.1.[6]

The field of quantum information science generally explores how information can be encoded in a quantum system, including the associated statistics, limitations, and unique affordances of quantum mechanics.

---

[6] See Appendix E for a discussion of research efforts by nation of origin.

BOX 2.1
Unique Properties of the Quantum World

The theory of quantum mechanics is a mathematical description of the world at very small scales and is the most accurate theory for understanding and predicting properties about the physical universe. Quantum interactions are quite unlike those experienced by people every day. Some of the defining principles of quantum mechanics are described below.

- *Wave-particle duality*—A quantum object generally has both wave- and particle-like properties. While the evolution of the system follows a wave equation, any measurement of the system will return a value consistent with it being a particle.
- *Superposition*—A quantum system can exist in two or more states at once, referred to as a "superposition" of states or a "superposition state." The wave function for such a superposition state can be described as a linear combination of the contributing states, with complex coefficients. These coefficients describe the magnitude and relative phases between the contributing states.
- *Coherence*—When a quantum system's state can be described by a set of complex numbers, one for each basis state of the system, the system state is said to be "coherent." Coherence is necessary for quantum phenomena such as quantum interference, superposition, and entanglement. Small interactions with the environment cause quantum systems to slowly decohere. The environmental interactions make even the complex coefficients for each state probabilistic.
- *Entanglement*—Entanglement is a special property of some (but not all) multiparticle superposition states, where measurement of the state of one particle collapses the state of the other particles, even if the particles are far apart with no apparent way to interact. This arises when the wave functions for different particles are not separable (in mathematical terms, when the wave function for the entire system cannot be written as a product of the wave functions for each particle). There is no classical analogue to this phenomenon.
- *Measurement*—Measurement of a quantum system fundamentally changes it. In the case where the measurement yields a well-defined value, the system is left in a state corresponding to the measured value. This is commonly referred to as "collapsing the wave function."

Harnessing these properties in a controlled way creates new potential paradigms for engineering.

QUANTUM COMPUTING: A NEW PARADIGM

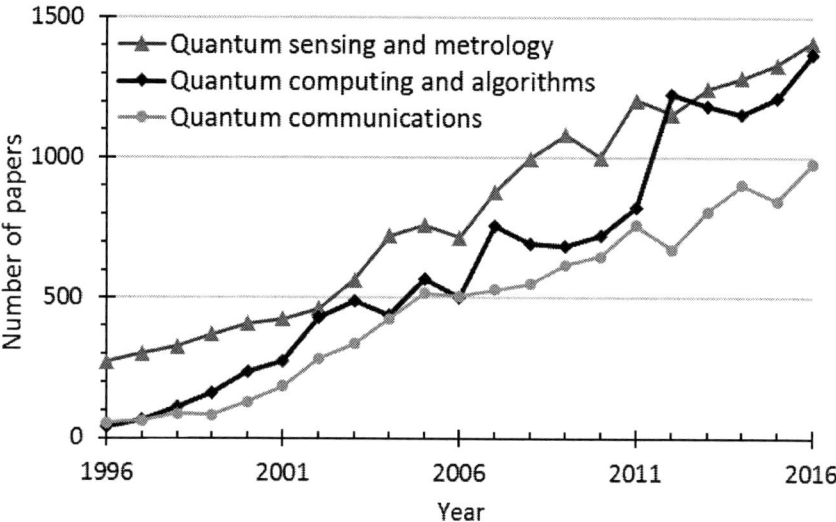

FIGURE 2.1 The number of research papers published per year in quantum computing and algorithms, quantum communications, and quantum sensing and metrology, respectively. See Appendix E for a discussion of research efforts in different nations. Data are the result of a bibliometric analysis conducted by a team at the Naval Surface Warfare Center Dahlgren Division. SOURCE: Data courtesy of Jacob Farinholt.

This area provides much of the foundation for quantum computing, communications, and sensing.

R&D in *quantum communication* focuses on the transport or exchange of information by encoding it into a quantum system. Quantum communication protocols are likely to be necessary for quantum computing—whether to transport information from one part of quantum computer hardware to another, or to enable communication between quantum computers. A subfield of quantum communication is *quantum cryptography*, in which quantum properties are used to design communication systems that may not be eavesdropped upon by an observer.[7]

---

[7] The most prominent example is quantum key distribution (QKD), a quantum measurement-based method of distributing cryptographic keys to use for standard (classical) encryption of data sent over classical communication channels. The best-known protocol, called BB84, was developed by Charlie Bennett and Gilles Brassard in 1984. This protocol has been experimentally deployed both via fiber optic cables and via satellite. It has even led to several companies and commercial products. While QKD and quantum cryptography in general do not remove the risk of side channel attacks and are currently more expensive than classical methods to deploy, theoretical and experimental research continues to advance.

Quantum sensing and metrology involve the study and development of quantum systems whose extreme sensitivity to environmental disturbances can be exploited in order to measure important physical properties (such as magnetic fields, electric fields, gravity, and temperature) with more precision than is possible with classical technologies. Quantum sensors are commonly based upon qubits and are implemented using many of the same physical systems[8] used in experimental quantum computers.

Quantum computing, the primary focus of this report, leverages the quantum mechanical properties of interference, superposition, and entanglement to perform computations that are roughly analogous to (although they operate quite differently from) those performed on a classical computer. In general, a quantum computer is defined as a physical system that comprises a collection of coupled qubits that may be controlled and manipulated in order to implement an algorithm such that measurement of the system's final state yields the answer to a problem of interest with a high probability. The qubits of a quantum computer themselves must be sufficiently isolated from the environment for their quantum state to remain coherent for the duration of a computation.

Finding: Research in quantum mechanics has already led to fundamental advances in physics and to promising new technologies—for example, in quantum sensing. Such advances and applications are likely to drive further work that will help to deepen human knowledge of quantum phenomena and lead to improved methods for quantum engineering.

The foundations of classical and quantum computing are compared in the remainder of this chapter, in order to illustrate the fundamental differences between their components, and to provide a basic overview of the properties of quantum computation.

2.3 BITS AND QUBITS

In order to provide insight into how quantum properties enable a new computing paradigm, and how to meet the ensuing challenges, this section provides a brief overview of the foundations of classical computing, including how machines process information, which is represented by bits. The analogous quantum systems are then presented, and their properties compared and contrasted.

---

[8] For example, trapped ions, superconducting circuits, neutral atoms, nitrogen vacancies in diamond; these technologies are discussed in more detail later in this chapter and in Chapter 5.

2.3.1 Classical Computing: From Analog Signals to Bits and Digital Gates

The powerful classical computing systems that exist today are based upon a robust foundation of reliable physical components. Transistors, the basic building blocks for integrated circuits (ICs) in classical computers, communicate with each other through the use of electrical "signals." These signals are "analog" in nature, which means that their values can change smoothly, as with temperature, or speed.[9] In a circuit, transistors are connected via wires, which conduct the electrical signals from one device to the other. Unfortunately, these electrical signals also interact with their environment, and this interaction can disrupt or "perturb" their value. Such perturbation is called "noise," and it can be broken down into two components. The first, "fundamental noise," results from energy fluctuations arising spontaneously within any object that is above absolute zero in temperature. The second, "systematic noise," results from signal interactions that in theory could have been modeled and corrected, but either were not modeled at all, were not modeled correctly, or were left deliberately uncorrected at the hardware level. This systematic noise arises from many sources. For example, abstractions are used to reduce design complexity, which is essential when creating complex systems. Yet these abstractions often introduce systematic noise, since by hiding implementation details, the designers do not know the precise details of the implementation they are using. Even when information hiding is not a problem, systematic noise still arises from manufacturing variations. While a designer can consider the nominal signal interactions, variations in the manufacturing process—which, as a matter of practice, is not perfectly precise—would create a system slightly different from the one designed. These residual differences also give rise to systematic noise. In order to work properly, a circuit must be robust to the noise these variations cause.

When a circuit is analog (that is, when small changes in its input or parameters cause small changes in its output) the effects of noise are usually additive, accumulating as a signal passes through each successive circuit. While the noise added at each stage may be small enough that it does not disrupt a given process, the cumulative noise can ultimately become large enough to affect the accuracy (or fidelity) of the result. Consequently, electronic analog computers were never very popular or very complex, and they fell out of use after the 1950s and 1960s.

To get around the noise problem with analog circuits, most ICs use transistors to create circuits which operate on digital, binary signals (called

---

[9] By analogy, to get to 60 miles per hour in a car from a stop, the car's speed continuously increases from 0 to 60 miles per hour and hits all speeds between those limits.

"bits"), rather than analog signals. These circuits, called "digital gates" or simply "gates," view the electrical signal as a binary value, as either 0 or 1, rather than viewing it as a real number that changes smoothly from 0 to 1. Some gates, called "registers" or "memories," store the value of a bit, while others process a number of input bit values to create a new output value. By restricting the set of values a signal can carry, gates can reject noise that was added to the signal, providing what is called "noise immunity." This is achieved by treating all signals that have electrical values close to the nominal 0 level as a zero, and signals around the 1 level as a one, and provide an output value that doesn't depend on the exact input voltage. Figure 2.2 shows the input/output relationship for an analog amplifier, and a digital logic gate (an inverter), which shows how the inverter is able to reject noise that is a third the size of the output swing.

Building ICs entirely out of digital gates simplifies the design process for digital systems significantly by creating a robust circuit framework that is insensitive to most fabrication or design variation. Thus, the designers can ignore all the circuit issues and think about gates simply as functions (known as Boolean functions) that take in binary values and output binary values. The kinds of functions that operate this way are completely

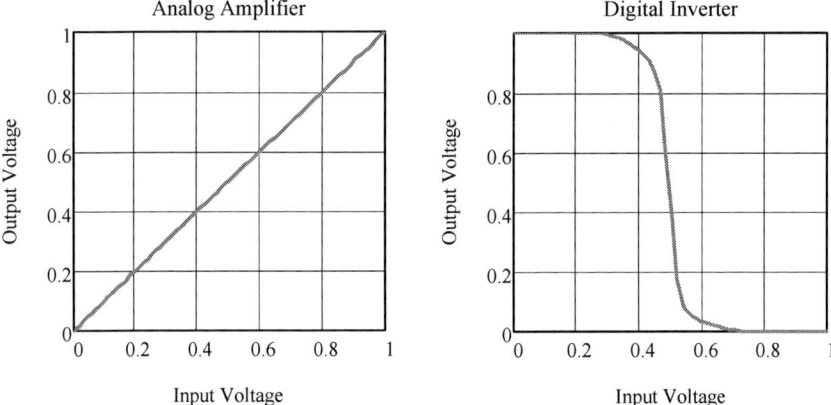

FIGURE 2.2 Input and output relationships for examples of an analog amplifier and a digital inverter. For the analog circuit, small changes in the input voltage will cause small changes in the output voltage. For the digital inverter, when the input is close to 0 V or 1 V, variations in the input voltage make no difference in the output voltage. This attenuation of the input noise around the two Boolean states (0 V and 1 V) for the digital inverter is called noise immunity. SOURCE: Data generated using HSPICE, using 45 nm transistors models from the predictive technology modeling effort at Arizona State University; see Nanoscale Integration and Modeling (NIMO) Group, "Introduction: Predictive Technology Model," http://ptm.asu.edu/.

TABLE 2.1 Primitive Boolean Operations

Boolean Operation	Inputs		Output	Symbolic Notation
	x	y		
AND	0	0	0	$x \wedge y$
	0	1	0	
	1	0	0	
	1	1	1	
OR	0	0	0	$x \vee y$
	0	1	1	
	1	0	1	
	1	1	1	
XOR	0	0	0	$x \oplus y$
	0	1	1	
	1	0	1	
	1	1	0	
NOT	0		1	$\sim x$
	1		0	

NOTE: Primitive Boolean operations, implemented through digital logic gates, are the building blocks of contemporary computation. A universal set of basis operations can be constructed from just two of these operations: NOT and one of either AND or OR.

described by the well-established rules of Boolean algebra. These rules describe how any complicated Boolean function can be decomposed into a small series of simpler operations, such as those listed in Table 2.1. This translation allows today's hardware designers to describe their designs at a relatively high abstraction level and to use an automated design tool to map them to the required logic gates, a process called "logic synthesis." Since the number of basic building blocks is limited, all IC manufacturers provide a set of predesigned and tested logic gates, their "standard cell library," that may be incorporated into a chip's design and built in silicon using their manufacturing technology.

Using both digital logic and standard libraries for these logic gates also makes designs robust—that is, they have negligible error rates. IC manufacturers provide checking tools that analyze a design to ensure that its systematic noise is smaller than the noise margin of their gates, ensuring that the logical abstraction can be implemented by the underlying components.

Even with the large noise margin in digital gates, noise can sometimes be large enough to disrupt the Boolean values stored in memories. To get high density and high performance, these structures typically have larger device variations and smaller noise margins, so occasionally the noise is large enough to corrupt a digital output. To correct for this, a layer of error protection is added. The data is "encoded," using an error correction code (ECC), adding some bits that add redundancy to the values stored in the memory. This code is checked on each read, making it possible to detect memory errors. Efficient ECCs have been developed that, with small overheads (adding 8 bits to a 64-bit value, which is <15 percent overhead), can detect and correct any single-bit error in a memory operation and detect double-bit errors. Efficient error correction schemes are critical to the success and reliability of today's classical computing systems. This type of algorithmic error correction is even more important in quantum computing, since quantum gates have little intrinsic noise immunity, as the next section will show.

The digital design flow also helps with other aspects of the design, such as testing and removing errors from the design, a process generally called "debugging." In ICs, there are two types of errors that need to be dealt with: design errors and manufacturing defects. Given the complexity of modern systems, errors (bugs) inevitably occur in the design, so methods to find these errors and correct them is a key aspect of any design strategy. When the circuit is integrated on a small piece of silicon, it is hard or impossible to look at internal signals to try to track the error. To mitigate this, the synthesis tools that map the high-level design description into gates add additional hardware to the design to provide internal test points that enable this type of design debugging. These internal test points also enable tools to automatically generate tests that can confirm that the manufactured chip performs the exact same Boolean function as specified in the design, greatly simplifying manufacturing tests.

As the next sections will show, while quantum computers have bit-like structures (called "qubits") and gates, they behave very differently from classical bits and digital gates. The qubits possess both digital and analog character that provide their potential computational power. Their analog nature implies that unlike classical gates, the quantum gates have no noise margin (input errors are passed directly to output of the gate), but their digital nature provides a means to recover from this critical drawback. Thus, the digital design approach and abstractions developed for classical computing cannot be used directly for quantum computing. Quantum computing may borrow ideas from conventional computing; however, it will ultimately need its own method to mitigate the effects of processing variations and noise, and it will have to develop its own approach to debug design errors and manufacturing defects.

2.3.2 The Quantum Bit, or "Qubit"

When creating conventional ICs, designers take great pains to minimize the effect of quantum phenomena, which typically manifest as noise or other errors that affect transistor performance, especially as devices get smaller and smaller. Quantum computing in all its forms takes a very different approach by embracing rather than trying to minimize quantum phenomena, using quantum rather than classical bits.

A quantum bit, or qubit, has two quantum states, analogous to the classical binary states. While the qubit can be in either state, it can also exist in a "superposition" of the two (as described earlier in the example of a quantum coin). These states are often represented in so-called Dirac notation, where the state's label is written between a | and a ⟩. Thus, a qubit's two component, or "basis," states are generally written as $|0\rangle$ and $|1\rangle$. Any given qubit wave function may be written as a linear combination of the two states, each with its own complex coefficient a_i: $|\psi\rangle = a_0|0\rangle + a_1|1\rangle$. Since the probability of reading a state is proportional to the square of its coefficient's magnitude, $|a_0|^2$ corresponds to the probability of detecting the state $|0\rangle$, and $|a_1|^2$ to the probability of detecting $|1\rangle$. The sum of the probabilities of each possible output state must be one hundred percent, mathematically expressed in this case as $|a_0|^2 + |a_1|^2 = 1$.

While a classical bit is entirely specified either as 1 or 0, a qubit is specified by the continuum of the values a_0 and a_1, which are actually analog—that is, the relative contribution from each possible state can be any value between zero and one, provided the total probability is one. Of course, this richness exists before the qubit's state is measured, or "read out." The result of a measurement looks just like a classical bit, a 0 or a 1, with the associated probability of getting each value proportional to the square of the absolute value of the coefficient of the corresponding state, $|a_0|^2$ or $|a_1|^2$. Furthermore, upon measurement, the qubit's coefficient (or amplitude) becomes one in the state that is read and zero in the other; all information about the amplitudes is destroyed upon measurement.[10] Measurement outcomes for a single qubit are listed in Table 2.2 and explained in more detail in Box 2.2.

---

[10] However, if one were to initialize a qubit in a specific state an arbitrary number of times, and measure it each time, one would be able to create a histogram of the number of times that a measurement yields each output, which would enable one to statistically approximate the relative probabilities associated with each state, and so infer the absolute value of the coefficient (equivalent to the square root of the calculated probability).

TABLE 2.2 Measurement Outcomes and Probabilities for a Single Qubit Given Its Initial State for Several Examples

Premeasurement State (Wave function) of Qubit	Measurement Outcome	Probability of Outcome	Postmeasurement State of Qubit
$\|\psi\rangle = \|0\rangle$	0	100%	$\|\psi\rangle = \|0\rangle$
$\|\psi\rangle = \|1\rangle$	1	100%	$\|\psi\rangle = \|1\rangle$
$\|\psi\rangle = \frac{1}{\sqrt{2}}\|0\rangle + \frac{1}{\sqrt{2}}\|1\rangle$	0	50%	$\|\psi\rangle = \|0\rangle$
	1	50%	$\|\psi\rangle = \|1\rangle$
$\|\psi\rangle = \frac{1}{2}\|0\rangle + \frac{\sqrt{3}}{2}\|1\rangle$	0	25%	$\|\psi\rangle = \|0\rangle$
	1	75%	$\|\psi\rangle = \|1\rangle$
$\|\psi\rangle = \frac{1}{2}\|0\rangle + \frac{\sqrt{3}e^{-i\pi/4}}{2}\|1\rangle$	0	25%	$\|\psi\rangle = \|0\rangle$
	1	75%	$\|\psi\rangle = \|1\rangle$

BOX 2.2
Measurement of a Single Qubit

When a qubit is in the state $|\psi\rangle = |0\rangle$, the result of measurement will be 0 with a probability of 100 percent, which is not unlike what happens with a classical bit. Similarly, measurement of a qubit in state $|\psi\rangle = |1\rangle$ will yield an outcome of 1 with a probability of 100 percent.

For a qubit in a superposition state, the outcome is less simple—the outcome of measurement, even of a known state, cannot be predicted with certainty. For example, the superposition state $|\psi\rangle = \frac{1}{\sqrt{2}}|0\rangle + \frac{1}{\sqrt{2}}|1\rangle$ has an equal probability (50 percent) of yielding either outcome (probability being the square of the amplitude, or ½). Repeated preparation and measurement of this state will yield a random sequence of outcomes approaching an equal incidence of each as the number of trials increases, as would a classical coin flip. Accordingly, this state can be thought of as a "quantum coin."

After measuring a certain value, the qubit is left in the state corresponding to that value. For example, if the outcome of measurement is 1, the postmeasurement qubit is in the state $|\psi\rangle = |1\rangle$, regardless of the state it was in prior to measurement.

2.3.3 Multiqubit Systems

Consider a system of two bits. Classically, two bits can exist in four possible configurations, 00, 01, 10, and 11. In order to compute the output of a two-bit Boolean function for each of these possible inputs using a classical circuit, one would need to generate each corresponding pair of signals, and either send each in turn into a gate corresponding to the function, or direct each signal into its own copy of four identical gates corresponding to the function of interest.

On the other hand, if one used a quantum computer, all four possibilities could be encoded into the state of the two qubits via superposition of the four quantum basis states $|00\rangle$, $|01\rangle$, $|10\rangle$, and $|11\rangle$. The computation could be executed using a single quantum gate, which would operate on all of the states in parallel, at the same time. It is easy to see why a multiqubit system might be powerful. However, as alluded to previously—and as the next two sections will show—extracting any corresponding value out of the quantum system is hard.

Another way to think about the potential power of a collection of qubits is to look at the amount of information needed to fully specify the state of the system of qubits. A conventional digital two-bit system requires two bits of information to represent its state. In contrast, a two-qubit system exists in a superposition of four states ($|00\rangle$, $|01\rangle$, $|10\rangle$, and $|11\rangle$), requiring four complex constants, (a_{00}, a_{01}, a_{10}, and a_{11}) to fully describe the quantum state, rather than two bits. Different values of the four coefficients encode the results of all possible types of previous operations done on these two qubits, as well as the probability of ending up in each state if the system is measured. For a three-qubit system, eight coefficients are required to specify to contributions from the basis states ($|000\rangle$, $|100\rangle$, $|010\rangle$, $|001\rangle$, $|110\rangle$, $|101\rangle$, $|011\rangle$, and $|111\rangle$) to the three-qubit wave function. Following this logic, an n-qubit system requires 2^n coefficients, a_i, to be specified, rather than n bits as in a classical computer. This exponential scaling of the quantum state is what allows 32 qubits to represent all 2^{32} possible outputs of a 32-bit function and illustrates the richness of a quantum computer, and the difficulties in modeling these machines classically as they increase in size.

This view also points out that, while qubits have "bit" in their name, they are neither digital nor purely binary. The state of a qubit system is encoded in the a_i coefficient values, a set of analog signals (actually complex numbers), which are not robust to noise. In a digital system with only two legitimate levels, say 0 and 1, it is easy to remove noise in the system, as the values will all be close to 0 or 1, with minor deviations. For example, an input signal value of 0.9 is almost certainly a 1, so a gate can "remove" the noise by treating this input value as a 1 before computing its output. In an analog signal, for which any value between 0 and 1 might be meaningful and allowed, there is no way to know whether the signal is correct or if it has been corrupted by noise. For example, 0.9 could mean 1 with some error, or it could mean 0.9 with no error. In this situation, the best guess (that results in the smallest net error) is always to assume the error is zero and to treat the noisy value as the actual signal. This means that noise in a physical implementation of a qubit system perturbs the actual a_i values and affects the "fidelity" of the resulting quantum computation. Quantum gates have no noise margins, since their inputs (the initial a_i values) and their outputs (the final a_i values) are analog values. Since no analog gate perfectly matches its specifications (it is impossible to be perfectly precise), each gate operation will also add noise to the overall system, in a quantity that depends on the precision of the gate operations.

Normally, this lack of noise immunity would mean that the "compute depth"—the number of sequential operations that can be performed accurately—of a quantum computer would be limited, as with any analog computer. However, quantum gates are not completely analog: measurement of a qubit always returns a binary value. This digital relationship between inputs and outputs means that logical error correction can be applied to quantum machines that use quantum gates as their basic operations. These algorithms are called quantum error correction (QEC) and can be run on a noisy, gate-based quantum computer to reduce errors and emulate a noiseless system. As with classical error correcting codes mentioned in Section 2.3.1, QEC must add redundancy, and in the quantum case this redundancy must be entangled with the rest of the system state, in order to recover from error. Unlike classical codes, which have small overheads, QEC codes tend to have very high overheads, and can increase the number of qubits required to execute an error-free computation by many orders of magnitude. QEC algorithms are described in more detail in Section 3.2.

2.4 COMPUTING WITH QUBITS

The analog nature of qubit states and quantum gates dramatically changes the necessary design approaches and circuit architectures for quantum computers. (See Figure 2.3.) In conventional computer design, the robustness of the digital signal and gates to noise make it easy to optimize the design for performance—that is, to maximize the number of operations that can be performed in parallel (at the same time). A single IC can contain hundreds of millions of gates placed in different locations. Each wire connects the output of a gate (a 1 or a 0) to the gates that use that electrical signal as an input. While manufacturing variations make each gate a little different, and the electrical signals on the wires can interact with and introduce systematic noise in each other, the noise immunity

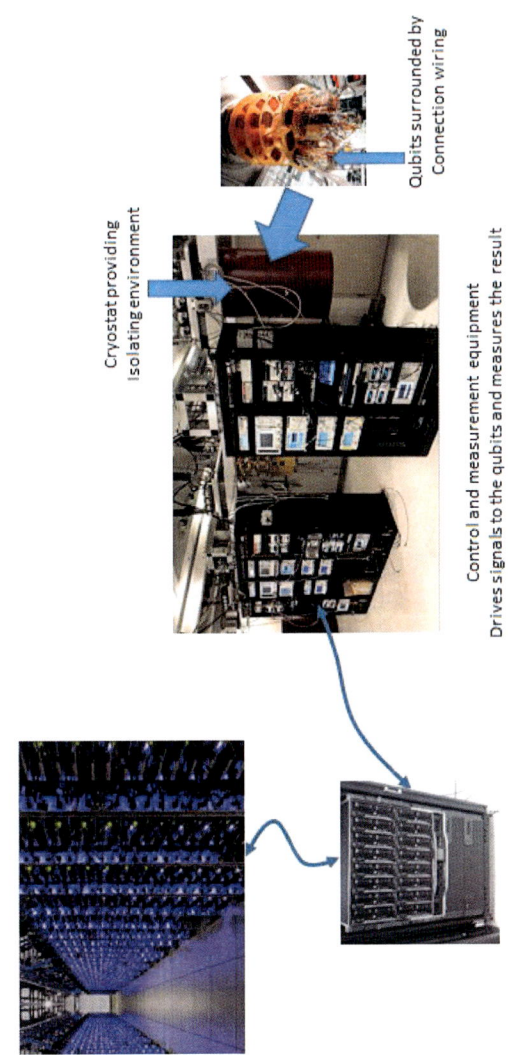

FIGURE 2.3 The basic parts needed to create and run a quantum computer, using parts of a contemporary superconducting qubit system as an example. The qubit chip is placed in a large structure that allows it to be cooled to 20 mK (image is from the Google effort), while supporting the needed control wiring. This large structure is then put into a cryostat, which cools the qubit chip. The control wires are then connected to a set of test and measurement equipment (equipment is from Will Oliver's Lab), which drives the qubits. This test equipment is driven from a control processor layer, which may consist of multiple processors in the case of a large quantum computer. The control processor is connected to a larger computer server (shown is part of a Google data center), which provides user access to the quantum computer, and the needed software support services.

of the digital gates used is sufficient to negate the effect of all these noise sources. Thus, even with the parallel operation of millions of gates, the resulting system behaves as intended, producing the same output as the Boolean model of the design.

Because quantum signals are analog and sensitive to noise, an entirely different approach is used in the design of quantum systems. Here, the key design goal is to minimize the introduction of noise into the qubit, which precludes sending the qubit state through noisy channels, such as a long wire.[11] Thus, these systems generally focus on building qubits, or containers for the qubits, along with the associated support circuitry required to do various operations on the qubits' states, including entangling qubits with other qubits in the same vicinity. In quantum systems, the operations (gates) tend to come to the qubits, while in classical machines, the bits go to the gates.

In addition to this difference in architecture, since quantum computers operate on different types of values than classical computers, they cannot use the same logical gate abstractions that were developed to manipulate classical bits. New abstractions for computations using qubits are required, providing a way to implement specified changes in quantum states. As with all quantum systems, the state of a qubit can be changed by changing its energy environment, which is the physical manifestation of its Hamiltonian.

There are two main approaches to quantum computing. The first generates the desired result by initializing the state of a quantum system and then using direct control of the Hamiltonian to evolve the quantum state in a way that has a high probability of answering the question of interest. In these systems, the Hamiltonian is often smoothly changed, so the quantum operations are truly analog in nature and cannot be fully error corrected,[12] and will be referred to as "analog quantum computing." This approach includes adiabatic quantum computing (AQC), quantum annealing (QA), and direct quantum simulation. The second approach, called "gate-based quantum computing," is similar to today's classical approaches, in that the problem is broken down into a sequence of a few very basic "primitive operations," or gates, which have well-defined "digital" measurement outcomes for certain input states. This digital property means that these type of designs can in principle use system-level error

---

[11] Qubits also must obey a no-cloning rule, which also precludes sending a qubit state to two different gates at the same time. This will be discussed further in Section 2.5.

[12] While methods for reducing the effects of noise have been developed and deployed for analog QCs, a theory for analog QC QEC has been proposed only for AQC; this is not expected to be easily achieved, and full error correction would require boundless resources. Thus, no practical method of achieving an error-free machine has been established for analog QCs. These issues are addressed further in Section 3.2.

correction to achieve fault tolerance. However, as noted above, the set of primitive quantum operations are distinct from classical primitives.

2.4.1 Quantum Simulation, Quantum Annealing, and Adiabatic Quantum Computation

Analog quantum computing involves a system of qubits in an initial quantum state, and changes to the Hamiltonian such that the problem is encoded in the final Hamiltonian and the final state corresponds to the answer. If the system remains in the ground state of the changing Hamiltonian, this approach is referred to as adiabatic quantum computing (AQC). When this requirement is relaxed—for example, if the quantum computer is also allowed to interact with a thermal environment, or if it is allowed to evolve too quickly—this protocol is called "quantum annealing." For a sufficiently complex choice of Hamiltonians, AQC is formally equivalent in computational power to the gate-based quantum computing model. For existing quantum annealing devices, the choice of Hamiltonians is limited, and these devices are not formally equivalent to universal quantum computers. Direct quantum simulation is where the Hamiltonian between qubits is set to model a quantum system of interest, so its evolution simulates that system.

As mentioned above, in these analog quantum computing approaches, not only are the values of the qubits analog but also the quantum operations are done by smoothly changing the Hamiltonian. This nondiscrete set of quantum operators confounds conventional approaches to system level error correction. While a model for QEC has been proposed for AQCs in particular [2], it would be challenging to implement in practice, since removing all errors would require unbounded resources. As a result, one tries to minimize the effect of noise in such systems via quantum error and noise suppression [3].

Decoherence plays a very different role in digital quantum computers and analog quantum computers. In digital quantum computers, decoherence is rarely desirable.[13] In the case of an analog quantum computer—and, in particular, a quantum annealer—decoherence plays a more subtle role. On the one hand, energy relaxation (dissipation) is desirable, because it enables the system to find the ground state, as required for the method to yield correct outputs. For larger-scale problems, an annealer will almost certainly leave its ground state during the annealing protocol, either as a result of changing the Hamiltonian too quickly, or due to thermal excitation from the environment. In these cases, dissipation to the environment is clearly advantageous, as it tends to bring the annealer back to its

---

[13] Except possibly during state preparation and projective measurement.

ground state. However, if there is too much dissipation, the system will no longer behave quantum mechanically and thus cease to be a quantum computer. Furthermore, phase coherence is also required for "coherent co-tunneling," a quantum process that enables more efficient relaxation to the ground state through coordinated flipping of qubits. In practice, a balance must be achieved in order for annealers to be effective. Analog quantum computing is discussed in more detail in Chapters 3 and 5.

2.4.2 Gate-Based Quantum Computing

In a gate-based approach to quantum computing, each primitive operation (gate) is performed by precisely changing the Hamiltonian of one or more qubits for the specific amount of time required to achieve the desired transformation. This is done by changing the physical environment, for example, via a laser pulse or application of some other electromagnetic field, depending on the way in which the qubits are built.[14] Since these primitive operations are analogous to logic gates in classical computing, systems built using this approach are called "digital quantum computers."

The rules of quantum mechanics constrain the set of possible quantum gate operations in a few interesting ways. First, the operations must be "lossless"—that is, they must not dissipate any energy, since energy dissipation means that the system is connected to the environment to allow heat to flow out, which would result in unacceptable decoherence. Since losing information dissipates energy [4], quantum gates must be reversible, which means that not only can you compute the gate's outputs from its inputs, you can also compute the gate's inputs from its outputs (the gate's computation can be run backward, or reversed). To be reversible, a function must always have as many outputs as it had inputs.

Second, while the operations will change the coefficients, or "amplitude distribution," of the different possible states, the sum of the squares of their absolute values (the sum of their probabilities) always remains one. One mathematical way to visualize the operations of quantum gates is to represent the state of 'n' qubits as a vector in a high dimensional space (2^n complex dimensions), where the value of the vector in each dimension is given by the complex coefficients a_i. Conserving probability forces the length of the vector to be constant and equal to 1, so the state of the system can be any place on the unit hypersphere (the extension of a sphere to higher dimensions). All quantum gates are simple rotations of the state vector to a new position on the hypersphere. As the number

---

[14] See Chapter 5 for further discussion of current approaches to physical implementations of qubits.

of qubits increases, the dimension of the space grows exponentially, but the state vector remains unit length, and the operations remain the different rotations possible on the hypersphere (which are all reversible). Operations that preserve the vector length are said to be "unitary." Box 2.3 shows the sphere generated by a single qubit.

As with classical logic, gates with a large number of inputs are hard to create, but can be constructed, or "synthesized," using a series of simpler gates, each of which takes a smaller number of inputs. In practice, quantum gates typically designed to operate on inputs of one, two, or three qubits. Also like classical logic, a small number of base quantum gates can be used to create all possible quantum gate functions. A common set of basic quantum gates and their representations is shown in Figure 2.4. Of particular significance is the Hadamard gate for superposition, which evolves a qubit in the $|0\rangle$ state to an equal superposition of $|0\rangle$ and $|1\rangle$, where both have the same relative phase ($\frac{1}{\sqrt{2}}|0\rangle + \frac{1}{\sqrt{2}}|1\rangle$), and evolves the $|1\rangle$ state to an even superposition of $|0\rangle$ and $|1\rangle$, but with opposite phases ($\frac{1}{\sqrt{2}}|0\rangle - \frac{1}{\sqrt{2}}|1\rangle$). The two-qubit CNOT gate performs an XOR logic operation, but it must pass one of the inputs to the output to make the computation reversible.

Because quantum gates map initial a_is of a set of input qubits into a new set of a_is, these gates are often written mathematically in the form of a matrix. In this representation, the a_i for each of the input states are stacked on top of each other to form a vector, and the result of the matrix vector multiplication results in a vector which represents the a_is of the output state. An n-input logic operation, or "gate," can be described mathematically as a $2^n \times 2^n$ unitary matrix that operates on n input qubits (encoding the initial 2^n a_is) producing n output qubits (encoding the 2^n new a_is).

It is known that the gates T, Hadamard, and CNOT, where T is a rotation by $\pi/4$ (90 degrees), forms a universal gate set [5] (that is, any unitary function can be approximated to arbitrary precision using a computer built from only gates in this set) [6].[15]

Unlike unitary operations that are the basis for implementing a quantum algorithm, the measurement operation strongly couples the quantum state to the measurement device, which produces a binary output and is

---

[15] For rotation of a general angle θ, single-qubit rotations cannot be expressed exactly in this gate set; thus, it is necessary to decompose the desired operation into a sequence of operations. Such "decomposition" of a given operation into a sequence of simple gates also enables a general circuit to be compiled as a sequence of simpler primitive gates that can more easily be implemented in hardware. It is worth noting that known algorithms for some applications, for example in computational chemistry, rely heavily upon general angle rotations; for these cases in particular, it is thus very important to have methods which can create, or synthesize, these operations using a small number of primitive gate operations. Better synthesis algorithms generate the target gates from fewer primitive gates.

BOX 2.3
Visualizing the State of a Qubit

The state of a single qubit is represented by $|\psi\rangle = a_0|0\rangle + a_1|1\rangle$. The probability condition $|a_0|^2 + |a_1|^2 = 1$ restricts the values that a_0 and a_1 can take. We can account for this constraint by setting the magnitude of a_0 to $\cos\frac{\theta}{2}$ and the magnitude of a_1 to $\sin\frac{\theta}{2}$, since $(\sin\frac{\theta}{2})^2 + (\cos\frac{\theta}{2})^2 = 1$. Accounting for the phase component of a complex number means $a_0 = e^{i\alpha}\cos\frac{\theta}{2}$ and $a_1 = e^{i(\alpha+\varphi)}\sin\frac{\theta}{2}$. As a result, the state of the qubit can be represented using three independent real numbers α, θ, and φ: $|\psi\rangle = e^{i\alpha}(\cos\frac{\theta}{2}|0\rangle + e^{i\varphi}(\sin\frac{\theta}{2}|1\rangle)$. It turns out that the global phase α has no physical significance whatsoever, and a single-qubit state can be fully described by two real numbers $0 \leq \theta < \pi$ and $0 \leq \varphi < 2\pi$. The description of an arbitrary single-qubit state can be mapped onto a point on the surface of a unit sphere (called a "Bloch sphere"), where the north and south pole correspond to the states $|0\rangle$ and $|1\rangle$, respectively. θ gives the latitude and φ gives the longitude of the positive of the quantum state on the Bloch sphere, as shown in Figure 2.3.1.

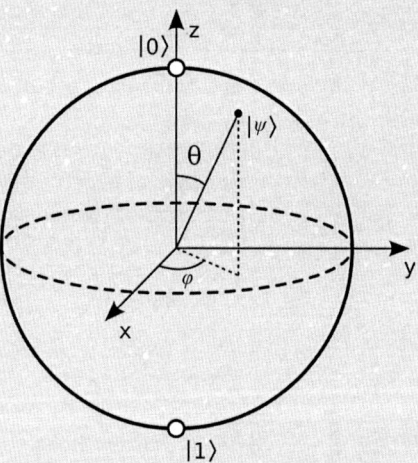

FIGURE 2.3.1 A picture of the Bloch sphere, which represents the set of all possible states for a single qubit. The qubit angles θ and φ are shown in the figure. Single-qubit gates rotate the qubit state to another point on this sphere. SOURCE: Smite-Meister, https://commons.wikimedia.org/w/index.php?curid=5829358.

Gate name	# Qubits	Circuit Symbol	Unitary Matrix	Description
Hadamard	1	—[H]—	$\frac{1}{\sqrt{2}}\begin{bmatrix} 1 & 1 \\ 1 & -1 \end{bmatrix}$	Transforms a basis state into an even superposition of the two basis states.
T	1	—[T]—	$\begin{bmatrix} 1 & 0 \\ 0 & e^{i\pi/4} \end{bmatrix}$	Adds a relative phase shift of $\pi/4$ between contributing basis states. Sometimes called a $\pi/8$ gate, because diagonal elements can be written as $e^{-i\pi/8}$ and $e^{i\pi/8}$.
CNOT	2		$\begin{bmatrix} 1 & 0 & 0 & 0 \\ 0 & 1 & 0 & 0 \\ 0 & 0 & 0 & 1 \\ 0 & 0 & 1 & 0 \end{bmatrix}$	Controlled-not; reversible analogue to classical XOR gate. The input connected to the solid dot is passed through to make the operation reversible.
Toffoli (CCNOT)	3		$\begin{bmatrix} 1 & 0 & 0 & 0 & 0 & 0 & 0 & 0 \\ 0 & 1 & 0 & 0 & 0 & 0 & 0 & 0 \\ 0 & 0 & 1 & 0 & 0 & 0 & 0 & 0 \\ 0 & 0 & 0 & 1 & 0 & 0 & 0 & 0 \\ 0 & 0 & 0 & 0 & 1 & 0 & 0 & 0 \\ 0 & 0 & 0 & 0 & 0 & 1 & 0 & 0 \\ 0 & 0 & 0 & 0 & 0 & 0 & 0 & 1 \\ 0 & 0 & 0 & 0 & 0 & 0 & 1 & 0 \end{bmatrix}$	Controlled-controlled-not; a three-qubit gate that switches the third bit for states where the first two bits are 1 (that is, switches $\|110\rangle$ to $\|111\rangle$ and vice versa).
Pauli-Z	1	—[Z]—	$\begin{bmatrix} 1 & 0 \\ 0 & -1 \end{bmatrix}$	Adds a relative phase shift of π between contributing basis states. Maps $\|0\rangle$ to itself and $\|1\rangle$ to $-\|1\rangle$. Sometimes called a "phase flip."
Z-Rotation	1	—[$R_z(\theta)$]—	$\begin{bmatrix} e^{-i\theta/2} & 0 \\ 0 & e^{i\theta/2} \end{bmatrix}$	Adds a relative phase shift of (or rotates state vector about z-axis by) θ.
NOT	1		$\begin{bmatrix} 0 & 1 \\ 1 & 0 \end{bmatrix}$	Analogous to classical NOT gate; switches $\|0\rangle$ to $\|1\rangle$ and vice versa.

FIGURE 2.4 Commonly used 1-, 2-, and 3-qubit quantum gates, along with their corresponding unitary matrices, circuit symbols, and a description of their effects. The T, Hadamard, and CNOT gates are known to form a universal quantum gate set. SOURCE: Adapted from M. Roetteler and K.M. Svore, 2018, Quantum computing: Codebreaking and beyond, *IEEE Security & Privacy* 16(5):22-36.

not reversible. Measurement is necessary in order to extract information from the quantum computer; however, measurement collapses the system wave function and returns only n bits of information from the n-qubit quantum register, that is, it returns one classical result. The information that was held in the a_is of the 2^n states that the register encoded up until the instant of measurement is lost. The outputs of measurement of a two-qubit system are illustrated in Table 2.3 and discussed in Box 2.4 [7].

2.5 QUANTUM COMPUTER DESIGN CONSTRAINTS

As alluded to in previous sections, the large potential power of a quantum computer comes with four major constraints. The first major constraint is that the number of coefficients required to describe a state of a quantum computer increases exponentially with the number of qubits only when the qubits all become entangled with each other. While adding a qubit to a system does double the number of quantum states, if this qubit has not interacted with the rest of the system, the description of the quantum state can be factored and represented as the product of the added qubit's state, times the state of the rest of the system. This factored state requires only two additional coefficients (the state of the added qubit) compared to the original quantum system. To get the power of quantum computing, qubits must be entangled—that is, the state of any qubit must be correlated with the states of the other qubits. To form such a dependence between two qubits, they need to interact either directly or indirectly via an intermediate quantum system—whether a photon, phonon, or another qubit—which at some point interacts with each qubit to be entangled.[16]

Even though the generation of direct interaction between qubits that are physically separated (that is, nonadjacent) inside the quantum processor, like complex gates, can be hard to achieve,[17] it can be decomposed into a number of simpler primitive gate operations directly supported by the hardware. This indirect coupling can be performed through a chain

---

[16] If qubit A is entangled with qubit B, and at some later time qubit B becomes entangled with qubit C, it is likely that qubit A is now also entangled with qubit C. To see this, assume all qubits start in the |0> state, and qubit A is then operated on by a Hadamard gate. It is the control input to a CNOT gate for qubit B, and qubit B is then the control terminal for qubit C. Measurement of A, B, or C will give zero 50 percent of the time, and one 50 percent of the time. But once one of the qubits is measured, the state of the other qubits will be known with 100 percent probability.

[17] To prevent the qubit energy from coupling with the environment, it is held in localized, well-isolated spots. Distributing the energy over a wide area for two qubits to interact would also expose those qubits to a lot of environment, which in today's technologies greatly shortens the coherence time.

TABLE 2.3 Measurement Outcomes and Probabilities for Some Possible States of a Two-Qubit System, Given Its Initial State

Premeasurement State (Wave Function) of System	Measurement Outcome	Probability of Outcome	Postmeasurement State of System
$|\psi\rangle = |00\rangle$	00	100%	$|\psi\rangle = |00\rangle$
$|\psi\rangle = |01\rangle$	01	100%	$|\psi\rangle = |01\rangle$
$|\psi\rangle = \frac{1}{\sqrt{2}}|00\rangle + \frac{1}{\sqrt{2}}|11\rangle$	00	50%	$|\psi\rangle = |00\rangle$
	11	50%	$|\psi\rangle = |11\rangle$
$|\psi\rangle = \frac{1}{2}|00\rangle + \frac{1}{2}|10\rangle + \frac{1}{2}|01\rangle + \frac{1}{2}|11\rangle$	00	25%	$|\psi\rangle = |00\rangle$
	10	25%	$|\psi\rangle = |10\rangle$
	01	25%	$|\psi\rangle = |01\rangle$
	11	25%	$|\psi\rangle = |11\rangle$
$|\psi\rangle = \frac{1}{2}|01\rangle + \frac{\sqrt{3}}{2}|10\rangle$	01	25%	$|\psi\rangle = |01\rangle$
	10	75%	$|\psi\rangle = |10\rangle$

> **BOX 2.4**
> **Measurement and Entanglement in a Two-Qubit System**
>
> Wave functions for multiqubit systems are constructed as linear combinations of all possible classical states, which serve as so-called basis states, in the language of linear algebra. There are four possible classical states for a two-bit system, so the wave function for a two-qubit system has the general form
>
> $$|\psi_{ij}\rangle = a_{00}|00\rangle + a_{01}|01\rangle + a_{10}|10\rangle + a_{11}|11\rangle,$$
>
> where the magnitude squared of a state's coefficient corresponds to its probability of measurement.
>
> Consider the state where only a_{00} is nonzero, $|\psi\rangle = |00\rangle$. Measuring the first particle yields 0 with 100 percent certainty, and the same with the second particle. In this case, each qubit can be described independently by its own wave function: $|\psi_i\rangle = |0\rangle_i$ and $|\psi_j\rangle = |0\rangle_j$. The whole system can be written as the product of the individual qubits $|\psi\rangle = |\psi_i\rangle \cdot |\psi_j\rangle = |0\rangle_i |0\rangle_j$, which is the same as writing $|\psi_{ij}\rangle = |00\rangle$.
>
> Now consider the superposition state $|\psi_{ij}\rangle = \frac{1}{\sqrt{2}}|00\rangle + \frac{1}{\sqrt{2}}|11\rangle$. What happens if the first qubit is measured? If the outcome is 1, the wave function collapses into a combination of only those states with this value for the first qubit, or $|\psi_{ij}\rangle = |11\rangle$. Subsequently, the second qubit has a 100 percent probability of being found in the same state. On the other hand, measuring the first qubit as 0 guarantees that the second one will be as well, according to the same logic. Further inspection will reveal that, regardless of which qubit is measured first, measuring the second will always yield the same value that was observed for the first. The particles are inextricably correlated in that the state of one is dependent upon the other, and measurement of one intrinsically determines the state of the other—whether or not the second is measured. This condition is called "entanglement," and is inherently quantum mechanical. In mathematical terms, entanglement arises when there is no way to write the multiqubit wave function as the product of one-qubit wave functions. This particular state is an example of a "Bell state," a specific category of entangled state. Entangled states are inherently quantum mechanical and are key to the power of quantum computation.

of operations, using intermediate qubits or other quantum systems to facilitate the interaction. However, as in classical computing this indirect coupling creates an overhead in the machine, the first major design constraint. This cost of communication is well understood in classical computing and contributes to the very high gate counts in modern machines. In many quantum computing implementations, generating this long-range interaction will consume some of the qubits in the machine, and the number of useful qubits will be less than the number of physical qubits in the machine. This need to break down long-range interactions also means that some of the two-qubit operations taken from the universal gate set will take multiple primitive gate operations to perform. These overheads are most significant in the early stages of a technology's development when qubits and gate operations are limited.

A second constraint comes from the fact that it is impossible to make a copy of a quantum system, because of the so-called no-cloning principle [8,9]. While the state of a set of qubits can be moved to another set of qubits, this has the effect of deleting that information from the original qubits; arbitrary quantum information may be moved but not copied. Since making and storing copies of intermediate states or partial results in memory is an essential part of classical computing and the way we think about programming, quantum computers require a different approach to algorithm design. Also, computing tasks often require the ability to access stored data, and many quantum algorithms require a means to access stored classical bits in a way that reveals which bits are being queried and loaded into quantum memory.

The third main constraint comes from the lack of noise immunity of quantum operations. Since small imperfections in the input signals or gate operations are not removed by the basic gate operations, as they are in classical logic gates, these small errors will accumulate over time, perturbing the system's state. These errors affect the accuracy of the calculation, and, when large enough, can lead to measurement errors, or even a loss of quantum coherence (and thus loss of any quantum advantage). This noise comes from imperfect isolation from the environment, uncorrected variations in physical preparation or manufacture of the qubits themselves (or the devices that contain or maintain them), and imperfections in the signals used to perform the desired qubit operations. Taken together, these imperfections generally degrade the quality of a qubit operation. These effects are still significant even when using strategies to minimize and avoid noise that leads to errors.

The quality of a gate operation is measured either by the error rate, defined by the probability that the gate operation yields an incorrect outcome, or by the fidelity, the probability that the operation yields the correct outcome (Box 2.5). For state-of-the-art systems in 2018, the best error rates are in the 10^{-3} to 10^{-6} range for single qubit gates [10-13] and in the 10^{-2} to 10^{-3} range for two qubit (entangling) gates [14-17] in superconducting and trapped ion qubits. In current machines, this quality degrades as the number of qubits in the machine increases; the capabilities of today's systems are discussed in more detail in Chapter 5.

The final constraint is the inability to actually observe the full state of the machine after it has completed its operation. For example, if the quantum computer initializes a set of qubits into a superposition of all qubit-state combinations, and then applies a function to this input state, the resulting quantum state will have information about the value of

> **BOX 2.5**
> **Defining and Quantifying Qubit Fidelity/Error Rates**
>
> Quantum computers require high qubit and gate fidelity for successful operation. This report will use gate error rates as a measure of the qubit fidelity of a computer. Gate error rate is a metric that characterizes the robustness of a gate operation subject to a broad set of error sources. Essentially, it is a measure of how closely actual gate operations match—on average—theoretically ideal versions of those operations. A gate error rate of 1 percent indicates that a given type of gate operation will yield the correct result upon measurement, on average, 99 out of 100 times it is tried.
>
> These errors arise from a number of different mechanisms that add "noise" to the qubit. One source of noise is the loss of qubit coherence, and since qubit state consists of both a magnitude and phase, "noise" can affect both aspects of qubit state. It is impossible to completely isolate any system from its environment, so over time the energy of the qubit will tend to equilibrate with the environment—excited states will lose energy and become the ground state if the environment is cold. This means that the probability (magnitude of the amplitude of the excited state squared) of the excited state decreases over time. Physical processes also add random phase shifts to the quantum state over time, which reduces the phase coherence of the qubit states. Since quantum operations require phase alignment for proper operation, this phase decoherence also leads to qubit errors over time. For simple noise, energy relaxation and phase decoherence proceed via exponential decays, with time constants referred to as T_1 and T_2, respectively. Since energy relaxation is also a phase-breaking process, the coherence time T_2 captures both energy relaxation and dephasing processes, and T_2 must be much longer than the time needed to implement a required number of quantum gates to create a useful quantum computer.
>
> In addition to the fundamental qubit coherence errors, given the analog control signals used to perform qubit gate operations, each gate operation is not perfect, and

the function for each possible input value. Yet measuring this quantum system directly will not yield this information. Instead, since all the input cases were equally likely, the measurement will return only one of the 2^n possible outputs. The key to a successful quantum algorithm is to manipulate the system so the states that correspond to the sought-after solution have much higher probability of being measured than any other possible output. This condition is intrinsic to quantum algorithm primitives such as the quantum Fourier transform and amplitude amplification, which are described in more detail in Chapter 3. These operations amplify the coefficient of the state whose index indicates the answer sought, such that the meaningful answer is highly likely to be observed in the readout measurement; however, they can require a nontrivial amount of time, reducing the overall speedup of the quantum algorithm.

The characteristics of quantum phenomena both provide a QC's computational power, and greatly constrain how it can be used.

performing this operation can affect other qubit states in the system (this interference is called "crosstalk"). This means that in a sequence of gate operations, there is a chance that the output generated is incorrect, and that these operations increase the error rate for future operations. The probability of generating the correct result (correctly performing all the gate operations to create the result) again decreases exponentially with the number of gate operations. Thus, from the measured system error rate, one can extract an average error rate per gate. Two-input qubit gates are more complex than single-qubit operations, since the state of the two qubits must interact in this operation, yielding higher error rates; error rates for both single- and two-qubit gates are often provided for a more complete picture. When error rates are used as the gate fidelity metric, this rate accounts for the decoherence that occurs during the gate time, and any other errors caused by the gate operation.

Given that the user of a quantum computer is interested in estimating the fidelity of the results, extracting effective gate error rates using the process of randomized benchmarking (RBM) is of great value. In general, RBM implements a random assortment of gates and compares the resulting state with the predicted state for that sequence. The error in the final state increases as the length of the sequence increases, with the rate of increase in error per gate providing a measure of an error rate for the selected group of gates. Interleaved RBM aims to characterize the error rate of a specific gate by injecting this gate periodically in the random assortment and comparing the resulting error with the same assortment minus the specific gate of interest. RBM and its variations provide a relatively efficient means to estimate the average gate error rates in a particular device. These estimates are not skewed by the presence of any initialization and measurement errors and are the basis for establishing the proposed metric 1 in Chapter 7. However, it should be noted that RBM provides a device's net error rate, without revealing specific error channels.

2.6 THE POTENTIAL FOR FUNCTIONAL QUANTUM COMPUTERS

As previously noted, computation built upon quantum rather than classical interactions presents the opportunity for a new type of computing machine. It has the potential to address some computational problems that are currently intractable on even the most powerful supercomputers today, and on any future classical computer. For example, in addition to excitement for potential cryptanalytic applications, there is much interest in applications involving the simulation of quantum systems of relevance for chemistry, materials science, and biology, in particular with potential applications to new materials development.

Experimentalists around the world are working to develop both gate-based and analog computers that could carry out useful computations, using a range of underlying qubit technologies. The rest of this report will discuss progress that has been made to devise useful applications for these machines, and to create the hardware and software platforms needed to create a quantum computer. Because quantum computing devices are generally at early stages, and because the capabilities of devices will depend upon their type and maturity levels, it is useful to define several different categories of quantum computers for easy reference and comparison, as outlined below:

- *Analog quantum computer (quantum annealer, adiabatic QC, direct quantum simulation)*. Such a system would operate through coherent manipulation of qubits, by changing the analog values of the system's Hamiltonian, without using quantum gates. For example, computation on a "quantum annealer" is conducted by preparing a set of qubits in some initial state, and slowly changing the energy they experience until the Hamiltonian defines the parameters of a given problem, so that the final state of the qubits corresponds, with a high probability, to the answer of the problem. An "adiabatic quantum computer" (AQC) operates by initializing the qubits into the ground state of the starting Hamiltonian, and then changing the Hamiltonian slowly enough that the system remains in its lowest-energy, or ground state throughout the process. An AQC, although not gate-based, has the same theoretical processing power as a gate-based quantum computer, but does not have a practical means for full error correction.
- *Noisy intermediate-scale quantum (NISQ) gate-based computer* [18]. Such a system would operate through gate-based operations on a coherent collection of qubits without the full quantum error correction required to suppress all errors; calculations would need to be designed to be feasible on quantum systems with some noise, and be completed in few enough steps (a shallow enough logical depth) such that gate errors and decoherence of the qubits don't obscure the results. The report will also refer to these systems as "digital NISQ" computers.
- *Fully error-corrected gate-based quantum computers*. Such a system would operate through gate-based operations on qubits, implementing quantum error correction to correct any system noise (including errors introduced by imperfect control signals or device fabrication, or unintended coupling of qubits to each other or to the environment) that occurs during the time frame of the calculation. In such systems, the error probability rates are reduced so significantly that the machine appears reliable for all computations. The design of these machines should allow them

to scale to hold thousands of these fully error corrected or logical qubits.

Gate-based quantum computers can have many physical realizations. However, any realizations must satisfy the celebrated DiVincenzo criteria, which stipulate that they have the following [19]:

1. Well-characterized quantum two-level systems that can be employed as qubits.
2. An ability to initialize the qubits.
3. Decoherence times that are long enough to be able to carry out the computation or error correction.
4. A set of quantum operations on the qubits, known as "quantum gates," that is universal for quantum computation.
5. An ability to measure quantum bits one by one, without disturbing the others.

Quantum annealers need all of the above except for item 4, since they do not use gates to express their algorithms. However, decoherence (item 3) plays a very different role in quantum annealing than in the gate model—in particular, some decoherence is tolerable in quantum annealing [20,21], and some amount of energy relaxation is necessary for quantum annealing to succeed [22,23]. To date, progress has been made toward building analog quantum and digital NISQ computer systems, while fully error-corrected systems are much more challenging.

In order to build a functional quantum computer, one must create a physical system that encodes qubits and control and manipulate these qubits precisely in order to carry out computations. Today, experimentalists are building and operating these systems in carefully controlled environments in laboratories. Two leading technologies for quantum computing—trapped ions and superconducting qubits—use very different strategies for embodying and operating on qubits. Trapped ion systems use two internal states of an atom as their fundamental quantum element. The atoms are each stripped of an outer electron, leaving them positively charged so that their positions can be controlled with electric fields in devices called "ion traps." Both the ions and the traps are contained in ultra-high vacuum chambers to minimize interaction with the environment, and lasers are used to cool the motion of the ions down to very low temperatures (0.1-1 mK). Although the ion traps typically operate at room temperature, they can also be cooled to cryogenic temperatures (4-10 K) to improve the vacuum environment or reduce the impact of intrinsic electrical noise on the ion's motion. The state of each ion can be changed by using precisely controlled laser pulses or microwave radiation. These pulses can be arranged to couple the states of two or more ions together to create entanglement between the ions. An example of a laboratory apparatus containing an ion trap system and control units is provided in Figure 2.5.

Superconducting systems are built using a very different approach. Instead of using a natural quantum system, this approach uses the unique properties of superconducting materials to create a circuit that acts as an artificial atom.[18] Since this circuit can be defined lithographically like an integrated circuit, it is possible to build arrays of these artificial atoms using a process similar to that used for manufacturing ICs. Microwave radiation is again used to manipulate the state of these "atoms," and adjacent "atoms" can be electronically coupled together to create entangled

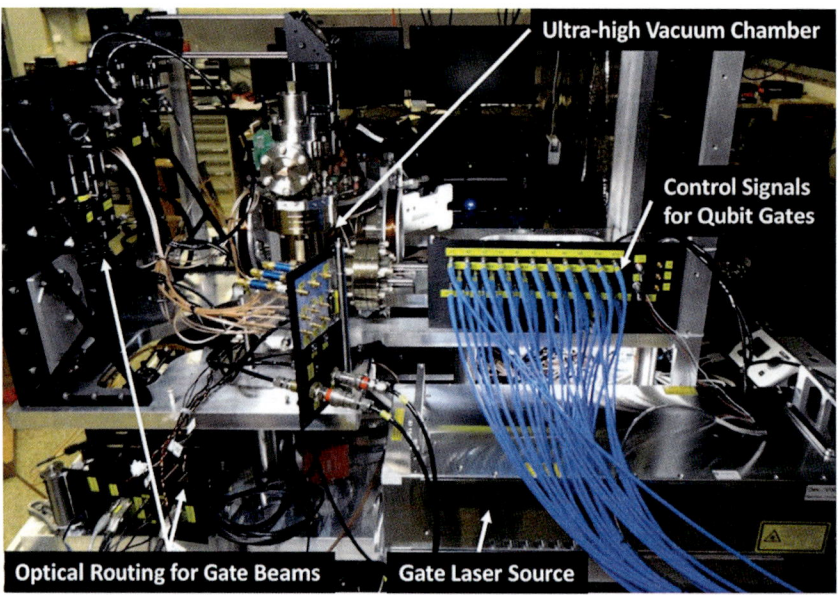

FIGURE 2.5 Laboratory apparatus for a contemporary ion trap system, operating at room temperature. The trapped ion qubits are housed inside the ultra-high vacuum chamber. The quantum logic gates on the qubits are carried out using the laser beams from the gate laser source, which is modulated by the control signals (RF signals delivered through the blue cables) and routed to the ions with the optical setup in the system. SOURCE: Courtesy of Professor Christopher Monroe, University of Maryland.

---

[18] This circuit essentially is a nonlinear oscillator, which means that, like an atom, it supports different energy states, and the separation between the energy states changes with energy level, so that the gap between the states of interest is unique, and the states of interest can be interrogated exclusively.

FIGURE 2.6 Laboratory apparatus for a contemporary superconducting qubit system. SOURCE: Courtesy of Dr. William Oliver, Lincoln Laboratory.

states. Unfortunately, the energy levels in these circuits are still very small, and these circuits are always in contact with the material that they are built on. Isolating these circuits therefore requires cooling them to approximately 10 mK. Figure 2.6 provides a snapshot of an experimental superconducting quantum computer in a laboratory, including some of the apparatus required to maintain the temperature of the qubit environment and control the quantum system.

Interest in quantum computing has increased as the coherence times and fidelity of quantum operations have improved for the underlying quantum systems. Chapters 3 and 4 describe the potential capabilities of a quantum computer. Chapters 5 and 6 explore in greater depth the hardware and software technologies for building quantum computers, along with the coherence and fidelity levels that have so far been achieved.

2.7 NOTES

[1] J. Preskill, 2018, "Quantum Computing in the NISQ Era and Beyond," arXiv:1801.00862.
[2] See, for example, K.C. Young, M. Sarovar, and R. Blume-Kohout, 2013, Error suppression and error correction in adiabatic quantum computation: Techniques and challenges, *Physical Review X* 3:041013;

A. Mizel, 2014, "Fault-Tolerant, Universal Adiabatic Quantum Computation," https://arxiv.org/abs/1403.7694;

S.P. Jordan, E. Farhi, and P.W. Shor, 2006, Error-correcting codes for adiabatic quantum computation, *Physical Review A* 74:052322; K.L. Pudenz, T. Albash and D.A. Lidar, 2014, Error-corrected quantum annealing with hundreds of qubits, *Nature Communications* 5:324;

W. Vinci, T. Albash and D.A. Lidar, Nested quantum annealing correction, 2016, *npj Quantum Information* 2:16017.

[3] See, for example, A.D. Bookatz, E. Farhi, and L. Zhou, 2015, Error suppression in Hamiltonian-based quantum computation using energy penalties, *Physical Review A* 92:022317;

M. Marvian and D.A. Lidar, 2017, Error suppression for Hamiltonian-based quantum computation using subsystem codes, *Physical Review Letters* 118:030504.

[4] R. Landauer, 1961, Irreversibility and heat generation in the computing process, *IBM Journal of Research and Development* 5(3):183-191.

[5] M. Nielsen and I. Chuang, 2016, *Quantum Computation and Quantum Information*, Cambridge University Press, p. 189.

[6] M. Roetteler and K.M. Svore, 2018, Quantum computing: Codebreaking and beyond, *IEEE Security and Privacy* 16:(5):22-36.

[7] Ibid.

[8] W.K. Wootters and W.H. Zurek, 1982, A single quantum cannot be cloned, *Nature* 299(5886):802-803.

[9] D. Dieks, 1982, Communication by EPR devices, *Physics Letters* 92A(6):271-272.

[10] T.P. Harty, D.T.C. Allcock, C.J. Ballance, L. Guidoni, H.A. Janacek, N.M. Linke, D.N. Stacey, and D.M. Lucas, 2014, High-fidelity preparation, gates, memory, and readout of a trapped-ion quantum bit, *Physical Review Letters* 113:220501.

[11] R. Blume-Kohout, J.K. Gamble, E. Nielsen, K. Rudinger, J. Mizrahi, K. Fortier, and P. Maunz, 2017, Demonstration of qubit operations below a rigorous fault tolerance threshold with gate set tomography, *Nature Communications* 8:4485.

[12] E. Mount, C. Kabytayev, S. Crain, R. Harper, S.-Y. Baek, G. Vrijsen, S.T. Flammia, K.R. Brown, P. Maunz, and J. Kim, 2015, Error compensation of single-qubit gates in a surface-electrode ion trap using composite pulses, *Physical Review A* 92:060301.

[13] S. Gustavsson, O. Zwier, J. Bylander, F. Yan, F. Yoshihara, Y. Nakamura, T.P. Orlando, and W.D. Oliver, 2013, Improving quantum gate fidelities by using a qubit to measure microwave pulse distortions, *Physical Review Letters* 110:0405012.

[14] J.P. Gaebler, T.R. Tan, Y. Lin, Y. Wan, R. Bowler, A.C. Keith, S. Glancy, K. Coakley, E. Knill, D. Leibfried, and D.J. Wineland, 2016, High-fidelity universal gate set for $^9Be^+$ ion qubits, *Physical Review Letters* 117:060505.

[15] C.J. Ballance, T.P. Harty, N.M. Linke, M.A. Sepiol, and D.M. Lucas, 2016, High-fidelity quantum logic gates using trapped-ion hyperfine qubits, *Physical Review Letters* 117:060504.

[16] R. Barends, J. Kelly, A. Megrant, A. Veitia, D. Sank, E. Jeffrey, T.C. White, et al., 2014, Logic gates at the surface code threshold: Supercomputing qubits poised for fault-tolerant quantum computing, *Nature* 508:500-503.

[17] S. Sheldon, E. Magesan, J. Chow, and J.M. Gambetta, 2016, Procedures for systematically turning up cross-talk in the cross-resonance gate, *Physical Review A* 93:060302.

[18] J. Preskill, 2018, "Quantum Computing in the NISQ Era and Beyond," arXiv:1801.00862.

[19] D.P. DiVincenzo, 2000, The physical implementation of quantum computation, *Fortschritte der Physik* 48:771-783.

[20] M.H.S. Amin, D.V. Averin, and J.A. Nesteroff, 2009, Decoherence in adiabatic quantum computation, *Physical Review A* 79(2):022107.

[21] A.M. Childs, E. Farhi, and J. Preskill, 2001, Robustness of adiabatic quantum computation, *Physical Review A* 65(1):012322.

[22] M.H.S. Amin, P.J. Love, and C.J.S. Truncik, 2008, Thermally assisted adiabatic quantum computation, *Physical Review Letters* 100(6):060503.

[23] N.G. Dickson, M.W. Johnson, M.H. Amin, R. Harris, F. Altomare, A.J. Berkley, P. Bunyk, et al., 2013, Thermally assisted quantum annealing of a 16-qubit problem, *Nature Communications* 4:1903.

3

Quantum Algorithms and Applications

A bedrock of the field of algorithms lies in the principle that the total number of computational steps required to solve a problem is (roughly) independent of the underlying design of the computer—remarkably, to a first approximation what is designated a single step of computation is a matter of convenience and does not change the total time to solution. This basic principle, called the extended Church-Turing thesis, implies that to solve a computational problem faster, one may (1) reduce the time to implement a single step, (2) perform many steps in parallel, or (3) reduce the total number of steps to completion via the design of a clever algorithm.

The discovery that quantum computers violate the extended Church-Turing thesis [1,2]—by solving certain computational tasks with exponentially fewer steps than the best classical algorithm for the same task—shook up the foundations of computer science, and opened the possibility of an entirely new way of solving computational problems quickly.[1] The practical potential of quantum computers was illustrated soon thereafter when Peter Shor created quantum algorithms for factoring large numbers and computing discrete logarithms that were exponentially faster than

---

[1] Note that quantum computers do not violate the original Church-Turing thesis, which defines the limits of what it is possible to compute at all (independent of time required to perform the computation). See D. Deutsch, 1985, Quantum theory, the Church-Turing Principle and the universal quantum computer, *Proceedings of the Royal Society of London A* 400(1818):97-117. The extended Church-Turing thesis is sometimes referred to as "the feasibility thesis" or the "computational complexity-theoretic Church-Turing thesis."

any developed for a classical computer [3-4].[2] These quantum algorithms generated serious concern in the security community, since the classical hardness of these two problems lie at the core of the public key "cryptosystems" that protect the vast majority of society's digital data.

Indeed, algorithms for factoring large numbers have been studied over the centuries by mathematicians and very intensely over the last few decades by computer scientists. The main issue in these, and most other computational problems, is combinatorial explosion: the exponential number of potential solutions that the algorithm must choose between. In the case of factoring an n bit number N, the possible prime divisors of N include all prime numbers less than N, and there are $\exp(n)$ many such primes. Indeed, the fastest classical algorithm for actually finding the prime divisors of N takes $\exp(O(n^{1/3}))$ steps, while Shor's quantum algorithm took only $O(n^3)$ steps, later improved to $O(n^2 \log[n])$.

A very general goal of the field of algorithms is to solve a computational task by an algorithm whose number of steps (colloquially called its "running time") scales polynomially in the size, n, of the input, thereby bypassing the combinatorial explosion. Computational tasks for which such polynomial time (classical) algorithms exist are referred to as belonging to the complexity class P. The corresponding complexity class, bounded-error quantum polynomial time (BQP), contains all those computational tasks that a quantum computer would be able to solve in polynomial time. By contrast, algorithms whose running time scales exponentially in the size of the input very quickly become prohibitively expensive as the input size is scaled.

It is important to realize that quantum computers do not uniformly speed up all computational problems. One of the most important classes of computational problems, the NP-complete problems [5], have been described as looking for a needle in an exponentially large haystack. About the same time as Shor's announcement, Bennett et al. [6] proved that quantum algorithms require exponential time to solve NP-complete problems in the black box model—that is, if the algorithm ignores the detailed problem structure—and are therefore unlikely to provide exponential speedups for such problems. More precisely, if N denotes the size of the haystack, Bennett et al. showed that any quantum algorithm to find the needle must take at least $N^{1/2}$ steps. A few years later, Grover showed that there is a quantum algorithm that can find the needle in $O(N^{1/2})$ steps [7]. The class NP is characterized by the requirement that a classical computer should be able to check the correctness of a solution in polynomial time (no matter how hard it is to actually find the solution). NP-complete

---

[2] Shor's algorithm for factorization scales asymptotically as $O(n^3)$, compared to $O(\exp[n^{1/3}])$ for the best classical approach, the general number field sieve algorithm.

problems are the hardest problems in NP, and include the famous Traveling Salesman Problem, as well as thousands of problems from every field in science. It is widely conjectured that P ≠ NP (this is one of the famous seven Clay Millennium Problems), and that any classical algorithm must require exp(n) steps to solve NP-complete problems [8].

The design of quantum algorithms follows completely different principles from those of classical algorithms. To begin with, even classical algorithms have to be cast in a special form—as reversible algorithms—before they can be run on a quantum computer. Algorithms that achieve quantum speedups use certain quantum algorithmic paradigms or building blocks that have no classical counterparts.

There is an extensive literature on quantum algorithms that has been developed in the quarter century since the first algorithms discussed above. All of these algorithms rely on a handful of quantum building blocks that are described in the next section and are designed to run on an idealized quantum computer. Real quantum devices are noisy, so an elaborate theory of quantum error correcting codes and fault-tolerant quantum computing has been developed to convert noisy quantum computers to ideal quantum computers. However, this conversion incurs an overhead both in number of qubits as well as running time.

The field is now entering the era of noisy intermediate-scale quantum (NISQ) devices [9]—the race to build quantum computers that are sufficiently large (tens to hundreds or a few thousand qubits) that they cannot be efficiently simulated by a classical computer, but are not fault tolerant and so cannot directly implement the algorithms developed for ideal quantum computers. While the enormous interest and funding for building NISQ computers has undoubtedly moved up the calendar for scalable, fault-tolerant quantum computers, significant work remains before each milestone is met.

The biggest upcoming challenges are algorithmic; in the near-term, this includes the search for computational tasks that such computers can speed up. Developing algorithms that run on NISQ computers are as important as creating the physical devices, since without both, the machine is not useful. In the longer term, much work remains to be done in the field of quantum algorithms for ideal (scalable, fault-tolerant) quantum computers. The next section describes major building blocks for quantum algorithms, as well as known algorithms for idealized quantum computers that provide speedups over the best classical algorithms for the same computational tasks. The subsequent section describes quantum error-correction and fault-tolerance techniques for converting a noisy quantum computer to an idealized quantum computer. The chapter concludes with a discussion of the major algorithmic challenge presented by NISQ computers, and the most promising leads in the search for such algorithms.

Finding: Progress in quantum algorithms is essential for quantum computing success. In the near term, developing algorithms that work on NISQ machines is critical.

3.1 QUANTUM ALGORITHMS FOR AN IDEAL GATE-BASED QUANTUM COMPUTER

The power of quantum algorithms ultimately derives from the exponential complexity of quantum systems—the state of a system of n entangled qubits is described by (and can thus encode) $N = 2^n$ complex coefficients, as discussed in the previous chapter. Moreover, the application of each elementary gate on, say, two qubits updates the 2^n complex numbers describing the state, thereby seeming to perform 2^n computations in a single step. On the other hand, at the end of the computation, when the n qubits are measured, the result is just n classical bits. The challenge of designing useful and advantageous quantum algorithms derives from the tension between these two phenomena—one must find tasks whose operational solutions both make use of this parallelism and yield a final quantum state that has a high probability of returning valuable information upon measurement. Successful approaches take advantage of the phenomenon of quantum interference for generating useful results. In the following, some of the major building blocks for quantum algorithms are described, as well as several foundational quantum algorithms and how they can be used to solve different kinds of abstract problems.

3.1.1 The Quantum Fourier Transform and Quantum Fourier Sampling

One of the most basic building blocks for quantum algorithms is the quantum Fourier transform (QFT) algorithm. The Fourier transform, a critical step in many classical calculations and computations, is an operation that transforms one representation of a signal of interest into a different representational form. The classical Fourier transform turns a signal represented as a function of time into its corresponding signal represented as a function of frequency. For example, this could mean transforming a mathematical description of a musical chord in terms of air pressure as a function of time into the amplitudes of the set of musical tones (or notes) that combine to form the chord. This transformation is reversible via the inverse Fourier transform, so involves no information loss—a key requirement for any operation on a quantum computer. Concretely, the input is an N-dimensional vector with complex entries $(a_1, a_2, ..., a_N)$, and the output is an N-dimensional vector with complex entries $(b_1, b_2, ..., b_N)$ which is obtained by multiplying the input vector with the $N \times N$ Fourier transform matrix.

Given the utility of the Fourier transform, many clever algorithms have been developed to implement it on classical computers. The best, the fast Fourier transform (FFT), takes O(NlogN) time, which is only slightly longer than it takes to read the input data [O(N)]. While the classical FFT is quite efficient, quantum Fourier transform (QFT) is exponentially faster, requiring only $O(\log^2 N) = O(n^2)$ time (where $N = 2^n$) in its original formulation, later improved to $O(n \log n)$ [10].

Before describing the QFT, it is important to understand how the input and output are represented as quantum states. The input $(a_1, a_2, \ldots a_N)$ is represented as the quantum state $\Sigma_i a_i | i \rangle$, and the output $(b_1, b_2, \ldots b_N)$ is represented as the quantum state $\Sigma_i b_i | i \rangle$. Thus, the input and output are represented as states of just n qubits, where $n = \log N$. This is shown in Figure 3.1. Exponential speedup is possible only if the input data has already be encoded into a compact quantum state, or can be encoded into this state in $O(\log N)$ steps. The quantum circuit that carries out this transformation has total number of gates that scales as $O(n \log n)$. Another caveat is that one of course cannot access the amplitudes b_i through measurement. Indeed, if the output of the QFT is measured, it yields the index i with probability $|b_i|^2$. Thus, measuring this algorithm's output only yields the index of a probable output, which is called quantum Fourier sampling (QFS). QFS is an important primitive in quantum algorithms, and entails applying the QFT and measuring the output state, resulting in the sampling of an index i from a certain probability distribution.

First, since O(N) time is required to read the input data, the quantum algorithm can be completed only in $O(\log^2 N)$—that is, it can yield speedup only compared to its classical analogue—if the input data is preencoded into logN qubits and not read in directly from a file of data. These logN qubits are in a superposition of N quantum states, and the coefficient on each state represents the data sequence to be transformed. This is shown in Figure 3.1. Applying the QFT algorithm to this input changes the state of the log N qubits such that the new coefficients are the Fourier Transform of the input coefficients. Of course, since the output is a quantum state, there is no way to directly read these values. When the output is measured, only one of the N possible classical output states is observed. The probability that any of the N states will be observed is the square of the absolute value of the coefficient of that state, which is also the square of its Fourier transform value. Performing a QFT on a set of qubits and then measuring their final state accomplishes the same task as what is referred to classically as Fourier sampling.

It turns out that sampling the output of the Fourier transform is useful in some cases for finding structure in a sequence of numbers, as illustrated in Figure 3.1. Notice that the coefficients of the input data are periodic, with four periods in this sequence. This periodicity causes the amplitude of state $|100\rangle$ to be much larger than all the others, so with high

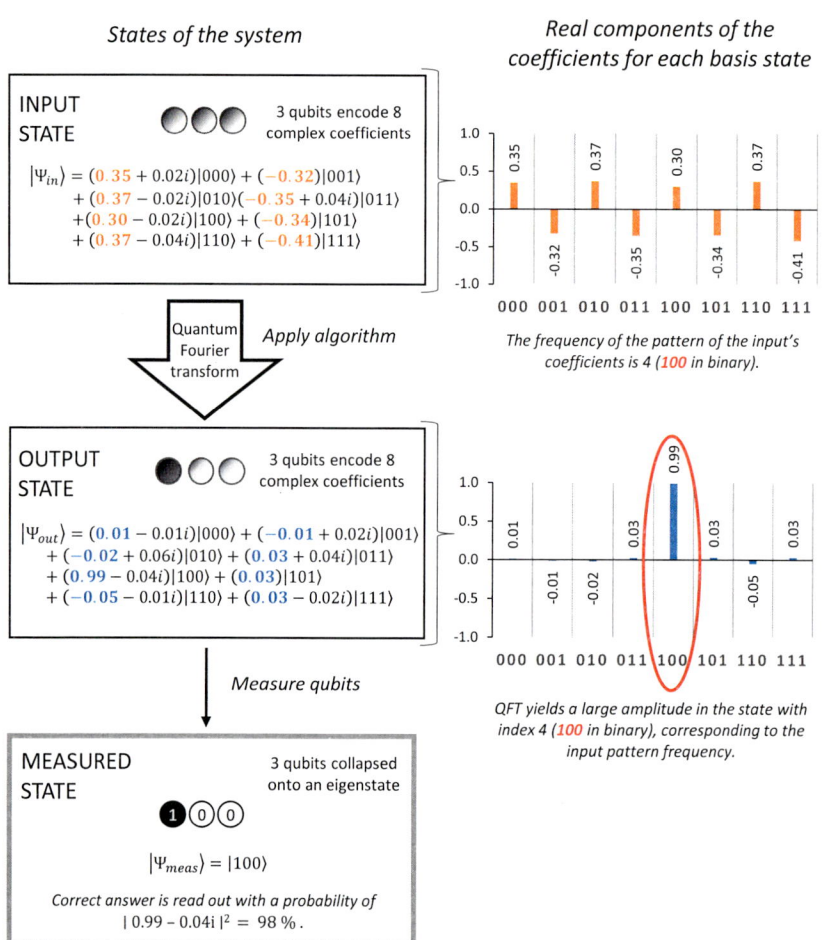

FIGURE 3.1 An illustrative example of the quantum Fourier transform (QFT) applied to a three-qubit system. The three qubits must be initially prepared such that the eight ($2^3 = 8$) complex coefficients encode the system state corresponding to the sequence of values to be transformed. Since the number of coefficients, N, is 2^n, where n is the number of qubits, only $\log(N)$ bits are needed: 3 qubits can represent the 8 complex values shown. The QFT effectively finds patterns in the input sequence and identifies their frequency of repetition. In this example, all the input states have similar probability, with the real components of coefficients alternating sign four times. The coefficients of the output state (shown on the right) capture this pattern: the coefficient of the ith state, a_i, is large if there are i cycles in the input sequence. (Actually, for a sequence of N, the highest number of repetitions possible is $N/2$, or 4 in the example. The values of 5, 6, and 7 "alias" back to tones that repeat 3, 2, and 1 times respectively, so these tones can be represented by either location.) Thus, in this example all outputs are all small except for one state, 100, corresponding to the input pattern frequency. Thus, measuring this output is likely to provide the index of this strong pattern in the input sequence.

probability, measuring the final system state will return 100 (binary for 4), revealing the input sequence repeated 4 times, or had a repeat distance of 2. This example illustrates the power and pitfalls of quantum computing. If the initial input superposition already exists, the Fourier transform can be performed on the superposition coefficients exponentially faster than would be possible classically. However, at the end of this operation, one samples only one of the N states, rather than obtaining the entire set of output coefficients. Furthermore, it is not clear in general how to create the input superposition without taking $O(N)$ time—although this becomes less of a problem if QFT is performed on a preloaded input quantum state as one step in a longer algorithm.

The QFT, which cleverly leverages the characteristics of quantum computation, is useful in constructing a host of quantum algorithms. Examples include quantum factoring, finding hidden structure, and quantum phase estimation.

3.1.2 Quantum Factoring and Finding Hidden Structures

Shor's discovery of polynomial time algorithms for factoring and calculating discrete logarithms [11] was a major breakthrough for the field of quantum algorithms, both because of the apparent speedup compared to the classical algorithms and because of the implications of this speedup for known applications. At their heart, both algorithms may be seen as an ingenious way of exploiting the exponential speedup in the QFT, even given the input and output limitations of Fourier sampling.

To be able to use the power of the QFT, Shor first converted the problem of finding the factors of a number to a problem that involves finding a repeating pattern—exactly what the FT detects. Shor was able to show that the factoring problem was equivalent to the problem of finding the period in a sequence of numbers, albeit a sequence of numbers that is exponentially longer than the number of bits of the corresponding number to be factored. Thus, while this equivalency does not provide any help in solving the problem on a classical computer (since it would need to generate this sequence of 2^n numbers for an n-bit number to factor, which would take an exponential amount of time), it is a perfect problem for a quantum computer. In a quantum computer, the exponentially long sequence can be encoded into merely n qubits, and generated in a time that is polynomial in n. Once that sequence is generated, the QFT can be used to find the period. The fact that the returned result is only a sample of the output FT amplitudes is not limiting, since the desired information is highly likely to be what a measurement would sample.

Shor's algorithm, if deployed on a perfect quantum computer, would make it possible to compute the secret key of the most widely used public key cryptosystems, RSA. In addition, it would be able to compute the secret key of other widely used public-key cryptosystems, such as Diffie-Hellman and elliptic curve cryptography. The implications of quantum computing for cryptography are discussed in more detail in Chapter 4.

Shor's quantum algorithm for factoring and discrete log can both be regarded as examples of finding hidden algebraic structure, related to a well-known mathematical problem called the "hidden subgroup problem" [12,13]. Currently, there are quantum approaches for solving some cases of this problem efficiently, specifically for so-called Abelian and closely related groups (characterized by their symmetry properties). On the other hand, the problem is expected to be hard for the so-called dihedral symmetry group. This hard problem is closely related to another, called the shortest vector problem—the basis of the learning with errors (LWE) cryptosystem, one of the proposed post-quantum (that, is, quantum-resistant) cyphers described in Chapter 4.

3.1.3 Grover's Algorithm and Quantum Random Walks

While the QFT underlies many quantum algorithms, another class of algorithms take advantage of a different method, called the "quantum random walk." This method is analogous to classical random walk methods, which probabilistically simulate progress in traversing some terrain.

Grover's algorithm addresses the specific problem of finding the unique inputs to a given function that will yield a certain output [14].[3] Classically, this is a basic NP-hard search problem—that is, there are no known polynomial time solutions. In the absence of information about the nature of the function, the fastest known classical algorithm for this problem is exhaustive search, or exploration of all possible inputs to find the answer—a process that takes $O(N) = O(2^n)$ steps, where n is the number of bits required to represent the input. Grover's algorithm solves this problem in $O(\sqrt{N})$ steps. While this is only a polynomial speedup over the best classical approach, it could nonetheless be significant in practice. As will be discussed in the next chapter, this could be sufficient to compromise additional cryptographic operations. Moreover, this is the optimal quantum algorithm for this problem, in light of the result of Bennett et al. [15] showing that any quantum algorithm must take at least $\sqrt{N}$ steps to solve this problem in the black box model.

The problem with the classical exhaustive search approach is that the systematic testing of each possible answer is a blind guess-and-check: each query provides no information about the answer until it is actually found. To get around this problem, Grover's algorithm proceeds by

---

[3] The problem can be more formally phrased as follows: If f is an efficiently computable binary function that operates on strings of length n, find x such that $f(x) = 1$.

iterating a set of two operations on the qubits. The first effectively flags the state corresponding to the correct answer by changing the sign of its coefficient. The second, called the Grover diffusion operator, is then able to slightly increase the magnitude of this coefficient. Together, the two steps comprise a so-called Grover iteration, each application of which increases the probability that the correct answer will be read-out upon measurement. This procedure to increase the amplitude of the state(s) containing the correct answer is an example of a general algorithmic approach called amplitude amplification [16], which is useful in a number of quantum algorithms.

The sequence of amplitude amplification operations can be viewed as a sort of quantum random walk; however, Grover's algorithm does the "walk" backward, from a distributed state (analogous to all possible endpoints of a random walk from a given starting point) back to a state focused around the single correct component (analogous to the starting point of the walk). A classical random walk approach can explore an area proportional to the square root of the number of steps; the quantum random walk can explore an area proportional to the number of steps. Hence, the quantum algorithm provides quadratic speedup.

This technique is very versatile and has led to a number of quantum algorithms providing polynomial speedups for specific computational tasks. For example, there is a quantum walk-based algorithm for solving the basic problem of determining whether the player making the first move has a winning strategy in a combinatorial game (such as chess). The naïve classical algorithm involves an exponential search of the possible moves and outcomes, called the "game tree," while the quantum algorithm provides the quadratic speedup described above. More generally, the quantum algorithm provides a quadratic speedup for evaluating any AND-OR formula [17,18].

While Grover's algorithm is often referred to as quantum "search," this is not really a valid application of the technique. To perform a true quantum search, the set of data to be searched must first be represented as a superposition of quantum states and for a quantum algorithm to provide any speedup, this representation would need to be created in a time much less than the number of data points, N—somewhere between $O(1)$ to $O(\log N)$. In the classical case, this data would simply be stored in random access memory (RAM) and called when needed. However, while RAM is a key element of classical computing, there is currently no robust practical RAM equivalent that generates the needed quantum superposition state for a quantum computer.

It has been proposed that a quantum version of random access memory (RAM), or QRAM, could generate this data in $O(\log N)$ time [19], although this has not been practically demonstrated. To achieve this, a classical data storage unit would be supplemented with quantum logic around the memory cells. A classical analogue to this structure, called a content addressable memory, or CAM, exists, and solves this search problem in O(log N) time. However, with CAM and with QRAM, getting the data into the device in the first place still takes O(N) time, so either approach will only be useful when multiple queries are performed on the same data set—that is, the utility of CAM and QRAM, if it can be built, grows in direct proportion to the number of times the input can be reused.

3.1.4 Hamiltonian Simulation Algorithms

Simulating the dynamics of quantum systems is the most natural and obvious application of quantum computers and was the motivation for Richard Feynman's pioneering exploration of quantum computing [20]. Quantum algorithms can exponentially outperform classical ones when simulating a system with many quantum degrees of freedom, with applications including problems in chemistry, materials science, condensed matter, nuclear physics, and high-energy physics.

The general objective in simulating a quantum system is to determine its structure or behavior, given knowledge of its components and the environment in which it exists. For example, a simulation could be used to elucidate the structure of a substance, or the behavior over time of a collection of interacting particles. These problems can have a variety of applications, from informing the development of new industrial materials to solving important physics problems. In general, these simulations require knowledge of the Hamiltonian (energy operator) describing all elements and interactions of the system. From there, one can either solve for the ground-state wave function for that system (in the time-independent picture), or, given some initial state of the system at a time t_0, compute a close approximation to the quantum state at a future time t. Scientists have been performing classical simulations of quantum systems for decades, either restricting attention to small systems or relying upon approximate methods that can trade accuracy for computational efficiency. Accurate models are so compute-intensive (given the intrinsic high dimensionality of quantum systems) as to be inadequate for all but small systems.

A quantum, rather than classical, simulation is naturally better equipped to explore the state space spanned by quantum systems. In principle, quantum simulation can proceed via at least three general approaches, each of which promises more efficient solutions in certain scenarios. The first approach involves implementation of time-evolution algorithms on a gate-based quantum computer, commonly referred to as "Hamiltonian simulation." The second is a variational approach for obtaining approximations to quantum states using quantum computers and will be discussed later in this chapter. Last, in the field of analog quantum simulation, dedicated quantum systems, although not full-blown quantum computers, are built to emulate specific Hamiltonians. While this hardware is likely to be much simpler than gate-based machine solving the same problem, the downside of the analog simulation approach is that the hardware has limitations on the Hamiltonians it can create, so the resulting system is special-purpose and the application and simulator need to be co-designed. In addition, unlike digital quantum computations that can be protected using fault-tolerant protocols, the ability to perform analog quantum simulation in realistic, noisy environments is less well understood.

In the time-evolution Hamiltonian simulation algorithms, the form of the Hamiltonian, and potentially its own dependence on time, as well as the initial state of the system must be provided as inputs. The algorithm begins by initializing the qubits into the initial system state or an approximation to it. Then, the system is advanced through time, or "propagated," according to its Hamiltonian, in discrete intervals, Δt, for the number of iterations required to arrive at the time of interest, t_f. In practice, the overall Hamiltonian is usually represented as a sum of smaller, so-called local Hamiltonians, each of which act on only a component of the larger system, which provides a useful decomposition (more generally, the Hamiltonian can be simulated efficiently provided it is sparse and the nonzero entries in any given row can be efficiently located and computed). For the process to proceed efficiently, the method of encoding of the initial state in qubits and of representing the time propagation as a gate sequence must be carefully chosen for the system in question. The first concrete quantum algorithms for gate-based Hamiltonian simulation were developed in the mid-1990s [21], and additional methods for different kinds of quantum systems has followed, along with algorithmic insights that have yielded significant reductions in time [22-28].[4]

Efficient Hamiltonian simulation on a quantum computer would enable important speedups for problems in quantum chemistry and materials simulation [29,30]. In particular, the electron correlation problem has been one of the most challenging problems for classical methods to tackle [31]. To understand and predict complex reaction mechanisms involved in, for example, a transition-metal catalyzed chemical transformation, requires extremely accurate electronic structure approaches. Classically, even molecules with fewer than one hundred strongly correlated electrons are beyond the scale of classical ab initio methods at chemical accuracy. Quantum computers promise exponential speedups for the simulation of the electronic structure problem and it has been shown that they would enable efficient elucidation of chemical reaction mechanisms [32]. Here,

---

[4] Specifically, discrete-time random walks; see A.M. Childs, 2010, On the relationship between continuous- and discrete-time quantum walk, *Communications in Mathematical Physics* 294(2):581-603.

a quantum computer could enable researchers to compute or confirm the energies of chemical intermediates and transition states, and in turn help to determine accurate activation energies for chemical processes, which are important for understanding the kinetics of chemical reactions [33]. Strongly correlated species involved in chemical reactions where classical approaches presently fail include problems such as photochemical processes, nitrogen fixation, C-H bond breaking, carbon dioxide fixation and transformation, hydrogen and oxygen production, and other transition-metal catalysis problems. These applications extend to important industrial applications including fertilizer production, polymerization catalysis and clean energy processes. [34]. Hamiltonian simulation is also used within quantum algorithms for solving complex correlated material problems [35], which may have application in, for example, the search for a high-temperature superconductor. Quantum computers promise an exponential speedup over classical approaches for time evolution of quantum systems. Thus, quantum computers may have the most impact in their application to problems in quantum chemistry, for example as applied in pharmaceutics, and materials science [36].

However, there are many types of Hamiltonians that will require new methods if they are to become efficiently solvable on a quantum computer. For example, to model the electronic structure for applications in quantum chemistry [37], the Hamiltonian of an n-orbital system involves $O(n^4)$ terms, which means a low-error quantum computer will be required for its computation. Classical approaches to solving such problems have leveraged an understanding of the system's physical structure to create tailored techniques [38]. Researchers have recently combined these techniques with the existing framework for quantum Hamiltonian simulation that has led to rapid progress in these quantum algorithms for such problems [39-47].

Hamiltonian simulation has also proven to be a powerful tool for developing quantum algorithms for problems with no immediate connection to quantum mechanics. A prominent example is the recent development of a new class of quantum algorithms that directly perform linear algebra on the quantum state; this is discussed next.

3.1.5 Quantum Algorithms for Linear Algebra

Linear algebra, a foundational area of mathematics, can be useful in a range of contexts, from the science of quantum mechanics to computer graphics design to methods in machine learning. The general task of linear algebra is to find the solution to a system of linear equations, that is, one or more equations of the form where the sum of a set of independent variables, each scaled by some coefficient, is equal to a constant value.

Mathematically speaking, such a problem can be written in matrix form as **A** $x = b$, where **A** is an $N \times N$ matrix whose elements are the coefficients on the variables in the equations, x is a column vector whose elements are each of the variables to be solved for, and b is a column vector of the constants.

A quantum algorithm for such applications, termed HHL after its developers Harrow, Hassidim, and Lloyd, makes use of methods from Hamiltonian simulation [48]. It assumes that the input vector b is given as a quantum state of log$N$ qubits $|b\rangle = \Sigma_i b_i |i\rangle$. It also assumes that the matrix **A** is sparse and its entries are accessible via an easy to compute function. Moreover, it computes the output vector **x** in the form of a quantum state of log$N$ qubits $|x\rangle = \Sigma_i x_i |i\rangle$. At the heart of the HHL algorithm lies one of the basic quantum algorithmic building blocks: Kitaev's quantum phase estimation algorithm. This is a procedure for exponentially fast estimation of the eigenvalue (or phase) of an eigenvector of a unitary operator. This is relevant to linear algebra, since inverting the matrix A is easy if its eigenvalues are known. The running time of the HHL algorithm scales as a polynomial in log$N$ and the condition number of A. Of course, the access to the solution x is restricted to information that can be readily accessed from the quantum state $|x\rangle$. For a given **A** and b, the algorithm would output a quantum state for which the values of the N coefficients are proportional to the N elements of solution x. Although the solution is present in the quantum computer, the rules of quantum mechanics also prevent it from being directly read out. However, if one is interested in only finding certain expectation values of the solution, one can obtain this result with a number of gates that has poly(log$N$) cost [49].

Linear algebra problems can be solved with a classical computer using memory and running time that scale as poly(N) so a quantum computer would use exponentially fewer resources and time for solving this more restricted problem. Recent related work has shown similar results for solving linear differential equations [50] and performing convex optimization [51], under the assumption that the input matrix **A** is very sparse—that is, that most of the coefficients are zero—since the algorithm's running time is polynomial in the number of nonzero elements per row.

As with the preceding algorithms, this exponential speedup comes with a number of important caveats. As previously mentioned, reading the output provides only an index i with probability proportional to $|x_i|^2$. Thus, one major issue in using this algorithm is finding settings where this limited information is useful. One example of such a setting is recommendation systems, where past ratings of several products by a group of users (specified by a matrix) are used to provide personalized recommendations to individual users. The recommendation is a product, which is specified by an index. A quantum algorithm for this problem was found with an exponential speedup over existing classical algorithms [52]. Recently, this quantum algorithm inspired a new classical algorithm which is only polynomially slower than the quantum algorithm [53].[5]

Another issue is that this exponential speedup is only true if both the input b and the matrix $\mathbf{A}$ are already encoded in $\log N$ qubits, or if they can be encoded into qubits in poly($\log N$) time. This precludes reading in this data, since simply reading the data to create this state would take at least $O(N)$ time. This exponential speedup is only possible if this data was already prepared as a quantum state before the start of the algorithm, or if some method is found to prepare it efficiently.

As previously mentioned, for exponential speedup the current ability for a quantum processor to read-in large amounts of data efficiently is a common challenge in quantum algorithm development; an efficient solution to this problem will likely be required for many algorithms to be useful in practice. Of course, even if this issue is not resolved, quantum algorithms can still provide polynomial speedup where classical algorithms require $O(N^2)$ or higher steps to process the input, since a quantum computer can read the data in $O(N)$ steps.

3.1.6 Required Machine Quality

The algorithms described in this section illustrate the types of tasks which when executed on a quantum computer would lead to an enormous computational advantage. For interesting problem sizes, they mostly require thousands of qubits, a few orders of magnitude larger than current machines. Unfortunately, these algorithms need to do a very large number of qubit gate operations, requiring order 10^{12} or even as high as 10^{18} operations.[6] In order for these results to be correct in the end, the gate error rate must be very small (on the order of 10^{-12} to 10^{-18}). As explained in Chapter 2, unlike today's classical computers, whose gates can achieve these low error rates by directly rejecting noise and producing outputs with less noise than contained in their inputs, quantum gates have much higher error rates. As shown in Chapter 5, current quantum computers have error rates in the 10^{-2}-10^{-3} range, and are unlikely to reach the required error needed to run these quantum algorithms natively. Quantum error correction is one way to overcome this limitation, and is described next.

---

[5] In this manner, progress in quantum algorithms has commonly spurred new advances in classical algorithms. This is discussed further in Chapter 7.

[6] See, for example, Figure 3.2 and Table 4.1 for runtime estimates for illustrative problems in chemistry and cryptanalysis.

3.2 QUANTUM ERROR CORRECTION AND MITIGATION

Two general approaches have been developed to reduce errors in quantum systems: correction and mitigation. Of the two, quantum error correction (QEC) is the only way to dramatically lower effective error rates. This approach involves encoding the quantum state using many redundant qubits, and the using a QEC code (QECC) that exploits this redundancy of information to emulate stable qubits with very low error rates, often called "fault-tolerant" or "logical" qubits. The state of some of these additional qubits are periodically measured and a classical computing device "decodes" this information to determine which qubits have errors. Given this information, the errors can be corrected. Each logical qubit requires a large number of physical qubits and many quantum gate operations (and classical computation) to achieve and maintain its state. Gate operations on the more robust logical qubit, which exists only as an abstraction, must be translated into operations on the underlying physical qubits. Thus, QEC incurs costs, or "resource overheads," of both additional qubits for each logical qubit, and additional quantum gates for each logical operation.

Quantum error correction is an active area of quantum algorithm research, with the goal of dramatically lower the overheads in qubits and time to achieve fully error free operation. Much of this research has focused on studying surface codes and the larger class of topological codes of which they are a part. Current codes for gates with error rates of 0.1 percent still have high overheads (15,000 times) to create a logical qubit. Until a breakthrough in either gate error rate or QEC code overhead, near-term machines will not be able to achieve logical qubits, leading to machines that must deal with noise and errors (NISQ computers). In the shorter term, researchers have turned to approaches for quantum error mitigation (QEM) and may use QEC to lower, but not eliminate errors, as error rates fall.

3.2.1 Quantum Error Mitigation Strategies

Compared to QEC, QEM has the more modest goal of reducing the effective error rate of the quantum calculation to support simple computations, or for non-gate-based quantum approaches to extend the coherence of imperfect qubits [54,55] for durations long enough to complete short algorithms. Since a lower error rate lowers the overhead when using QEC, many of these mitigation strategies would also be used with error correction.

Two useful error-mitigation approaches that are widely used today include the application of composite pulses and dynamical decoupling methods. Although such techniques do not suppress all types of errors, they can be designed to mitigate known systematic errors (composite pulses) or coherent dephasing errors (dynamical decoupling sequences).

For both analog and digital quantum computers, error suppression techniques are being developed based on "energy penalties" to suppress specific types of errors. These approaches work by encoding the qubits strategically in ways for which these errors are less energetically favorable and therefore less likely. In addition, both types of computers may take advantage of "decoherence-free subspaces," where multiqubit architectures are designed in ways that make the qubit system insensitive to certain channels of noise. Since these techniques suppress only certain types of errors, the error-rate improvement will depend on the system and may be modest.

QEM is expected to be particularly important for analog QCs, as full QEC is not currently understood to be practically achievable on these systems. While QEC is corrective—that is, it measures errors and then fixes them—QEM methods are preventative and attempt to reduce the adverse impacts of noise and the probability of errors.

3.2.2 Quantum Error Correction Codes

The first quantum error correction codes were developed in the mid-1990s [56,57]. Further work has provided practical insights into the error threshold—that is, the maximum allowable error rate of every physical gate in an actual device for which QEC will correct more errors than it introduces [58,59]. However, achieving both the number and fidelity of qubits required to successfully implement QEC and enable fault-tolerant computing has proven challenging.

In classical computing, one of the simplest types of error correction codes, called a "repetition code," copies each bit of information into several bits to preserve the information through redundancy. All gate operations are also replicated to maintain this redundancy. These bits all have the same value, unless an error occurs, which would result in one of the bits being set to the wrong value. Since the likelihood of any error arising is small, the correct value can be identified as that held by the majority of the copies. The "distance" of an error correcting code is the minimum number of errors that are needed to convert one valid representation of data to another valid data representation. A repetition by 3 code (each bit is either 000, or 111) is a distance 3 code, since one need change all three bits to go from one valid representation, 111, to another valid representation, 000. In general, a distance D code can correct $(D-1)/2$ errors, so the replication 3 code can correct one error. This makes sense, since if only a single error occurred, the majority of the bits will still represent the right value.

Approaches to QEC are similar to this classical approach. However, the precise implementation of QEC requires vastly different techniques than the classical repetition code because quantum information cannot be directly copied, as described in the no cloning theorem [60], and owing to the additional types of errors that can occur in quantum gates. Nonetheless, QEC protocols have been developed that enable the encoding of a logical qubit into a distributed fabric of physical qubits. Since these qubits hold the quantum state, none of them can be directly measured: any measurement would cause the quantum state to collapse and destroy the computation. Instead, two qubits, which should have the same value, are compared to each other, and all one reads out is whether these two qubits agree or disagree. This measurement does not reveal the value of the qubit, so it does not cause the quantum state to collapse. The qubits that are measured are sometimes called the "syndrome" or "ancilla" qubits (Box 3.1). From all these comparison measurements and knowledge about the QECC used, a classical computer can compute which qubits have errors, and what type of error a qubit has. Thus, it can provide the quantum operation that need to be applied to remove the errors in the quantum state. While these operations can be directly applied to the physical qubits, it is often more efficient for the software to "virtually" apply these corrections, modifying future operations to account for these errors rather than adding a separate step just to correct them. The classical algorithm, also called a "decoding algorithm" or "decoder," which takes syndrome measurements as its input and computes which qubits have errors grows

---

BOX 3.1
The Use of Ancilla Qubits for Quantum Error Correction

For error correction, one needs to replicate the state of a qubit onto a number of qubits. While the no cloning theorem prevents one from copying the state of a qubit directly onto another, one can create a redundant entangled qubit state of many qubits. The key is that the qubits to be entangled must start out in a known state. Qubits with a known state (for purposes of this discussion, it will be the state $|0\rangle$), called "ancilla qubits," may be added to a computation for this purpose. Since the state of ancilla qubits are known, it is possible to create a simple circuit that makes the output state of all these ancilla qubits match the protected qubit: run each ancilla through a controlled-NOT gate, where the control is driven by the qubit that needs to be replicated. Assume that there is a qubit with state ψ that we want to protect, where $|\psi\rangle$ represents an arbitrary superposition state $|\psi\rangle = a_0|0\rangle + a_0|1\rangle$. In the CNOT gate, the ancilla $|0\rangle$ state will remain a $|0\rangle$ state by the $|0\rangle$ component of $|\psi\rangle$, but it will be converted to $|1\rangle$ by the $|1\rangle$ component of $|\psi\rangle$. The result of this operation is the newly entangled two-qubit state $a_0|00\rangle + a_1|11\rangle$, creating a system in which the ancilla qubit is now perfectly entangled with the first qubit. Adding more ancillas increases the distance of the repetition code.

in complexity as the distance increases to handle higher error rates. If the error rate is close to the error threshold, not only are the overheads very high but the decoding algorithm is more complex as well. If the error rates are low or there are very few logical qubits required to run the algorithm, then a small lookup table can be used as the decoder.

The computational complexity of the error decoder might be an issue, since running QEC tightly couples the qubits of a quantum computer and the classical control processor that decodes the errors and selects the next quantum gate operations to be performed. At a high level, the following operations are needed. First, the control processor sends a quantum operation to the qubits, and some time is needed to perform the operations. Second, the syndrome qubit must be measured and sent back to the control processor. Third, the control processor must then use these measurements to decode which errors are present, and, fourth, update its future operations to account for these errors. It is simplest for the quantum computer if the classical computer can decode the error state without slowing down the next quantum operation. For a superconducting QC, this means the classical computer has only a few hundred nanoseconds (on the order of a thousand instructions on a modern processor) to decode the errors. If this is not possible, either custom hardware, to speed up the computation, or changing the QEC algorithm to allow additional quantum operations to occur before the error information is decoded, could be used to address the issue. If these techniques are not done, the added time will slow down the effective speed of a quantum computer, with delays between gates leading to additional decoherence and higher error rates.

3.2.3 Quantum Error Correction Overhead

The number of physical qubits required to encode a fault-tolerant, logical qubit depends on the error rates of the physical quantum device and the required distance, or the protection capacity, of the quantum error-correcting code chosen. As a simple example, consider the so-called Steane quantum error correction code. This approach encodes a single logical qubit into seven physical qubits, and is has a distance of three,[7] which means that it can correct a single error. To achieve a higher-distance protocol (one which can correct additional errors) using the Steane code, one can use a recursive approach called "concatenation." This essentially entails applying the Steane code to a set of physical qubits, and then applying it again to the corrected qubits, using the output of the first

---

[7] One needs more than 3 qubits for a distance 3 code since the syndrome measurements cannot reveal any information about the actual quantum state (which would force it to collapse).

level of corrections as the better qubits to be used in a subsequent level. Multiple levels can be stacked until the desired degree of error protection is achieved. In general, concatenating a QECC that encodes k qubits into n physical qubits and has distance d, written as $[[n, k, d]]$, scales to a $[[n^r, k, d^*]]$ code for r levels of concatenation, where $d^* \geq d^r$. That is, n^r it requires physical qubits per logical qubit. For example, three levels of concatenation of the Steane code would require 343 physical qubits to encode a single logical qubit and achieve a distance of at least 27. This qubit overhead is smaller than many other QEC approaches. However, a Steane code requires error rates lower than 10^{-5}, which is much lower than current machines. Other concatenation codes have higher qubit overheads but can accommodate higher error rates. Finding better codes is an active area of research.

Another approach to a QECC, the so-called surface code, is less sensitive to physical qubit error rate, with the potential to protect against errors even for quantum device error rates as high as 10^{-2} (1 percent), meaning it corrects more errors than it adds if all gates and measurements fail at most 1 in 100 times on average. The surface code's error threshold of one percent applies for a device architecture where each physical qubit interacts only with its four nearest-neighboring qubits, which—as Chapter 5 will show—is common in some current quantum computer designs.

However, a high error threshold comes at the price of high overhead. A distance d surface code requires a lattice of $(2d - 1) \times (2d - 1)$ physical qubits in order to encode a single logical qubit. As apparent from the formula, a surface code with a distance of three—the smallest possible code—requires 25 physical qubits to encode a logical qubit.[8] While a distance three code will not fully correct all errors, since two errors generate an incorrect output, this code reduces the effective error rate. As QCs grow in size and decrease in error rates, these smaller codes can be used to improve the effective error rate of the machine, but with a significant reduction in the number of effective qubits.

Of course, to completely remove errors, most quantum algorithms are extensive enough to require a distance of greater than three. For example, to fault-tolerantly perform Shor's algorithm or Hamiltonian simulation for quantum chemistry, the required distance is closer to 35, meaning that approximately 15,000 physical qubits are required to encode a logical qubit, assuming a starting error rate of 10^{-3} [61,62]. Beyond the Steane and surface codes, other more resource-efficient QECCs have been developed;

---

[8] There are some improvements to the encoding cost; however, they are minimal, enabling a distance 3 surface code to use only 13 or 17 qubits. See, for example, Y. Tomita and K.M. Svore, 2014, Low-distance surface codes under realistic quantum noise, *Physical Review A* 90:062320.

however, in 2018 such codes either lack efficient decoding algorithms or require error rates that are too low for the NISQ era. Work in this area is essential to reach the goal of creating a fully error corrected quantum computer.

In addition to the physical qubit overhead of QEC, in order to operate on fault-tolerant, logical qubits, there must be software available at compile time to convert the desired gate on the logical qubits to gates on the actual physical qubits that encode them. This translation would occur directly in the compilation of a quantum algorithm, with each logical qubit and each logical operation replaced according to a QECC and a distance-specific fault-tolerant replacement rule. The replacement rule accounts for the implementation of both the logical gate and the error correction algorithm, including the syndrome measurements and the corresponding classical decoding algorithm. The number of gates and time-steps required to implement each logical gate depends on the logical gate and the QEC algorithm; details of such calculations may be found elsewhere [63].

Finding: Quantum error correction (QEC) algorithms would enable the emulation of a perfect quantum computer using noisy physical qubits in order to deploy practical algorithms. However, QEC incurs significant overheads in terms of both the number of physical qubits required to emulate a logical qubit and the number of primitive qubit operations required to emulate a logical quantum operation.

Arguably the most daunting and costly challenge in quantum error correction is that of achieving a fault-tolerant "universal" set of operations. Existing QEC schemes have developed very cost efficient replacement rules and other methods for achieving fault-tolerant logical gate operations in the so-called Clifford group (consisting of the Pauli operations, controlled-NOT [CNOT], Hadamard [H], the phase gate S, and their products), as well as measurement in the computational basis. However, achieving universality also requires fault-tolerant implementation of non-Clifford gates (such as the Toffoli gate, or the $\pi/8$ gate also known as T). To do so, one can invoke a variety of techniques. For example, so-called magic state distillation enables improvement of the error rate of a logical non-Clifford operation such as the logical T gate. Another more newly developed technique, "code switching," switches back and forth between a code that is efficient for Clifford gates and a code that is optimized for non-Clifford gates to achieve universality. Both approaches incur overhead in the form of additional physical qubits, quantum gates, and classical decoding complexity. The substantial overhead introduced going from fault-tolerant Clifford gates to a universal set of fault-tolerant gates has been a major driver of research in quantum error correction codes and fault-tolerance schemes.

In the case of magic state distillation, several methods have been developed to lower the overhead cost [64]. In its simplest form, albeit not the optimal form in terms of resource overhead, magic state distillation for the T gate can transform a physical T gate with error rate to a logical T gate with an error rate of roughly $35p^3$. If this is still too high to be able to implement an algorithm of interest, then the procedure can be recursed, achieving $35(35p^3)^3$, and so on for r rounds resulting in $35^r p^{3r}$. In turn, each round requires 15 qubits to perform one improved T gate; thus, r rounds require 15^r qubits (physical or logical qubits may be used, depending on the desired output error rate on the T gate). Thus, while the QEC protocol is costly for Clifford operations and logical qubit encoding, the most costly procedure by far is the fault-tolerant implementation of the non-Clifford gate required for universality [65]. To convey a sense of the resource requirements of Clifford- and non-Clifford gates, Table 3.1 provides estimates of the requirements for carrying out an error-corrected quantum simulation of the molecular system FeMoco. This example should be seen as a snapshot of capabilities as of 2017. Progress

TABLE 3.1 Estimates of the Resource Requirements for Carrying Out Error-Corrected Simulations of a Chemical Structure (FeMoco in Nitrogenase) Using a Serial Algorithmic Approach for Hamiltonian Simulation and the Surface Code for Error Correction

Physical qubit error rate	10^{-3}	10^{-6}	10^{-9}
Physical qubits per logical qubit	15,313	1,103	313
Total physical qubits in processor	1.7×10^6	1.1×10^5	3.5×10^4
Number of T state factories	202	68	38
Number of physical qubits per factory	8.7×10^5	1.7×10^4	5.0×10^3
Total number of physical qubits including T state factories	1.8×10^8	1.3×10^6	2.3×10^5

NOTE: The table illustrates the trade-offs, for three specific physical qubit error rates, between the number and quality of the physical qubits required to achieve a fault-tolerant implementation of the algorithm. Estimates are based on a requirement of 111 logical qubits for the algorithm instance and physical gate frequencies of 100 MHz. Note that the requirements for distillation (T factories) are far greater than those for the rest of the error corrections. The cost of achieving an error-free, non-Clifford gate is orders of magnitude higher than encoding the qubits and their other Clifford operations with this particular QECC (surface code and magic state distillation).
SOURCE: Adapted from M. Reiher, N. Wiebe, K.M. Svore, D. Wecker, and M. Troyer, 2017, Elucidating reaction mechanisms on quantum computers, *Proceedings of the National Academy of Sciences of the U.S.A.* 114:7555-7560.

in quantum chemistry and simulation algorithms is ongoing, and these numbers will likely be improved.[9]

Finding: The performance of an error-corrected quantum algorithm will be limited by the number of operations which are the most expensive to error correct required for its implementation—for example, in the case of surface code QECC, the "non-Clifford Group" operations require many primitive gate operations to error correct and dominates the overall time (number of operations) that an algorithm requires.

Research continues on developing new quantum error-correcting codes and new quantum fault-tolerance schemes with the aim of dramatically lowering the resource overheads required to achieve fault-tolerant quantum computation. Much of this work has coalesced on studying surface codes and variants thereof, a class of code called topological codes [66].[10] Owing to the numerous unresolved questions about surface codes, researchers continue to find better ways of using these codes [67], and better ways of evaluating and decoding these codes [68]. When experimental systems reach the size at which interesting fault-tolerance experiments can be run, and these machines can interleave quantum operations and measurement, QEC schemes can be tested in order to verify the theory and analyses. The real benefit of these experiments will be that researchers working on QEC will see the effects and sources of "real" system errors, rather than using theoretical noise models. Insights about the actual errors could enable the development of more efficient QEC codes tailored for the error statistics of the actual machine. Again, minimizing the overhead is critical for deploying fault-tolerance schemes, especially on early quantum devices which will have a limited number of high-quality qubits.

Early demonstration of limited QEC operation on devices dates to as early as 2005, and the basic features of such protocols have been implemented on both superconducting qubit and trapped ion qubit devices. Such experiments have not yet yielded fault-tolerant logical qubits, given the generally poor gate fidelity of physical qubit operations [69-71]. Recently, quantum error detection codes—smaller precursors to QECs—have been implemented in available quantum processors, with some evidence of success [72,73]. As will be discussed in Chapter 7, successful

---

[9] For a recent review of progress in the field, see S. McArdle, S. Endo, A. Aspuru-Guzik, S. Benjamin, and X. Yuan, 2018, "Quantum Computational Chemistry," preprint arXiv:1808.10402.

[10] Topological codes are relatively good performers in terms of noise tolerance and qubit overhead, and they have the advantage of being naturally geometrically local in two dimensions, making them a promising class of codes for physical implementation—although some of the important variants live naturally in three or more dimensions.

demonstration of QEC to emulate practical, fault-tolerant logical qubits remains a significant milestone yet to be reached.

3.3 QUANTUM APPROXIMATION ALGORITHMS

Given that the high cost of error correction will preclude its use in early quantum computers, researchers have looked for other approaches for taking advantage of early quantum computers. A promising approach is to forgo the desire to obtain an exact solution for the computational problem and instead use an approximate, or heuristic approach to solve the problem. This approach has given rise to a number of quantum and hybrid quantum-classical algorithms for tasks that range from the simulation of many-body systems such as molecules and materials [74-82] to optimization [83] and machine learning applications [84-86]. The goal of these methods is to provide approximate but useful solutions to the problem at hand, with lower resource requirements than other approaches.

3.3.1 Variational Quantum Algorithms

Many problems of interest, in particular, problems in quantum chemistry, can be framed as so-called eigenvalue problems. According to the variational principle of quantum mechanics, the computed energy of the ground (lowest-energy) state of a quantum chemical system decreases as the approximations to the solution improve, asymptotically approaching the true value from above. This principle has given rise to iterative classical algorithms for solving these problems, where a crude guess of the solution is the input, and a somewhat-improved approximation is the output. This output is then used as the guess for the next iteration, and, with each cycle, the output gets closer and closer to the true solution, but never overshooting.

This approach can be split between a classical and a quantum algorithm, with the optimization step performed by the quantum processor, and subsequently read out, with a classical control unit deciding whether to perform another iteration. The ability to separate the quantum processing among many small, independent steps—with coherence required only over the course of a single step—makes these approaches a clever way to minimize the qubit fidelity requirements and obtain a useful result. For this reason, quantum variational algorithms have been suggested as applications for digital NISQ computers. It is worth noting that, of course, these algorithms are readily carried out using fully error-corrected quantum computers as well.

One specific example is the variational quantum eigensolver (VQE) [87-95], where the problem is broken into the sum of set of smaller problems that can each be approximated independently, with the sum of all outputs corresponding to the approximate solution of interest. The process is repeated until a heuristic stopping criteria is reached, usually corresponding to the achievement of an energy threshold. The computational power of VQE depends on the form of the assumed quantum state, or *ansatz*, employed. Some *ansatz* are purely defined by convenient circuit forms that can be readily accessible by hardware, whereas others are designed to capture specific types of quantum correlations. The VQE algorithm is believed to become competitive with a classical computer at the similar task of approximating the wave function and properties of a many-body system of interest when the number of qubits in the quantum register and the depth of the quantum circuit employed generate states that are intractable to prepare in a classical computer. The specific number of gates and qubits where this occurs is heavily dependent on the type of algorithm, but a very rough estimate for quantum simulation applications could consist of hundreds of qubits and tens of thousands of quantum gates [96].

A related approach is the quantum approximate optimization algorithm (QAOA) [97], an algorithm for preparing a variational guess of a wave function that satisfies an optimization problem, such as the satisfiability problem. The algorithm follows a similar procedure as the VQE algorithm—namely, a series of preparation and measurement experiments followed by optimization by a classical computer. The resulting quantum state, when sampled, provides approximate or exact solutions to the computational problem.

3.3.2 Analog Quantum Algorithms

In addition to algorithms that require a gate-based quantum computer, there are set of approaches that work by directly representing the task in terms of a Hamiltonian, which may or may not vary with time. The desired result is encoded in the system state at the end of the simulation run. "Direct quantum simulation," where the Hamiltonian created is analogous to that of the quantum system being explored, is one example of this type of approach, and a type of analog quantum computation. Examples of direct quantum simulation include the realization of spin Hamiltonians [98] or the study of quantum phase transitions [99-101].

Quantum annealing and, more specifically, adiabatic quantum optimization, also take this "analog" approach and provide a general-purpose schema for designing quantum algorithms without requiring the abstraction layer of logical operations, or gates. These two approaches are closely related: adiabatic quantum optimization is simply quantum annealing at zero temperature. Adiabatic quantum computation is interesting because one can in principle convert any gate-based quantum computation to an equivalent adiabatic quantum computation (although it might not be an efficient solution method) [102]. These methods require mapping an optimization problem of interest into a Hamiltonian, H_f, such that finding the lowest energy, or ground state, of a system defined by that Hamiltonian is equivalent to solving the problem.

The algorithm for quantum adiabatic optimization is implemented as follows: a set of qubits begins with a Hamiltonian H_i for which the ground state is known, and H_i is then slowly transformed into H_f. Since a quantum system will remain in its ground state if the Hamiltonian is changed slowly enough (adiabatically), this procedure drags the system from the ground state of H_i to the ground state of H_f. Measurement of the final state provides the answer sought with a high probability [103,104].

There was a great deal of excitement about the prospects of such algorithms following work by Farhi et al. [105], giving evidence suggesting that these algorithms could be fast on random instances of 3SAT, a logic satisfiability problem that is equivalent to many other hard problems. The theoretical analysis of this algorithm was quite challenging, since its running time was governed by the spectral gap (the difference in energy of states near the ground state), of the time evolving Hamiltonian. A sequence of papers analyzed this gap in a number of cases, establishing there are classes of 3SAT formulae and other NP-complete problems for which the spectral gap for an adiabatic algorithm is exponentially small, which means for these problems this approach will take time exponential in the size of the problem [106,107]. As a result, the formal power of this type of computing is still not known. Thus, the approach to establishing the speedup of quantum annealing algorithms is largely empirical; researchers literally compare the time required to complete a given task on a quantum annealer with the best times of optimal classical computer systems for arriving at the same result.

All real quantum computers operate at a finite temperature. When that temperature corresponds to an energy greater than the spectral gap, an analog quantum computer can only implement quantum annealing rather than quantum adiabatic computation. Quantum annealing is particularly attractive from the viewpoint of experimental realization, with the caveat that theoretical analysis of these algorithms is difficult, and there is no clear theory of fault-tolerance for this model. Adiabatic optimization devices, in particular the D-Wave machines, have overcome significant engineering challenges and scaled rapidly to thousands of qubits, albeit with some trade-offs in qubit fidelity. While it initially looked like these devices demonstrated promising speedups for some applications, further work on new classical algorithms for these specific problems have erased these speedups [108]. Recent work suggests that this reflects the relatively high temperature at which the D-Wave processors operate [109] and the presence of certain analog errors in these devices [110], although this does not rule out the possibility that there could be other fundamental limitations of quantum annealers.

3.4 APPLICATIONS OF A QUANTUM COMPUTER

As is apparent from the preceding discussions, many quantum algorithms have been developed, both for gate-based quantum computers and for quantum annealers. A comprehensive online catalogue of quantum algorithms is maintained by the U.S. National Institute of Standards and Technology (NIST) [111]. While this collection includes a host of algorithms that theoretically offer quantum speedup, this speedup is often the result of a few basic techniques at their core—in particular, quantum Fourier transform, quantum random walks, and Hamiltonian simulation. Furthermore, most algorithms require a large number of high-quality qubits in order to be useful, most likely requiring quantum error correction—far beyond the quantum resources available in known prototypical devices. In addition, the current inability to load large quantities of input data efficiently suggest that many of these would be difficult to implement in practice.

Furthermore, algorithms are generally not in and of themselves applications; rather, they are building blocks that must be combined in order to perform a useful task. As experimental efforts at realizing quantum computers gain momentum, the near-term challenge is to identify or create quantum applications and the algorithms they require—preferably useful ones which provide dramatic speedup over classical approaches—that can be deployed on non-error-corrected devices.

3.4.1 Near-Term Applications of a Quantum Computer

The potential near-term utility of a quantum computer is currently an active area of research. It is expected that such applications are likely to be those that require few qubits, can be implemented with a relatively shallow code (that is, they require relatively short sequences of gates), and can work on NISQ computers. The approximate algorithms discussed in Section 3.3 are considered to be leading prospects for implementation on near-term analog or digital NISQ machines. While there are many potential commercial[11] applications for this class of machine, as of the time of publication of this report (2018), none are certain to provide an

---

[11] A commercial application is one where someone is willing to pay money for the answer it can provide. It is an application that would bring revenue into quantum computing.

advantage over classical approaches when run on a NISQ computer. All of the researchers who spoke to the committee, including those from startups, agreed this was a critical area for research.

Finding: There is no publicly known application of commercial interest based upon quantum algorithms that could be run on a near-term analog or digital NISQ computer that would provide an advantage over classical approaches.

3.4.2 Quantum Supremacy

A necessary milestone on the path to useful quantum computers is quantum supremacy—a demonstration of any quantum computation that is prohibitively hard for classical computers, whether or not the computation is useful. In essence, quantum supremacy is an experimental demonstration that quantum computers violate the extended Church-Turing thesis. Quantum supremacy would also address skepticism about the viability of quantum computers, as well as provide a test of quantum theory in the realm of high complexity. To achieve this, one would need both to create a quantum computer large enough to demonstrate supremacy and to find a simple problem that it can perform but that is hard for a classical machine to compute. A common type of such problems is those where operations are performed on qubits to generate an entangled quantum state, and then to sample that state to estimate its probability distribution [112].

The first proposal for a good test problem is owing to Aaronson and Arkhipov in 2010, in their boson sampling proposal [113], building on earlier work on the classical complexity of sampling problems [114,115].[12] They were able to prove that computing the output probabilities of a random system of noninteracting bosons was in a complexity class (#P-hard) corresponding to computations thought to be difficult for classical computers to run. Moreover, under the plausible conjecture that these probabilities remain #P-hard to approximate, it would follow that classical computers cannot even sample a random output of a typical linear-optical network. For a quantum computer, providing such a sample (referred to as "qubit sampling") could amount to demonstration of quantum supremacy. While boson sampling has been popular with experimentalists, and small-scale implementations have already been achieved in a number of labs, including a 6-photon experiment [116], it remains

---

[12] The term "quantum supremacy" was coined by John Preskill in 2012, although work in this area began earlier.

challenging to push these experiments to the roughly 50 photons necessary to establish quantum supremacy [117].

A different approach for demonstrating quantum supremacy in superconducting qubits was proposed by the Google theory group in 2016 [118]. It was experimentally inspired, with quantum supremacy playing the role of a milestone on the way to building superconducting NISQ computers. Concretely, the proposal—Random Circuit Sampling (RCS)—called for implementing a random quantum circuit and measuring the output of the circuit. They conjectured that sampling from the output distribution of such random circuits is a hard problem classically. Recently, strong complexity-theoretic evidence for the classical hardness of RCS, on par with that for boson sampling, was given by Bouland et al. [119].

There are two main parts to a quantum supremacy proposal: the first is the definition of a computational task that could be experimentally realized in the near term, but which is prohibitively difficult for any algorithm running on a classical computer. The second is an efficient method for verifying that the quantum device actually carried out the computational task. This is particularly complicated, since the proposed algorithms are computing samples from a certain probability distribution (namely, the output distribution of the chosen quantum circuit). The first simplification to get around this validation problem is to choose n, the number of qubits, to be small enough ($n \approx 50$) so that a classical supercomputer can actually calculate the output distribution of the chosen quantum circuit. This still leaves the challenge of verifying that the outputs of the quantum device are actually drawn from this (or a close-by) distribution. This too can be difficult to prove.

For this, the RCS supremacy model [120] proposes the computation of a score in the form of the cross-entropy between the distribution sampled from the device and the true output distribution of the chosen quantum circuit. It turns out that the cross-entropy score verifies that the two distributions are close, provided a simple condition is met—namely, that the entropy of the distribution sampled from the device is at least as large as the entropy of the true output distribution of the chosen quantum circuit. [121]. Unfortunately, it is not possible to verify this entropy condition using any reasonable number of samples—although it holds for many noise models, such as local depolarizing noise. A different proposal for verification uses the concept of heavy output generation (or HOG) [122] and can be provably shown to verify supremacy under a (nonstandard) complexity assumption. Last, a third verification proposal, binned output generation (BOG), simultaneously verifies HOG and cross-entropy, and is information theoretically optimal in some formal model [123].

A proof-of-concept test for this quantum supremacy algorithm was performed in 2017 on a 9-qubit device [124]. The error rate was shown to be proportional to the number of operations multiplied by the number of qubits, with an average error per 2-qubit gate of about 0.3 percent. Simple extrapolation to a qubit device with around 50 qubits indicates that a quantum supremacy result should be possible with this architecture, and the Google hardware team (and others) are working hard to achieve this goal.

The approaches leave two questions unanswered. The first is how to perform verification without the entropy assumption (or a nonstandard complexity assumption). The second is the possibility of establishing quantum supremacy beyond the limit of the computing power of classical supercomputers, currently understood[13] to correspond to on the order of about 50 qubits. A recent proposal shows how to provably carry out quantum supremacy based on post-quantum cryptography. Specifically, based on the hardness of the learning with errors (LWE) problem, the proposal gives a way of provably testing quantum supremacy for quantum computers with arbitrarily large numbers of qubits [125].

Finding: While several teams have been working to demonstrate quantum supremacy, this milestone has not yet been demonstrated (as of the time of publication of this report). Its achievement will difficult to establish definitively, and this target may continue to move as improvements are made to classical approaches for solving the chosen benchmark problem.

In summary, the pursuit of quantum supremacy has already achieved an interesting goal: the development of theoretical tools useful for rigorously analyzing the computational hardness of certain quantum problems that may soon be experimentally implementable. However, owing both to the uncertain nature of the hardness results (i.e., the reliance on nonstandard hardness conjectures) and to the restrictive nature of the noise models addressed by these results, there is much work remaining to be done.

3.4.3 Applications for an Ideal Quantum Computer

In the event of development of a robust, large-scale error-corrected quantum computer, the existing algorithms with known speedup are likely to be useful for solving any number of practical problems, or parts

---

[13] While the exact number depends upon the specifications and approximations of the particular simulation, and this number will increase as classical methods improve, it is expected to remain at this order of magnitude for a significant amount of time. Recently, researchers have used a new classical approach to perform a single instance of the quantum supremacy task that would be achievable by a 70-qubit quantum device; however, this does not correspond to the full 100,000-instance quantum supremacy experiment proposed for a 50-qubit device, which has not yet proven achievable on a classical computer.

of problems. Perhaps the best-understood application of quantum algorithms is in the field of cryptography (specifically, defeating it), an application based directly on mathematics; these applications will be discussed in the next chapter. Quantum simulation, for both foundational and applied science, is also commonly raised as a potential "killer app," especially in the field of quantum chemistry [126].

The electronic structure problem has received much attention, owing to its centrality to the fields of chemistry and materials science. This problem requires solving for the ground state energies and wave functions of electrons interacting in the presence of some external field, usually arising from atomic nuclei. Electronic structure defines chemical properties and the rates and products of chemical reactions. While classical computing approaches to this problem (such as density functional theory) are quite effective in many contexts (such as predicting molecular geometries), they often fail to reach the level of accuracy required to predict chemical reaction rates or distinguish between competing phases of correlated materials. This is especially true when the system involves transition metal elements (which are present in most catalysts). Quantum computers could enable efficient solutions to this problem in the classically intractable regime. In fact, one early quantum algorithm offers exponential speedup over classical approaches to calculation of chemical reaction rate constants [127]. This and other algorithms could open the door to significant insights about chemical reactions and phases of matter that have long eluded description by a systematic and predictive theory. Such results could also have commercial applications in areas such as energy storage, device displays, industrial catalysts, and pharmaceutical development.

3.5 THE POTENTIAL ROLE OF QUANTUM COMPUTERS IN THE COMPUTING ECOSYSTEM

While quantum chemistry, optimization (including machine learning), and defeating cryptography are the best-understood potential applications of an ideal quantum computer, the field is still in early stages—in terms of both algorithms, as discussed in this chapter, and devices, as will be discussed in Chapter 5. Existing algorithms may be modified or implemented in ways not yet anticipated; new algorithms will likely emerge as research continues. As a result, except for cryptography, it is not possible to predict the implications of quantum computers on various commercial sectors—the field is so young that these changes are not even on the horizon. For cryptography, the potential of a future quantum computer running Shor's algorithm is sufficient to affect action today. These issues are described in Chapter 4.

As is clear from this chapter's discussions, the ability to deploy known quantum algorithms could render some previously intractable problems efficiently solvable. However, even a large error-corrected quantum computer would not be generally superior to a classical computer. In fact, quantum computers do not speed up many classes of problems, and the maturity of the classical computing ecosystem (including hardware, software, and algorithms) means that for these classes of problem, classical computing will remain the dominant computing platform. Even applications accelerated by a quantum computer, the parts accelerated are likely to comprise only a small component of the broader task in question. For the foreseeable future, a quantum processor is thus likely to be useful for performing only certain parts of certain tasks, with the remaining operations more efficiently carried out on a classical computer. Thus, a quantum computer is expected to serve as a co-processor to, rather than a replacement for, a classical computer. Furthermore, as will be discussed in Chapter 5, the physical implementation of any quantum computation will require a host of complex gating operations to be performed upon qubits maintained in a controlled environment, which will require the use of classical computers.

Finding: Quantum computers are unlikely to be useful as a direct replacement for conventional computers, or for all applications; rather, they are currently expected to be special-purpose devices operating in a complementary fashion with conventional processors, analogous to a co-processor or accelerator.

3.6 NOTES

[1] E. Bernstein and U. Vazirani, 1997, Quantum complexity theory, *SIAM Journal on Computing* 26(5):1411-1473.
[2] D. Simon, 1997, On the power of quantum computation, *SIAM Journal on Computing* 26(5):1474-1483.
[3] P. Shor, 1994, "Algorithms for Quantum Computation: Discrete Logarithms and Factoring," pp. 124-134 in *35th Annual Symposium on Foundations of Computer Science, 1994 Proceedings*, https://ieeexplore.ieee.org.
[4] R.J. Anderson and H. Wolf, 1997, Algorithms for the certified write-all problem, *SIAM Journal on Computing* 26(5):1277-1283.
[5] R.M. Karp, 1975, On the computational complexity of combinatorial problems, *Networks* 5(1):45-68.
[6] C.H. Bennett, E. Bernstein, G. Brassard, and U. Vazirani, 1997, Strengths and weaknesses of quantum computing, *SIAM Journal on Computing* 26(5):1510-1523.
[7] L.K. Grover, 1996, "A Fast Quantum Mechanical Algorithm for Database Search," pp. 212-219 in *Proceedings of the Twenty-Eighth Annual ACM Symposium on Theory of Computing*, https://dl.acm.org/proceedings.cfm.
[8] S. Cook, 2006, "The P versus NP problem," pp. 87-104 in *The Millennium Prize Problems* (J. Carlson, A. Jaffe, A. Wiles, eds.), Clay Mathematics Institute/American Mathematical Society, Providence, R.I.
[9] J. Preskill, 2018, "Quantum Computing in the NISQ Era and Beyond," arXiv:1801.00862.

[10] L. Hales and S. Hallgren, 2000, "An Improved Quantum Fourier Transform Algorithm and Applications," pp. 515-525 in *41st Annual Symposium on Foundations of Computer Science, 2000 Proceedings*, https://ieeexplore.ieee.org.

[11] P.W. Shor, 1994, "Algorithms for Quantum Computation: Discrete Logarithms and Factoring," pp. 124-134 in *35th Annual Symposium on Foundations of Computer Science, 1994 Proceedings*, https://ieeexplore.ieee.org.

[12] R. Jozsa, 2001, Quantum factoring, discrete logarithms, and the hidden subgroup problem, *Computing in Science and Engineering* 3(2):34-43.

[13] A.Y. Kitaev, 1995, "Quantum Measurements and the Abelian Stabilizer Problem," preprint arXiv:quant-ph/9511026.

[14] L.K. Grover, 1996, "A Fast Quantum Mechanical Algorithm for Database Search," pp. 212-219 in *Proceedings of the Twenty-Eighth Annual ACM Symposium on Theory of Computing*, https://dl.acm.org/proceedings.cfm.

[15] C.H. Bennett, E. Bernstein, G. Brassard, and U. Vazirani, 1997, Strengths and weaknesses of quantum computing, *SIAM Journal on Computing* 26(5):1510-1523.

[16] G. Brassard, P. Hoyer, M. Mosca, and A. Tapp, 2002, Quantum amplitude amplification and estimation, *Contemporary Mathematics* 305:53-74.

[17] E. Farhi, J. Goldstone, and S. Gutmann, 2007, "A Quantum Algorithm for the Hamiltonian NAND Tree," preprint arXiv:quant-ph/0702144.

[18] A. Ambainis, A.M. Childs, B.W. Reichardt, R. Špalek, and S. Zhang, 2010, Any AND-OR formula of size N can be evaluated in time $N^{1/2}+O(1)$ on a quantum computer, *SIAM Journal on Computing* 39(6):2513-2530.

[19] V. Giovannetti, S. Lloyd, and L. Maccone, 2008, Quantum random access memory, *Physical Review Letters* 100(16):160501.

[20] R.P. Feynman, 1982, Simulating physics with computers, *International Journal of Theoretical Physics* 21(6-7):467-488.

[21] D.S. Abrams and S. Lloyd, 1997, Simulation of many-body Fermi systems on a universal quantum computer, *Physical Review Letters* 79(13):2586.

[22] D. Aharonov and A. Ta-Shma, 2003, "Adiabatic Quantum State Generation and Statistical Zero Knowledge," pp. 20-29 in *Proceedings of the Thirty-Fifth Annual ACM Symposium on Theory of Computing*, https://dl.acm.org/proceedings.cfm.

[23] D.W. Berry, A.M. Childs, R. Cleve, R. Kothari, and R.D. Somma, 2015, Simulating Hamiltonian dynamics with a truncated Taylor series, *Physical Review Letters* 114(9):090502.

[24] R. Babbush, D.W. Berry, I.D. Kivlichan, A. Scherer, A.Y. Wei, P.J. Love, and A. Aspuru-Guzik, 2017, Exponentially more precise quantum simulation of fermions in the configuration interaction representation, *Quantum Science and Technology* 3:015006.

[25] G.H. Low and I.L. Chuang, 2016, "Hamiltonian Simulation by Qubitization," preprint arXiv:1610.06546.

[26] See, for example, G.H. Low and I.L. Chuang, 2017, Optimal Hamiltonian simulation by quantum signal processing, *Physical Review Letters* 118(1):010501.

[27] R. Babbush, D.W. Berry, I.D. Kivlichan, A.Y. Wei, P.J. Love, and A. Aspuru-Guzik, 2016, Exponentially more precise quantum simulation of fermions I: Quantum chemistry in second quantization, *New Journal of Physics* 18:033032.

[28] D.W. Berry, A.M. Childs, and R. Kothari, 2015, "Hamiltonian Simulation with Nearly Optimal Dependence on All Parameters," pp. 792-809 in *Proceedings of the 56th IEEE Symposium on Foundations of Computer Science*, https://ieeexplore.ieee.org.

[29] S. McArdle, S. Endo, A. Aspuru-Guzik, S. Benjamin, and X. Yuan, 2018, "Quantum Computational Chemistry," preprint arXiv:1808.10402.

[30] D. Wecker, M.B. Hastings, N. Wiebe, B.K. Clark, C. Nayak, and M. Troyer, 2015, Solving strongly correlated electron models on a quantum computer, *Physical Review A* 92(6):062318.

[31] C. Dykstra, G. Frenking, K.S. Kim, and G.E. Scuseria, 2005, *Theory and Applications of Computational Chemistry: The First Forty Years*, Elsevier, Amsterdam.
[32] M. Reiher, N. Wiebe, K.M. Svore, D. Wecker, and M. Troyer, 2017, Elucidating reaction mechanisms on quantum computers, *Proceedings of the National Academy of the Sciences of the U.S.A.* 114:7555-7560.
[33] G. Wendin, 2017, Quantum information processing with superconducting circuits: A review, *Reports on Progress in Physics* 80(10):106001.
[34] M. Reiher, N. Wiebe, K.M. Svore, D. Wecker, and M. Troyer, 2017, Elucidating reaction mechanisms on quantum computers, *Proceedings of the National Academy of Sciences of the U.S.A.* 114:7555-7560.
[35] B. Bauer, D. Wecker, A.J. Millis, M.B. Hastings, and M. Troyer, 2016, Hybrid quantum-classical approach to correlated materials, *Physical Review X* 6:031045.
[36] See J. Olson, Y. Cao, J. Romero, P. Johnson, P.-L. Dallaire-Demers, N. Sawaya, P. Narang, I. Kivlichan, M. Wasielewski, and A. Aspuru-Guzik, 2017, "Quantum Information and Computation for Chemistry," preprint arXiv:1706.05413, for a good overview.
[37] R. Babbush, D.W. Berry, I.D. Kivlichan, A.Y. Wei, P.J. Love, and A. Aspuru-Guzik, 2017, Exponentially more precise quantum simulation of fermions in the configuration interaction representation, *Quantum Science and Technology* 3:015006.
[38] J. Olson, Y. Cao, J. Romero, P. Johnson, P.-L. Dallaire-Demers, N. Sawaya, P. Narang, I. Kivlichan, M. Wasielewski, and A. Aspuru-Guzik, 2017, "Quantum Information and Computation for Chemistry," preprint arXiv:1706.05413.
[39] I.D. Kivlichan, J. McClean, N. Wiebe, C. Gidney, A. Aspuru-Guzik, G. Kin-Lic Chan, and R. Babbush, 2018, Quantum simulation of electronic structure with linear depth and connectivity, *Physical Review Letters* 120:11501.
[40] R. Babbush, C. Gidney, D.W. Berry, N. Wiebe, J. McClean, A. Paler, A. Fowler, and H. Neven, 2018, "Encoding Electronic Spectra in Quantum Circuits with Linear T Complexity," preprint arXiv:1805.03662.
[41] G.H. Low and N. Wiebe, 2018, "Hamiltonian Simulation in the Interaction Picture," preprint arXiv:1805.00675.
[42] D.W. Berry, M. Kieferová, A. Scherer, Y.R. Sanders, G.H. Low, N. Wiebe, C. Gidney, and R. Babbush, 2018, Improved techniques for preparing eigenstates of fermionic Hamiltonians, *npj Quantum Information* 4(1):22.
[43] D. Wecker, M. B. Hastings, N. Wiebe, B.K. Clark, C. Nayak, and M. Troyer, 2015, Solving strongly correlated electron models on a quantum computer, *Physical Review A* 92(6):062318.
[44] D. Poulin, M.B. Hastings, D. Wecker, N. Wiebe, A.C. Doherty, and M. Troyer, 2014, "The Trotter step size required for accurate quantum simulation of quantum chemistry," *arXiv preprint arXiv:1406.49*.
[45] M.B. Hastings, D. Wecker, B. Bauer, and M. Troyer, 2014, "Improving Quantum Algorithms for Quantum Chemistry," preprint arXiv:1403.1539.
[46] D. Poulin, A. Kitaev, D.S. Steiger, M.B. Hastings, and M. Troyer, 2018, Quantum algorithm for spectral measurement with a lower gate count, *Physical Review Letters* 121(1):010501.
[47] D. Wecker, B. Bauer, B.K. Clark, M.B.. Hastings, and M. Troyer, 2014, Gate-count estimates for performing quantum chemistry on small quantum computers, *Physical Review A* 90(2):022305.
[48] A.W. Harrow, A. Hassidim, and S. Lloyd, 2009, Quantum algorithm for linear systems of equations, *Physical Review Letters* 103(15):150502.
[49] A.M. Childs and W.V. Dam, 2010, Quantum algorithms for algebraic problems, *Reviews of Modern Physics* 82(1):1.
[50] D.W. Berry, A.M. Childs, A. Ostrander, and G. Wang, 2017, Quantum algorithm for linear differential equations with exponentially improved dependence on precision, *Communications in Mathematical Physics* 356(3):1057-1081.

[51] F.G.S.L. Brandao and K. Svore, 2017, "Quantum Speed-Ups for Semidefinite Programming," https://arxiv.org/abs/1609.05537.

[52] I. Kerenidis and A. Prakash, 2016, "Quantum Recommendation Systems," preprint arXiv:1603.08675.

[53] E. Tang, 2018, "A Quantum-Inspired Classical Algorithm for Recommendation Systems," preprint arXiv:1807.04271.

[54] P.D. Johnson, J. Romero, J. Olson, Y. Cao, and A. Aspuru-Guzik, 2017, "QVECTOR: An Algorithm for Device-Tailored Quantum Error Correction," preprint: arXiv:1711.02249.

[55] A. Kandala, K. Temme, A.D. Corcoles, A. Mezzacapo, J.M. Chow, and J.M. Gambetta, 2018, "Extending the Computational Reach of a Noisy Superconducting Quantum Processor," arXiv:1805.04492.

[56] A.R. Calderbank and P.W. Shor, 1997, "Good quantum error-correcting codes exist," *Physical Review A*, 54:1098-1106, arXiv:quant-ph/9512032.

[57] A. Steane, 1996, Simple quantum error correcting codes, *Physical Review A* 54:4741, arXiv:quant-ph/9605021.

[58] See, for example, E. Knill, 2005, Quantum computing with realistically noisy devices, *Nature* 434:39-44.

[59] P. Aliferis, D. Gottesman, and J. Preskill, 2006, Quantum accuracy threshold for concatenated distance-3 codes, *Quantum Information and Computation* 6:97-165, arXiv:quant-ph/0504218.

[60] W.K. Wootters and W.H. Zurek, 1982, A single quantum cannot be cloned, *Nature* 299(5886):802-803.

[61] M. Reiher, N. Wiebe, K.M. Svore, D. Wecker, and M. Troyer, 2017, Elucidating reaction mechanisms on quantum computers, *Proceedings of the National Academy of the Sciences of the U.S.A.* 114:7555-7560.

[62] A.G. Fowler, M. Mariantoni, J.M. Martinis, and A.N. Cleland, 2012, Surface codes: Towards practical large-scale quantum computation, *Physical Review A* 86:032324.

[63] For details on low-distance codes, see Y. Tomita and K.M. Svore, 2014, "Low-distance Surface Codes under Realistic Quantum Noise," https://arxiv.org/pdf/1404.3747.pdf. For general replacement rules for the surface code, see, for example, A.G. Fowler, M. Mariantoni, J.M. Martinis, and A.N. Cleland, 2012, "Surface Codes: Towards Practical Large-Scale Quantum Computation, https://arxiv.org/abs/1208.0928. For concatenated and block codes, see, for example, P. Aliferis, D. Gottesman, and J. Preskill, 2005, "Quantum Accuracy Threshold for Concatenated Distance-3 Codes," https://arxiv.org/abs/quant-ph/0504218, and K.M. Svore, D.P. DiVincenzo, and B.M. Terhal, 2006, "Noise Threshold for a Fault-Tolerant Two-Dimensional Lattice Architecture," https://arxiv.org/abs/quant-ph/0604090.

[64] See, for example, M.B. Hastings, J. Haah, "Distillation with Sublogarithmic Overhead," https://arxiv.org/abs/1709.03543;

J. Haah and M.B. Hastings, 2017, "Codes and Protocols for Distilling T, controlled S, and Toffoli Gates," https://arxiv.org/abs/1709.02832;

J. Haah, M.B. Hastings, D. Poulin, and D. Wecker, 2017, "Magic State Distillation at Intermdediate Size," https://arxiv.org/abs/1709.02789; and

J. Haah, M.B. Hastings, D. Poulin. and D. Wecker, 2017, "Magic State Distillation with Low Space Overhead and Optimal Asymptotic Input Count," https://arxiv.org/abs/1703.07847.

[65] See, for example, Table II in M. Reiher, N. Wiebe, K.M. Svore, D. Wecker, and M. Troyer, 2017, "Elucidating Reaction Mechanisms on Quantum Computers," https://arxiv.org/pdf/1605.03590.pdf, for detailed numbers on the cost of the T implementation for understanding reaction mechanisms on a quantum computer using Hamiltonian simulation.

[66] H. Bombin and M.A. Martin-Delgado, 2006, Topological quantum distillation, *Physical Review Letters* 97:180501, arXiv:quant-ph/0605138.
[67] See, for example, J.E. Moussa, 2016, Transversal Clifford gates on folded surface codes, *Physical Review A* 94:042316, arXiv:1603.02286;

C. Horsman, A. G. Fowler, S. Devitt, and R. Van Meter, 2012, Surface code quantum computing by lattice surgery, *New Journal of Physics* 14:123011, arXiv:1111.4022;

S. Bravyi and A. Cross, 2015, "Doubled Color Codes," arXiv:1509.03239;

H. Bombin, 2015, Gauge color codes: Optimal transversal gates and gauge fixing in topological stabilizer codes, *New Journal of Physics* 17:083002, arXiv:1311.0879;

T.J. Yoder and I.H. Kim, 2017, The surface code with a twist, *Quantum* 1:2, arXiv:1612.04795.
[68] See, for example, S. Bravyi, M. Suchara, and A. Vargo, 2014, Efficient algorithms for maximum likelihood decoding in the surface code, *Physical Review A* 90:032326, arXiv:1405.4883;

G. Duclos-Cianci and D. Poulin, 2014, Fault-tolerant renormalization group decoder for abelian topological codes, *Quantum Information and Computation* 14:721-740, arXiv:!304.6100.
[69] J. Chiaverini, Di. Leibfried, T. Schaetz, M.D. Barrett, R.B. Blakestad, J. Britton, W.M. Itano, et al., 2004, Realization of quantum error correction, *Nature* 432(7017):602.
[70] D. Nigg, M. Mueller, E.A. Martinez, P. Schindler, M. Hennrich, T. Monz, M.A. Martin-Delgado, and R. Blatt, 2014, Quantum computations on a topologically encoded qubit, *Science* 1253742.
[71] S. Rosenblum, P. Reinhold, M. Mirrahimi, Liang Jiang, L. Frunzio, and R.J. Schoelkopf, 2018, "Fault-Tolerant Measurement of a Quantum Error Syndrome," preprint arXiv:1803.00102.
[72] N.M. Linke, M. Gutierrez, K.A. Landsman, C. Figgatt, S. Debnath, K.R. Brown, and C. Monroe, 2017, Fault-tolerant quantum error detection, *Science Advances* 3(10):e1701074.
[73] R. Harper and S. Flammia, 2018, "Fault Tolerance in the IBM Q Experience," preprint arXiv:1806.02359.
[74] A. Peruzzo, J.R. McClean, P. Shadbolt, M.-H. Yung, X.-Q. Zhou, P.J. Love, A. Aspuru-Guzik, and J.L. O'Brien, 2013, "A Variational Eigenvalue Solver on a Quantum Processor," arXiv:1304.3061.
[75] D. Wecker, M.B. Hastings, and M. Troyer, 2015, Progress towards practical quantum variational algorithms, *Physical Review A* 92:042303.
[76] J.R. McClean, J. Romero, R. Babbush, and A. Aspuru-Guzik, 2016, The theory of variational hybrid quantum-classical algorithms, *New Journal of Physics* 18:023023.
[77] P.J.J. O'Malley, R. Babbush, I.D. Kivlichan, J. Romero, J.R. McClean, R. Barends, J. Kelly, et al., 2016, Scalable quantum simulation of molecular energies, *Physical Review X* 6:031007.
[78] R. Santagati, J. Wang, A.A. Gentile, S. Paesani, N. Wiebe, J.R. McClean, S.R. Short, et al., 2016, "Quantum Simulation of Hamiltonian Spectra on a Silicon Chip," arXiv:1611.03511.
[79] G.G. Guerreschi and M. Smelyanskiy, 2017, "Practical Optimization for Hybrid Quantum-Classical Algorithms," arXiv:1701.01450.
[80] J.R. McClean, M.E. Kimchi-Schwartz, J. Carter, and W.A. de Jong, 2017, Hybrid quantum-classical hierarchy for mitigation of decoherence and determination of excited states, *Physical Review A* 95:042308.
[81] J.R. Romero, R. Babbush, J.R. McClean, C. Hempel, P. Love, and A. Aspuru-Guzik, 2017, "Strategies for Quantum Computing Molecular Energies Using the Unitary Coupled Cluster Ansatz," arXiv:1701.02691.
[82] Y. Shen, X. Zhang, S. Zhang, J.-N. Zhang, M.-H. Yung, and K. Kim, 2017, Quantum implementation of the unitary coupled cluster for simulating molecular electronic structure, *Physical Review A* 95:020501.

[83] See, for example, E. Farhi, J. Goldstone, and S. Gutmann, 2014, "A Quantum Approximate Optimization Algorithm," arXiv:1411.4028;
E. Farhi, J. Goldstone, and S. Gutmann, 2014, "A Quantum Approximate Optimization Algorithm Applied to a Bounded Occurrence Constraint Problem," arXiv:1412.6062;
E. Farhi and A.W. Harrow, 2016, "Quantum Supremacy through the Quantum Approximate Optimization Algorithm," arXiv:1602.07674.

[84] J. Romero, J. Olson, and A. Aspuru-Guzik, 2017, Quantum autoencoders for efficient compression of quantum data, *Quantum Science and Technology* 2:045001.

[85] M. Benedetti, D. Garcia-Pintos, Y. Nam, and A. Perdomo-Ortiz, 2018, "A Generative Modeling Approach for Benchmarking and Training Shallow Quantum Circuits," https://arxiv.org/abs/1801.07686.

[86] G. Verdon, M. Broughton, and J. Biamonte, 2017, "A Quantum Algorithm to Train Neural Networks Using Low-Depth Circuits," arXiv:1712.05304.

[87] A. Peruzzo, J.R. McClean, P. Shadbolt, M.-H. Yung, X.-Q. Zhou, P.J. Love, A. Aspuru-Buzik, and J.L. O'Brien, 2013, "A Variational Eigenvalue Solver on a Quantum Processor," arXiv:1304.3061.

[88] D. Wecker, M.B. Hastings, and M. Troyer, 2015, Progress towards practical quantum variational algorithms, *Physical Review A* 92:042303.

[89] J.R. McClean, J. Romero, R. Babbush, and A. Aspuru-Guzik, 2016, The theory of variational hybrid quantum-classical algorithms, *New Journal of Physics* 18:023023.

[90] P.J.J. O'Malley, R. Babbush, I.D. Kivlichan, J. Romero, J.R. McClean, R. Barends, J. Kelly, et al., 2016, Scalable quantum simulation of molecular energies, *Physical Review X* 6:031007.

[91] R. Santagati, J. Wang, A.A. Gentile, S. Paesani, N. Wiebe, J.R. McClean, S.R. Short, et al., 2016, "Quantum Simulation of Hamiltonian Spectra on a Silicon Chip," arXiv:1611.03511.

[92] G.G. Guerreschi and M. Smelyanskiy, 2017, "Practical Optimization for Hybrid Quantum-Classical Algorithms," arXiv:1701.01450.

[93] J.R. McClean, M.E. Kimchi-Schwartz, J. Carter, and W.A. de Jong, 2017, Hybrid quantum-classical hierarchy for mitigation of decoherence and determination of excited states, *Physical Review A* 95:042308.

[94] J.R. Romero, R. Babbush, J.R. McClean, C. Hempel, P. Love, and A. Aspuru-Guzik, 2017, "Strategies for Quantum Computing Molecular Energies Using the Unitary Coupled Cluster Ansatz," arXiv:1701.02691.

[95] Y. Shen, X. Zhang, S. Zhang, J.-N. Zhang, M.-H. Yung, and K. Kim, 2017, Quantum implementation of the unitary coupled cluster for simulating molecular electronic structure, *Physical Review A* 95:020501.

[96] P.-L. Dallaire-Demers, J. Romero, L. Veis, S. Sim, and A. Aspuru-Guzik, 2018, "Low-Depth Circuit Ansatz for Preparing Correlated Fermionic States on a Quantum Computer," arXiv:1801.01053.

[97] E. Farhi, J. Goldstone, and S. Gutmann, 2014, "A Quantum Approximate Optimization Algorithm," preprint arXiv:1411.4028.

[98] J. Smith, A. Lee, P. Richerme, B. Neyenhuis, P. W. Hess, P. Hauke, M. Heyl, D. A. Huse, and C. Monroe, 2015, "Many-Body Localization in a Quantum Simulator with Programmable Random Disorder," arXiv:1508.07026.

[99] A. Mazurenko, C.S. Chiu, G. Ji, M.F. Parsons, M. Kanász-Nagy, R. Schmidt, F. Grusdt, E. Demler, D. Greif, and M. Greiner, 2017, A cold-atom Fermi-Hubbard antiferromagnet, *Nature* 545:462-466.

[100] R. Harris, Y. Sato, A. J. Berkley, M. Reis, F. Altomare, M.H. Amin, K. Boothby, et al., 2018, Phase transitions in a programmable quantum spin glass simulator, *Science* 361(6398):162-165.

[101] A.D. King, J. Carrasquilla, J. Raymond, I. Ozfidan, E. Andriyash, A. Berkley, M. Reis, et al., 2018, Observation of topological phenomena in a programmable lattice of 1,800 qubits, *Nature* 560(7719):456.

[102] D. Aharonov, W. van Dam, J. Kempe, Z. Landau, S. Lloyd, and O. Regev, 2004, "Adiabatic Quantum Computation is Equivalent to Standard Quantum Computation," arXiv:quant-ph/0405098.

[103] T. Kadowaki and H. Nishimori, 1998, Quantum annealing in the transverse Ising model, *Physical Review E* 58(5):5355.

[104] T. Albash and D.A. Lidar, 2016, "Adiabatic Quantum Computing," preprint arXiv:1611.04471.

[105] E. Farhi, J. Goldstone, S. Gutmann, J. Lapan, A. Lundgren, and D. Preda, 2001, A quantum adiabatic evolution algorithm applied to random instances of an NP-complete problem, *Science* 292(5516):472-475.

[106] W. Van Dam, M. Mosca, and U. Vazirani, 2001, "How Powerful Is Adiabatic Quantum Computation?," pp. 279-287 in *42nd IEEE Symposium on Foundations of Computer Science, 2001 Proceedings*, https://ieeexplore.ieee.org.

[107] A.P. Young, S. Knysh, and V.N. Smelyanskiy, 2008, Size dependence of the minimum excitation gap in the quantum adiabatic algorithm, *Physical Review Letters* 101(17):170503.

[108] See, for example, A. Selby, http://www.archduke.org/stuff/d-wave-comment-on-comparison-with-classical-computers/;

S. Boixo, T.F. Rønnow, S.V. Isakov, Z. Wang, D. Wecker, D.A. Lidar, J.M. Martinis and M. Troyer, 2014, Evidence for quantum annealing with more than one hundred qubits, *Nature Physics* 10:218-224;

T.F. Rønnow, Z. Wang, J. Job, S. Boixo, S.V. Isakov, D. Wecker, J.M. Martinis, D.A. Lidar, M. Troyer, 2014, Defining and detecting quantum speedup, *Science* 345:420;

J. King, S. Yarkoni, M.M. Nevisi, J.P. Hilton, and C.C. McGeoch, "Benchmarking a Quantum Annealing Processor with the Time-to-Target Metric," https://arxiv.org/abs/1508.05087;

I. Hen, J. Job, T. Albash, T.F. Rønnow, M. Troyer, and D.A. Lidar, 2015, Probing for quantum speedup in spin-glass problems with planted solutions, *Physical Review A* 92:042325;

S. Mandrà, Z. Zhu, W. Wang, A. Perdomo-Ortiz, and H.G. Katzgraber, 2016, Strengths and weaknesses of weak-strong cluster problems: A detailed overview of state-of-the-art classical heuristics versus quantum approaches, *Physical Review A* 94:022337;

V.S. Denchev, S. Boixo, S.V. Isakov, N. Ding, R. Babbush, V. Smelyanskiy, J. Martinis, and H. Neven, 2016, What is the Computational Value of Finite-Range Tunneling?, *Physical Review X* 6:031015;

S. Mandrà, H.G. Katzgraber, and C. Thomas, 2017, The pitfalls of planar spin-glass benchmarks: Raising the bar for quantum annealers (again), *Quantum Science and Technology* 2(3);

J. King, S. Yarkoni, J. Raymond, I. Ozfidan, A.D. King, M.M. Nevisi, J.P. Hilton, and C.C. McGeoch, 2017, "Quantum Annealing amid Local Ruggedness and Global Frustration," https://arxiv.org/abs/1701.04579;

S. Mandrà and H.G. Katzgraber, 2018, A deceptive step towards quantum speedup detection, *Quantum Science and Technology* 3:04LT01;

T. Albash and D.A. Lidar, 2018, Demonstration of a scaling advantage for a quantum annealer over simulated annealing, *Physical Review X* 8:031016.

[109] T. Albash, V. Martin-Mayor, and I. Hen, 2017, Temperature scaling law for quantum annealing optimizers, *Physical Review Letters* 119(11):110502.

[110] T. Albash, V. Martin-Mayor, and I. Hen, 2018, "Analog Errors in Ising Machines," preprint arXiv:1806.03744.

[111] S. Jordan, 2018, "Algebraic and Number Theoretic Algorithms," National Institute of Standards and Technology, last updated January 18, 2018, http://math.nist.gov/quantum/zoo/.

[112] A.W. Harrow and A. Montanaro, 2017, Quantum computational supremacy, *Nature* 549(7671):203.

[113] S. Aaronson and A. Arkhipov, 2011, "The Computational Complexity of Linear Optics," pp. 333-342 in *Proceedings of the Forty-Third Annual ACM Symposium on Theory of Computing*, https://dl.acm.org/proceedings.cfm.

[114] M.J. Bremner, R. Jozsa, and D.J. Shepherd, 2010, Classical simulation of commuting quantum computations implies collapse of the polynomial hierarchy, *Proceedings of the Royal Society of London A* 467(2126):rspa20100301.

[115] B.M. Terhal and D.P. DiVincenzo, 2001, "Classical Simulation of Noninteracting-Fermion Quantum Circuits," arXiv:quant-ph/0108010.

[116] J. Carolan, C. Harrold, C. Sparrow, E. Martín-López, N.J. Russell, J.W. Silverstone, P.J. Shadbolt, et al., 2015, Universal linear optics, *Science* 349(6249):711-716.

[117] P. Clifford and R. Clifford, 2018, "The Classical Complexity of Boson Sampling," pp. 146-155 in *Proceedings of the Twenty-Ninth Annual ACM-SIAM Symposium on Discrete Algorithms*, https://www.siam.org/Conferences/About-SIAM-Conferences/Proceedings.

[118] S. Boixo, S.V. Isakov, V.N. Smelyanskiy, R. Babbush, N. Ding, Z. Jiang, M.J. Bremner, J.M. Martinis, and H. Neven, 2017, "Characterizing Quantum Supremacy in Near-Term Devices," arXiv:1608.00263.

[119] A. Bouland, B. Fefferman, C. Nirkhe, and U. Vazirani, 2018, "Quantum Supremacy and the Complexity of Random Circuit Sampling," arXiv:1803.04402.

[120] S. Boixo, S.V. Isakov, V.N. Smelyanskiy, R. Babbush, N. Ding, Z. Jiang, M.J. Bremner, J.M. Martinis, and H. Neven, 2017, "Characterizing Quantum Supremacy in Near-Term Devices," arXiv:1608.00263.

[121] A. Bouland, B. Fefferman, C. Nirkhe, and U. Vazirani, 2018, "Quantum Supremacy and the Complexity of Random Circuit Sampling," arXiv:1803.04402.

[122] S. Aaronson and L. Chen, 2017, "Complexity-Theoretic Foundations of Quantum Supremacy Experiments," pp. 22:1-22:67 in *32nd Computational Complexity Conference, CCC 2017* (R. O'Donnell, ed.), Volume 79 of LIPIcs, Schloss Dagstuhl—Leibniz-Zentrum für Informatik.

[123] A. Bouland, B. Fefferman, C. Nirkhe, and U. Vazirani, 2018, "Quantum Supremacy and the Complexity of Random Circuit Sampling," arXiv:1803.04402.

[124] C. Neill, P. Roushan, K. Kechedzhi, S. Boixo, S.V. Isakov, V. Smelyanskiy, R. Barends, et al., 2017, "A Blueprint for Demonstrating Quantum Supremacy with Superconducting Qubits," arXiv:1709.06678.

[125] Z. Brakerski, P. Christiano, U. Mahadev, U. Vazirani, and T. Vidick, 2018, "Certifiable Randomness from a Single Quantum Device," arXiv:1804.00640.

[126] K. Bourzac, 2017, Chemistry is quantum computing's killer app, *Chemical and Engineering News* 95(43):27-31.

[127] D.A. Lidar and H. Wang, 1999, Calculating the thermal rate constant with exponential speedup on a quantum computer, *Physical Review E* 59(2):2429.

4

Quantum Computing's Implications for Cryptography

Increases in computational power are desirable, except for applications that rely upon the computational complexity of certain operations in order to function, which is the case in cryptography. Cryptography is an indispensable tool used to protect information in computer systems and it is used widely to protect communications on the Internet. Practical quantum computing at scale would have a significant impact on several cryptographic algorithms currently in wide use. This section explains what these algorithms are for and how they will be affected by the advent of large-scale quantum computers. Given the computing power that such a quantum computer is expected to have, the cryptography research community has developed and is continuing to develop post-quantum (or "quantum-safe") cryptographic algorithms. These are candidate cryptographic algorithms that run on a classical computer and are designed to remain secure even against an adversary who has access to a scalable, fault-tolerant quantum computer.

While it may not be obvious to the general public, cryptography underlies many interactions and transactions on the World Wide Web. As one example, most connections to websites use "https," a Web protocol that encrypts both the information a user sends to a website, and the information that the website sends back—for example, credit card information, bank statements, and e-mail. Another example is protecting stored passwords in a computer system. Passwords are stored in a form that allows the computer system to check that a user-entered password is correct, without storing the actual password. Protecting stored passwords in this way prevents passwords from being "stolen" from the computer system in case of a security breach.

In today's Web-based world, it is relatively easy for a large company like Google to experiment with new types of cryptography. A company like Google can make changes to its browser and its servers to add support for a new protocol: when a Google browser connects to a Google server, it can elect to use the new protocol. However, removing an existing protocol is much harder, since before this can be done, *all* of the machines in the world that rely upon the old protocol must be updated to use the alternative protocol. This type of replacement has already had to be done when a widely deployed hash function, called MD5, was found to be vulnerable to attack. While alternatives were deployed rapidly, it took over a decade for the vulnerable hash function to be completely removed from use.[1]

This chapter explains the key cryptographic tools deployed throughout today's conventional computing systems, what is known about their susceptibility to attack via a quantum computer, alternative classical cryptographic ciphers expected to be resilient against quantum attack, and the challenges and constraints at play in changing a widely deployed cryptographic regime.

4.1 CRYPTOGRAPHIC ALGORITHMS IN CURRENT USE

Creating a secure communication channel between two people is usually done as a two-step process: two people are given a *shared secret key* in a process called *key exchange*, and then this shared secret key is used to encrypt their communication so it cannot be understood (decrypted) by anyone without the secret key. The message encryption is called *symmetric encryption*, since both parties used the same shared secret key to encrypt and decrypt the communications traffic.

4.1.1 Key Exchange and Asymmetric Encryption

The first step in encrypting communications between two parties—in this example, called Alice and Bob—is for them to obtain a shared (symmetric) key that is known to them but to no one else. To establish this shared key, the two parties engage in a key exchange protocol. The most widely used key exchange protocol, called the Transport Layer Security

---

[1] The attack on MD5 was discovered by Wang in 2005. Only in 2014 did Microsoft release a patch to disable MD5; see Microsoft, "Update for Deprecation of MD5 Hashing Algorithm for Microsoft Root Certificate Program," Microsoft Security Advisory 2862973, updated June 10, 2014, Version 3.0, https://docs.microsoft.com/en-us/security-updates/SecurityAdvisories/2014/2862973.

(TLS) handshake, is used to protect Internet traffic. During a key exchange protocol, the parties send a sequence of messages to each other. At the end of the protocol, they obtain a shared secret key that both of them know, but that no one else knows, including any adversary. This key can then be used for exchanging data securely using a symmetric encryption algorithm, which is discussed in Section 4.1.2.

Key exchange protocols rely upon the assumption that certain algebraic problems are intractable. One such problem that is widely used in practice is called the "discrete-log problem on elliptic curves." For the purpose of this discussion, it suffices to say that an instance of this problem of size n bits can be solved classically in exponential time in n, or more precisely in time $2^{n/2}$. No better classical algorithm is known (although it has not been proven that none exists). In practice, one typically sets the key size as 256, meaning that the best-known classical attack on the key exchange protocol runs in time $2^{256/2} = 2^{128}$—the same as the time required to attack 128-bit AES-GCM. This way, security of key exchange and security of symmetric encryption are comparable.

The impact of a quantum computer: Asymmetric cryptographic algorithms used in key exchange protocols appear to be the most vulnerable to compromise by known quantum algorithms, specifically by Shor's algorithm. Because Shor's algorithm provides an exponentially faster method for solving the discrete-log problem and for the problem of factoring large integers, an adversary able to deploy it on a quantum computer could break all the key exchange methods currently used in practice. Specifically, key exchange protocols based on variants of the Diffie-Hellman and the RSA protocols would be insecure. To break RSA 1024 would require a quantum computer that has around 2,300 logical qubits, and even with the overhead associated with logical qubits, this algorithm could likely be carried out in under a day (see Table 4.1). Because of the seriousness of this potential compromise, the National Institute of Standards and Technology (NIST) in 2016 began a process that is expected to last six to eight years [1] to select and standardize replacement asymmetric cryptographic algorithms that are quantum secure. Potential replacements to currently deployed key exchange systems are discussed later in this chapter.

4.1.2 Symmetric Encryption

Once Alice and Bob have established their shared secret key, they can use it in a *symmetric cipher* to ensure that their communication stays private. A widely used encryption method called the Advanced Encryption Standard-Galois Counter Mode (AES-GCM) has been standardized for this purpose by NIST. In its simplest form, this encryption method is based on a pair of algorithms: an *encryption algorithm* and a *decryption*

TABLE 4.1 Literature-Reported Estimates of Quantum Resilience for Current Cryptosystems, under Various Assumptions of Error Rates and Error-Correcting Codes

Cryptosystem	Category	Key Size	Security Parameter	Quantum Algorithm Expected to Defeat Cryptosystem	# Logical Qubits Required	# Physical Qubits Required[a]	Time Required to Break System[b]	Quantum-Resilient Replacement Strategies
AES-GCM[c]	Symmetric encryption	128 192 256	128 192 256	Grover's algorithm	2,953 4,449 6,681	4.61×10^6 1.68×10^7 3.36×10^7	2.61×10^{12} years 1.97×10^{22} years 2.29×10^{32} years	
RSA[d]	Asymmetric encryption	1024 2048 4096	80 112 128	Shor's algorithm	2,050 4,098 8,194	8.05×10^6 8.56×10^6 1.12×10^7	3.58 hours 28.63 hours 229 hours	Move to NIST-selected PQC algorithm when available
ECC Discrete-log problem[e-g]	Asymmetric encryption	256 384 521	128 192 256	Shor's algorithm	2,330 3,484 4,719	8.56×10^6 9.05×10^6 1.13×10^6	10.5 hours 37.67 hours 55 hours	Move to NIST-selected PQC algorithm when available
SHA256[h]	Bitcoin mining	N/A	72	Grover's Algorithm	2,403	2.23×10^6	1.8×10^4 years	
PBKDF2 with 10,000 iterations[i]	Password hashing	N/A	66	Grover's algorithm	2,403	2.23×10^6	2.3×10^7 years	Move away from password-based authentication

[a] These are rough estimates. The number of physical qubits required depends on several assumptions, including the underlying architecture and error rates. For these calculations, assumptions include a two-dimensional (2D) lattice of qubits with nearest neighbour interactions, an effective error rate of 10^{-5}, and implementing the surface code.

[b] These are rough estimates. In addition to the assumptions associated with estimation of the number of physical qubits required, a quantum computer with gates operating at a 5 MHz frequency was assumed.

[c] M. Grassl, B. Langenberg, M. Roetteler, and R. Steinwandt, 2015, "Applying Grover's Algorithm to AES: Quantum Resource Estimates," Proceedings of Post-Quantum Cryptography 2016, vol. 9606 of Lecture Notes in Computer Science, pp. 29-43, Springer; M. Mosca and V. Gheorghiu, 2018, "A Resource Estimation Framework for Quantum Attacks Against Cryptographic Functions," Global Risk Institute, http://globalriskinstitute.org/publications/resource-estimation-framework-quantum-attacks-cryptographic-functions/.

[d] T. Häner, M. Roetteler, and K.M. Svore, 2017, "Factoring using 2n+2 qubits with Toffoli based modular multiplication," Quantum Information and Computation, 18(7and8):673-684.; M. Mosca and V. Gheorghiu, 2018, "A Resource Estimation Framework for Quantum Attacks Against Cryptographic Functions," Global Risk Institute, http://globalriskinstitute.org/publications/resource-estimation-framework-quantum-attacks-cryptographic-functions/.

[e] The values given are for the NIST P-256, NIST P-386, and NIST P-521 curves.

[f] M. Roetteler, M. Naehrig, K.M. Svore, and K. Lauter, 2017, "Quantum Resource Estimates for Computing Elliptic Curve Discrete Logarithms," Advances in Cryptology — ASIACRYPT 2017, Lecture Notes in Computer Science 10625, Springer-Verlag, pp. 241-272.

[g] M. Mosca and V. Gheorghiu, 2018, "A Resource Estimation Framework for Quantum Attacks Against Cryptographic Functions—Part 2 (RSA and ECC)," Global Risk Institute, https://globalriskinstitute.org/publications/resource-estimation-framework-quantum-attacks-cryptographic-functions-part-2-rsa-ecc/.

[h] M. Mosca and V. Gheorghiu, 2018, "A Resource Estimation Framework for Quantum Attacks Against Cryptographic Functions—Improvements," Global Risk Institute, https://globalriskinstitute.org.

[i] The time estimate for password hashing is based upon the time estimate (as it appears in the preceding row of the table) for SHA256, which is often used iteratively in PBKDF2, a password hashing algorithm. Assuming 10,000 iterations of SHA256 (a common deployment practice) would take 10,000 times as long as a single iteration. The classical search space of one cycle is 2^{66}, which implies a running time for Grover of 2^{33}, or one-eighth that required for breaking SHA256 in Bitcoin. Thus, the current estimate of 2.3×10^7 years is obtained by multiplying the value obtained for SHA256 by 10,000 and dividing by 8.

NOTE: These estimates are highly dependent on the underlying assumptions and are subject to update in the final report.

algorithm that encode and decode a message. The encryption algorithm takes as input a key and a message, scrambles the bits of the message in a very precise way, and outputs a *ciphertext*, an encoded form of the message that looks like random bits. The decryption algorithm takes as input a key and a ciphertext, uses the key to reverse the scrambling and output a message. AES-GCM is designed so that analysis of the ciphertext provides no information about the message.

AES-GCM supports three key sizes: 128 bits, 192 bits, and 256 bits. Suppose that an adversary, Eve, intercepts a ciphertext that she wants to decrypt. Furthermore, suppose Eve knows the first few characters in the decrypted message, as is common in Internet protocols where the first few characters are a fixed message header. When using a 128-bit key in AES-GCM, Eve can try all 2^{128} possible keys by exhaustive search until she finds a key that maps the first bytes of the given ciphertext to the known message prefix. Eve can then use this key to decrypt the remainder of the intercepted ciphertext. For a 128-bit key, this attack takes 2^{128} trials, which even at a rate of a 10^{18} (1 quintillion) trials per second—which is faster than even a very large custom-built AES computer would run—will still take 10^{13} (10 trillion) years. For this reason, AES-GCM is frequently used with a 128-bit key. Longer keys, 192-bits and 256-bits, are primarily used for high-security applications where users are concerned about preprocessing attacks or potential undiscovered weaknesses in the AES-GCM algorithm that would enable a faster attack.

The impact of a quantum computer: AES is a perfect fit for Grover's algorithm, which was discussed in the previous chapter. The algorithm can identify the secret key over the entire 128-bit key space of AES-GCM in time proportional to the square root of 2^{128}—namely, time 2^{64}. Running the algorithm on a quantum computer is likely to require around 3,000 logical qubits and extremely long decoherence times.

How long would a quantum computer take to run the 2^{64} steps of Grover's algorithm, called Grover steps, to break AES-GCM? That is hard to answer today, since it depends on how long a quantum computer takes to execute each Grover step. Each Grover step must be decomposed into a number of primitive operations to be implemented reversibly. The actual construction of the quantum circuit for each Grover step can substantially increase the number of qubits and coherence times required for physical implementation. Using classical hardware, one can build a special purpose circuit that tries 10^9 keys per second. Assuming a quantum computer can operate at the same speed, it would need about 600 years to run Grover's algorithm for the necessary 2^{64} steps. It would therefore take a large cluster of such quantum computers to crack a 128-bit key in a month. In fact, this is an overly optimistic estimate, because this type of quantum computer requires logical qubits; this not only greatly increases the number of physical qubits required, but, as described in Section 3.2, operations on logical qubits require many physical qubit operations to complete. This overhead is high for "non-Clifford" quantum gates, which are common in this algorithm. As Table 4.1 shows, assuming 200-nanosecond gate times and current algorithms for error correction, a single quantum computer would require more than 10^{12} years to crack AES-GCM.

Even if a computer existed that could run Grover's algorithm to attack AES-GCM, the solution is quite simple: increase the key size of AES-GCM from 128-bit to 256-bit keys. Running Grover's attack on a 256-bit key is effectively impossible, since it requires as many steps as a classical attack on a 128-bit key. Transitioning to a 256-bit key is very practical and can be put to use at any time. Hence, AES-GCM can be easily made secure against an attack based on Grover's algorithm.

However, AES-GCM was designed to withstand known sophisticated *classical* attacks, such as linear and differential cryptanalysis. It was not designed to withstand a sophisticated quantum attack. More precisely, it is possible that there is some currently unknown clever quantum attack on AES-GEM that that is far more efficient than Grover's algorithm. Whether such an attack exists is currently an open problem, and further research is needed on this important question. If a sophisticated quantum attack exists—one that is faster than exhaustive search using Grover's algorithm—then increasing the AES-GCM key size to 256 bits will not ensure post-quantum security and a replacement algorithm for AES-GCM will need to be designed.

4.1.3 Certificates and Digital Signatures

Digital signatures are an important cryptographic mechanism used to verify data integrity. In a digital signature system, the signer has a secret signing key, and the signature verifier has a corresponding public key, another example of asymmetric encryption. The signer signs a message using its secret key. Anyone can verify the signature using the corresponding public key. If a message-signature pair is valid, then the verifier has some confidence that the message was authorized by the signer. Digital signatures are used widely, as illustrated in the following three examples.

First, digital signatures are necessary for establishing identity on the Internet using a digital certificate. Here, a certificate authority (CA) uses its secret signing key to issue an identity certificate to an individual or an organization. A certificate is a statement that binds an identity, such as nas.edu, to a cryptographic key. Anyone can verify a certificate, but only the CA can issue a certificate, by digitally signing it using a secret signing key. An adversary who can forge the CA's signature can, in principle, masquerade as any entity.

A second application for digital signatures is in payment systems, such as credit card payments or a cryptocurrency such as Bitcoin. With these systems, a payer who wants to make payments holds a secret signing key. When making a payment, the payer signs the transaction details. The signature can be verified by anyone, including the payee and all relevant financial institutions. An attacker who can forge signatures can effectively spend other people's funds.

For a third example, consider the verification of software authenticity. Here, a software vendor uses its secret signing key to sign software and software updates that it ships. Every client verifies these signatures before installing the software, as they do with subsequent software updates. This ensures that clients know the software provenance and do not install software that has been tampered with or malware created and distributed by malicious actors. An attacker who could forge signatures could distribute malicious software to unsuspecting clients, who might install it thinking that it is authentic.

The two most widely used signature algorithms are called RSA and ECDSA.[2] Roughly speaking, one algorithm is based on the difficulty of factoring large integers, and the other is based on the same discrete log problem used for key exchange. The parameters for both systems are chosen so that the best-known classical attacks run in time 2^{128}.

The impact of a quantum computer: An adversary who has access to a quantum computer capable of executing Shor's algorithm would have the ability to forge both RSA and ECDSA signatures. This adversary would be able to issue fake certificates, properly sign malicious software, and potentially spend funds on behalf of others. The attack is worse than just forging signatures; Shor's algorithm allows attackers to recover private keys, which facilitates forging signatures but also eliminates the security of all other uses of the keys. Fortunately, there are several good candidate signature schemes that are currently believed to be post-quantum secure, as discussed at the end of this chapter.

4.1.4 Cryptographic Hash Functions and Password Hashing

The final cryptographic primitive discussed here enables one to compute a short message digest, called a hash, from an arbitrarily long message. The hash function can take gigabytes of data as input and output a short 256-bit hash value. There are many desirable properties that we might want hash functions to satisfy. The simplest is called "one-wayness," or "collision-resistance," which means that for any given hash

---

[2] The former is named after its inventors, Rivest, Shamir, and Adelman. The latter stands for "elliptic curve digital signature algorithm."

output value T, it should be difficult to find an input message that would yield that hash.

Hash functions are used in many contexts; a simple example is their use in password management systems. A server that authenticates user passwords usually stores in its database a one-way hash of those user passwords. This way, if an attacker steals the database, it may be difficult for the attacker to recover the cleartext passwords. Currently, the most commonly used hash function is called SHA256. It outputs a 256-bit hash value no matter how large the input is. This hash function is the basis of many password authentication systems. To be precise, the actual hash function used to hash passwords is derived from SHA256 via a construction called PBKDF2 [2].

The impact of a quantum computer: A hash function that produces 256-bit outputs is not expected to be threatened by quantum computing. Even using Grover's algorithm, it is currently believed to be essentially impossible (with a depth on the order of 2^{144} T gates on 2400 logical qubits) to break a hash function like SHA256. However, *password hashing* is at a higher risk because the space of user passwords is not very large. The set of all 10-character passwords is only about 2^{66} passwords. An exhaustive search over a space of this size using a cluster of classical processors is possible, but very costly. Using Grover's algorithm, the running time shrinks to only 2^{33} (about 10 billion) steps, which at the speed of a modern classical processor takes only a few seconds. However, the need for QEC for deploying Grover's algorithm again suggests that, with current error correction algorithms (and reasonable assumptions about error rates and architectures), the time required for this attack is still too long to be practical, at more than 10^7 years, although the time frame could be reduced through reduction of QEC overheads.

If QEC is improved to the point where Grover's algorithm becomes a threat to password systems, then there will be a need to move away from password authentication. Other authentication methods, which do not rely on passwords or other static values that need to be stored in hashed form, have been developed and are being adopted in some applications. These methods include biometric authentication, cryptographic one-time values, device identification, and others. The development of quantum computers may further motivate the deployment of such systems. Another defense is to harden password management systems using secure hardware [3], as already implemented by major websites.

Another popular application of hash functions is called proof-of-work, used in many crypto currencies such as Bitcoin and Ethereum. Blocks of Bitcoin transactions are validated every 10 minutes by a process in which "miners" solve a certain computation challenge; the first miner to solve the problem is paid by the cryptocurrency system. Grover's algorithm would be suited to solving a Bitcoin challenge. However, as the second to last row in Table 4.1 shows, the overhead of implementing Grover's algorithm using physical qubits to solve the proof-of-work challenge is currently estimated to require well over 10 minutes, which would make the attack a nonthreat to the current Bitcoin ecosystem. If the overheads required for this implementation were significantly reduced, there could be some risk if or when fault-tolerant quantum computers become available; Bitcoin would thus also need to transition to a post-quantum secure digital signature system to avoid bitcoin theft.

4.2 SIZING ESTIMATES

A critical question for understanding the vulnerability of cryptographic tools is: *What scale of a quantum computer would be required to defeat the cipher?* The answer to this question is expected to vary with the details of how the quantum algorithm is deployed. Nonetheless, a rough approximation of the number of qubits required for defeating various protocols for a given key size is provided in Table 4.1. This table also estimates the number of physical qubits required (assuming an effective error rate of 10^{-5}), and the time required for the algorithm's execution, using a surface code for quantum error correction and a surface code measurement cycle time of 200 nanoseconds. These assumptions for gate fidelity and gate speed are well beyond the capabilities of multiqubit systems in 2018. The table clearly shows that the major threats posed by a sophisticated quantum computer are breaking key exchange and digital signatures. While these figures reflect the current state of knowledge, the committee cautions the reader that these assessments are based upon quantum algorithms that are currently known, as well as implicit assumptions about the architecture and error rates of a quantum computer. Advances in either area have the potential to change timings by orders of magnitude. For example, if physical gate error rates of 10^{-6} were to be achieved (e.g., by topological qubits), and the other assumptions remain the same, then the number of physical qubits required to break RSA-4096 would drop to 6.7×10^6, and the time would drop to 190 hours. Similarly, if the assumptions are *not* achieved, then implementing these algorithms might not be possible or might come at a greater cost—for example, if physical gate error rates of only 10^{-4} are achieved, then the number of physical qubits required to break RSA-4096 would increase to 1.58×10^8 and the time required would increase to 280 hours [4]. It is also possible that new algorithms could be developed (or could already have been developed outside of the public sphere) that would present different attack vectors—for that matter, the same can also be said about potential alternative classical attacks.

4.3 POST-QUANTUM CRYPTOGRAPHY

The cryptographic research community has been working to develop replacement algorithms that are expected to be secure against an adversary with access to a large-scale quantum computer. These replacement algorithms, when standardized, will be executable on off-the-shelf classical processors. Their security relies on mathematical problems that are believed to be intractable even for a large-scale quantum computer. These algorithms, currently being evaluated by NIST, are thus expected to remain secure even after large-scale quantum computers are widely available. Like all cryptography, the hardness of these problem cannot be proved, and must continue to be evaluated over time to ensure that new algorithmic approaches do not weaken the cypher.

4.3.1 Symmetric Encryption and Hashing

Post-quantum secure symmetric encryption and hash functions are obtained by simply increasing the encryption key size or hash output size. Adequate solutions already exist, and the primary remaining challenge is to verify, through additional research to identify possible quantum attacks, that the standardized schemes, such as 256-bit AES-GCM and SHA256, are indeed secure against an adversary who has access to a quantum computer.

Problems where an increase in the size of the hashed data is not possible (or where the hashed data's entropy does not increase much even if its size is increased), like password systems, would be difficult to secure in a world with fast quantum computers. If a quantum computer was as fast as a modern classical processor in logical operations per second, thanks to Grover's algorithm, a quantum computer would likely be able to identify the 10-character password in a few seconds. While the need for extensive error correction would make this attack much slower in practice, the availability of low-overhead approaches would place passwords at risk. Defending against this threat requires either moving away from password authentication or using a hardware-based password hardening scheme, as mentioned earlier.

4.3.2 Key Exchange and Signatures

The most significant challenges are post-quantum key-exchange and post-quantum digital signatures. For quantum resilience, existing schemes such as RSA and ECDSA will need to be abandoned and new systems will need to be designed. NIST has already initiated a Post-Quantum Cryptography project to facilitate this process, seeking proposals for new cryptographic algorithms [5]. In the first round of submissions, which ended in November 2017, NIST received over 70 submissions. The NIST process is scheduled to conclude by 2022-2024; its selections are likely to become frontrunners for broader standardization—for example, through the Internet Engineering Task Force (IETF), the International Organization for Standardization (ISO), and the International Telecommunication Union (ITU). Internet systems will likely begin incorporating post-quantum resistant cryptography once the NIST process concludes, if not sooner. Boxes 4.1 to 4.4 provide brief descriptions of a few candidate post-quantum key-exchange and signature systems, as well as pointing out some early experiments done with some of these systems.

BOX 4.1
Post-Quantum Candidates: Lattice Systems

A "lattice" is a discrete set of points in space that has the property that the sum of two points on the lattice is also on the lattice. Lattices come up naturally in several branches of mathematics and physics. One of the most well-known computational problems on lattices is to find a "short" vector in a given lattice. All current classical algorithms for this problem take exponential time in the dimension of the lattice, and there is some evidence to suggest that the problem also takes exponential time on a quantum computer.[1] Over the past two decades, cryptographers constructed many cryptosystems that are secure assuming that this shortest vector problem (SVP) is hard. In particular, there are good candidate key-exchange and signature algorithms based on SVP. If indeed SVP is difficult to solve on a quantum computer, then these systems are expected to be post-quantum secure.

To experiment with lattice-based systems, cryptographers developed several concrete schemes, such as New-Hope[2] and Frodo.[3] Google recently experimented with deploying the New-Hope system in the Chrome browser.[4] They report that the system adds less than 20 milliseconds per key exchange for 95 percent of Chrome users. While this additional delay is undesirable, the experiment shows that there is no significant impediment to deploying post-quantum key exchange based on lattice systems.

---

[1] O. Regev, 2009, "On lattices, learning with errors, random linear codes, and cryptography," *Journal of the ACM (JACM)* 56(6):34.

[2] E. Alkim, T. Pöppelmann, and P. Schwabe, 2016, "Post-Quantum Key Exchange—A New Hope," *USENIX Security Symposium* on August 10-12, 2016, in Austin, TX.

[3] J. Bos, C. Coestello, L. Ducas, I. Mironov, M. Naehrig, V. Nikolaenko, A. Raghunathan, and D. Stebila, 2016, "Frodo: Take Off the Ring! Practical, Quantum-Secure Key Exchange from LWE," *Proceedings of the 2016 ACM SIGSAC Conference on Computer and Communications Security*, October 24-28, 2016, in Vienna, Austria.

[4] M. Braithwaite, 2016, "Experimenting with Post-Quantum Cryptography," *Google Security Blog*, https://security.googleblog.com/2016/07/experimenting-with-post-quantum.html.

BOX 4.2
Post-Quantum Candidates: Coding-Based Systems

Coding theory is the science of designing encoding schemes that let two parties communicate over a noisy channel. The sender encodes a message so that the receiver can decode even if bounded noise has been added by the channel. Over the years it has become apparent that certain encoding schemes are difficult to decode efficiently. In fact, for certain encoding schemes, the best decoding algorithm takes exponential time on a classical computer. Moreover, the decoding problem appears to be difficult even for a quantum computer. Cryptographers have been able to use this hard problem to construct secure cryptosystems, assuming that decoding the relevant codes is difficult. The most well studied system, called the McEliece cryptosystem,[1] can be used for post-quantum key exchange. Recently, practical variants of this system, such as CAKE,[2] have emerged.

---

[1] D.J. Bernstein, T. Lange, and C. Peters, 2008, Attacking and defending the McEliece cryptosystem, *Post-Quantum Cryptography*, vol. 5299:31-46.

[2] P.S.L.M. Barreto, S. Gueron, T. Gueneysu, R. Misoczki, E. Persichetti, N. Sendrier, and J.-P. Tillich, 2017, "CAKE: Code-Based Algorithm for Key Encapsulation," in M. O'Neill (eds) *Cryptography and Coding: 16th IMA International Conference, IMACC 2017, Oxford, UK, December 12-14, 2017, Proceedings*: 207-226.

BOX 4.3
Post-Quantum Candidates: Supersingular Isogenies

The Google experiment with the New-Hope lattice-based key exchange suggests that the primary reason for the 20 millisecond delay is due to the extra traffic generated by the key exchange protocol. Building on this observation, a recent post-quantum key exchange candidate[1] generates far less traffic than any other candidate, but it requires more computing time at both ends. Since the additional traffic is the primary reason for the delay, this candidate may outperform other candidates in real-world Internet settings. This key exchange mechanism is based on beautiful mathematical tools developed to study elliptic curves. While there is no known quantum attack on the system, it is based on a computational problem whose quantum difficulty has only begun to be explored recently. More research is needed to gain confidence in the post-quantum security of this candidate.

---

[1] C. Costello, P. Longa, and M. Naehrig, 2016, "Efficient Algorithms for Supersingular Isogeny Diffie-Hellman," in M. Robshaw and J. Katz (eds.), *Advances in Cryptology—CRYPTO 2016*. CRYPTO 2016, Lecture Notes in Computer Science, vol. 9814, Springer, Berlin, Heidelberg.

> **BOX 4.4**
> **Post-Quantum Candidates: Hash-Based Signatures**
>
> Post-quantum secure digital signatures have been around since the 1980s. These systems are based on standard hash functions, and there is little doubt about their post-quantum security, when using a secure hash function. The downside of these schemes is that they generate relatively long signatures, and therefore can be used only in certain settings. One such setting is signing a software package or a software update. Because software packages tend to be large, the added length of the signature is of little consequence. Given the high confidence in the post-quantum security of these systems, it is likely that software vendors will transition away from RSA and elliptic curve digital signature algorithm (ECDSA) to hash-based signatures for software signing. Several concrete proposals and drafts for standardization already exist, such as the Leighton-Micali signature scheme (LMSS).[1]
>
> ---
> [1] T. Leighton and S. Micali, 1995, "Large Provably Fast and Secure Digital Signature Schemes from Secure Hash Functions," U.S. Patent 5,432,852.

Finding: While the potential utility of Shor's algorithm for cracking deployed cryptography was a major driver of early enthusiasm in quantum computing research, the existence of cryptographic algorithms that are believed to be quantum-resistant will reduce the usefulness of a quantum computer for cryptanalysis and thus will reduce the extent to which this application will drive quantum computing R&D in the long term.

4.4 PRACTICAL DEPLOYMENT CHALLENGES

It is important to remember that today's encrypted Internet traffic is vulnerable to an adversary who has a sufficiently large quantum computer running quantum error correction. In particular, all encrypted data that is recorded today and stored for future use, will be cracked once a large-scale quantum computer is developed.

Finding: There is strong commercial interest in deploying post-quantum cryptography even before such a quantum computer has been built. Companies and governments cannot afford to have their private communications decrypted in the future, even if that future is 30 years away. For this reason, there is a need to begin the transition to post-quantum cryptography as soon as possible.

Realistically, completing the transition to Internet-wide post-quantum cryptography will be a long and difficult process. Some computer systems remain operational for a very long time. For example, computer systems in cars sold today will still be on the road in 15, and perhaps even 20 years. A quantum-vulnerable algorithm can be deprecated only once the vast majority of Internet systems are updated to support new algorithms. Once a major site like Google deprecates an algorithm, old devices that support only that algorithm can no longer connect to Google. A good example of this timeline is the long process of deprecating the SHA1 hash function and the transition to SHA256. The SHA1 function was considered to be insecure since 2004. However, it took many years to disable it. Even as of 2018, it is still not universally decommissioned—some old browsers and servers still do not support SHA256.

The transition from SHA1 to SHA256 provides a map for the steps required to transition to post-quantum cryptography. First, post-quantum cryptographic algorithm standards for key-exchange and signatures will need to be developed and ratified. After adoption as an official standard, the new standard algorithms must be implemented in a wide variety of computer languages, popular programming libraries, and hardware cryptographic chips and modules. Then the new standard algorithms will need to be incorporated into encryption format and protocol standards such as PKCS#1, TLS, and IPSEC. These revised format and protocol standards will need to be reviewed and adopted by their respective standards committees. Then vendors will need to implement the new standards in hardware and software product updates. From there, it will likely take many years until the majority of Internet systems are upgraded to support the new standards—and quantum-vulnerable algorithms cannot be disabled until their replacements are widely deployed. After this is done, sensitive data in corporate and government repositories must be reencrypted, and any copies encrypted under the previous paradigm need to be destroyed—especially given that some organizations rely upon merely deleting encryption keys as a substitute for destroying files, which will not help against an attack by a quantum computer. Vulnerable public-key certificates must be reissued and redistributed, and any documents that must be certified from official sources must be re-signed. Last, the signing and verification processes for all software code must be updated, and the new code must be re-signed and redistributed. This process probably cannot be completed in less than 20 years; the sooner it is begun, the sooner it will conclude [6].

Since the invention of a scalable general-purpose quantum computer would constitute a total, simultaneous, instantaneous, worldwide compromise of all of today's public-key cryptographic algorithms, quantum-resistant cryptographic algorithms would need to be designed, standardized, implemented, and deployed before the first quantum computer goes online. But in fact, the quantum-resistant infrastructure must be in place even before a quantum computer goes live, because encrypted (or signed) data needs to be protected for longer than an instant.

For example, consider a company's 10Q filing. This quarterly tax document contains information that is sensitive until it is published; people who come into possession of a 10Q before it is public information know things about the company's financial condition that they could use to profit from insider trading (because the stock value will change once the 10Q information becomes public, and people who know the information in advance can predict the magnitude and direction of the change and buy or sell shares accordingly). A 10Q filing needs to stay secret for no more than three months; after the end of the quarter, it is filed and published, and the information is no longer sensitive—so it does not need to be secret. So for a 10Q filing, the required "protection interval" is three months.

Now, consider a government classified document. Under the 50-year rule, the contents should not be made public for at least 50 years. Hence, the document must be encrypted with an encryption scheme that is expected to remain secure for at least 50 years. The required "protection interval" is 50 years.

Three pieces of information are necessary to determine when a quantum-resistant cryptographic infrastructure should be put in place:

1. When will the current cryptographic infrastructure fail? (That is, when would a quantum computer of sufficient sophistication to deploy Shor's or Grover's algorithms go live?)
2. How long does it take to design, build, and deploy the new quantum-resistant infrastructure?
3. What's the longest protection interval of concern?

Once these three things have been identified, the required timing can be computed using a simple formula[3] illustrated in Figures 4.1 and 4.2, where:

- X is the "security shelf life" (the longest protection interval we care about, assuming that the data is protected starting today)
- Y is the "migration time" (the time it takes to design build, and deploy the new infrastructure)
- Z is the "collapse time" (the time it takes for a sufficiently large quantum computer to become operational, starting from today)

---

[3] This formula was introduced by committee member Michele Mosca: M. Mosca, 2015, Cybersecurity in an era with quantum computers: Will we be ready? *IACR Cryptology ePrint Archive* 2015:1075.

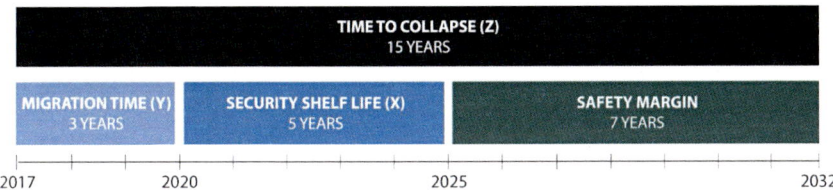

FIGURE 4.1 Example illustration of Mosca's model for a safe transition to post-quantum cryptography, for one example with hypothetical time frames. SOURCE: Adapted from M. Mosca, 2015, Cybersecurity in an era with quantum computers: Will we be ready? *IACR Cryptology ePrint Archive* 2015:1075.

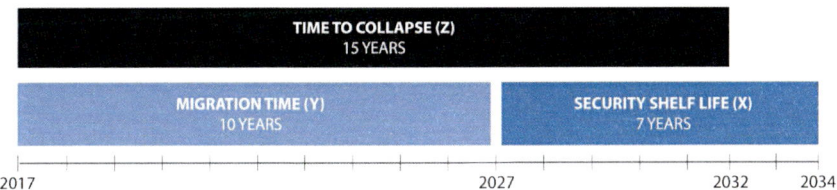

FIGURE 4.2 Example illustration of Mosca's model of a cryptographic transition timeline that is too long to ensure the desired level of security in deployed protocols. SOURCE: Adapted from M. Mosca, 2015, Cybersecurity in an era with quantum computers: Will we be ready? *IACR Cryptology ePrint Archive* 2015:1075.

The example in Figure 4.1 assumes that no quantum computer will exist for 15 years, that a quantum-resistant infrastructure can be designed, built, and deployed in only 3 years, and that the longest security shelf-life of concern is only 5 years. This optimistic scenario yields a safety margin of 7 years, suggesting that the start of earnest working on replacing our public-key cryptographic infrastructure could be delayed for several years.

A less optimistic scenario would set migration time at 10 years (the pessimistic estimate for completion of NIST's planned standardization interval of 2022-2024 plus up to 3 years for implementation and deployment), and security shelf life at 7 years (a common legally required retention interval for many kinds of business records). In this gloomier scenario, illustrated in Figure 4.2, there is no safety margin; if a large quantum computer goes online 15 years from today, sensitive data will remain at risk of compromise, with no effective protection technology available, for 3 years—*even if the work to replace our public-key cryptographic infrastructure begins today.*

The most realistic scenario is even more pessimistic. As noted in the preceding section, NIST's current schedule will result in the selection of a quantum-safe cryptographic algorithm suite around 2022-2024. Past experience with replacing the data encryption standard (DES) symmetric cryptosystem and various hash functions (SHA-1, MD5) suggests that the minimum time required to replace a widely deployed cryptographic algorithm, including retiring most consequential implementations of the broken algorithm, is about 10 years after design and standardization of the new algorithms are complete. Assuming a security shelf life of 7 years as in the previous scenario, the earliest safe date for the introduction of a quantum computer capable of breaking RSA 2048 is about 2040—if the work of replacing today's cryptographic libraries and crypto-dependent applications is begun as soon as NIST finishes its selection process. To put this another way, if a fault-tolerant quantum computer with 2,500 logical qubits is built any time in the next 25 years, some data will likely be compromised—even if work on the cryptographic fallout is begun today and continued diligently during the entire interval.

Much depends upon when such a device will come on the scene. The following two chapters provide a closer view of the current status of efforts to build a large-scale, fault-tolerant quantum computer. Chapter 5 describes progress in constructing quantum computing hardware and control systems, and Chapter 6 examines the software and architecture—including the classical co-processing—that will be required to implement algorithms on a mature device.

4.5 NOTES

[1] National Institute of Standards and Technology, 2018, "Post-Quantum Cryptography: Workshops and Timeline," last updated May 29, 2018, https://csrc.nist.gov/projects/post-quantum-cryptography/workshops-and-timeline.

[2] D. Martin, 2015, "Real World Crypto 2015: Password Hashing According to Facebook," *Bristol Cryptography Blog*, http://bristolcrypto.blogspot.com/2015/01/password-hashing-according-to-facebook.html.

[3] Ibid.

[4] V. Gheorghiu and M. Mosca, in preparation.

[5] National Institute of Standards and Technology, 2018, "Post-Quantum Cryptography," last modified May 29, 2018, http://csrc.nist.gov/groups/ST/post-quantum-crypto/.

[6] For additional discussion of the process and challenges associated with transitioning between cryptosystems, see National Academies of Sciences, Engineering, and Medicine, 2017, *Cryptographic Agility and Interoperability: Proceedings of a Workshop*, The National Academies Press, Washington, DC, https://doi.org/10.17226/24636.

5

Essential Hardware Components of a Quantum Computer

Having shown in the prior chapters the potential of quantum computing, this chapter focuses on the hardware, and Chapter 6 explores the software needed to implement these computational processes and capabilities in practice. Quantum hardware is an active area of research. More than 100 academic groups and government-affiliate laboratories worldwide are researching how to design, build, and control qubit systems, and numerous established and start-up companies are now working to commercialize quantum computers built from superconducting and trapped ion qubits.

Even although reports in the popular press tend to focus on development of qubits and the number of qubits in the current prototypical quantum computing chip, any quantum computer requires an integrated hardware approach using significant conventional hardware to enable qubits to be controlled, programmed, and read out. The next section divides this hardware by its functions, creating the four hardware layers every quantum computer contains, and describes the expected relationship between classical and quantum computing resources.

Finding: While much progress has been made in the development of small-scale quantum computers, a design for a quantum computer that can scale to the size needed to break current cryptography has not been demonstrated, nor can it be achieved by straightforward scaling of any of the current implementations.

As a result, it is not clear whether the current leading quantum technologies will be used to create this class of machines. To provide a sense of the capability and challenges of different approaches, this chapter describes the quantum technologies currently being used to create early demonstration systems—that is, trapped ion and superconducting qubits—and their scaling issues, while also highlighting other promising qubit technologies that are currently less developed.

5.1 HARDWARE STRUCTURE OF A QUANTUM COMPUTER

Since a quantum computer must eventually interface with users, data, and networks—tasks that conventional computing excels at—a quantum computer can leverage a conventional computer for these tasks whenever it is most efficient to do so. Furthermore, qubit systems require carefully orchestrated control in order to function in a useful way; this control can be managed using conventional computers.

To assist in conceptualizing the necessary hardware components for an analog or gate-based quantum computer, the hardware can be modeled in four abstract layers: the "quantum data plane," where the qubits reside; the "control and measurement plane," responsible for carrying out operations and measurements on the qubits as required; the "control processor plane," which determines the sequence of operations and measurements that the algorithm requires, potentially using measurement outcomes to inform subsequent quantum operations; and the "host processor," a classical computer that handles access to networks, large storage arrays, and user interfaces. This host processor runs a conventional operating system/user interface, which facilitates user interactions, and has a high bandwidth connection to the control processor.

5.1.1 Quantum Data Plane

The quantum data plane is the "heart" of a QC. It includes the physical qubits and the structures needed to hold them in place. It also must contain any support circuitry needed to measure the qubits' state and perform gate operations on the physical qubits for a gate-based system or control the Hamiltonian for an analog computer. Control signals routed to the selected qubit(s) set the Hamiltonian it sees, which control the gate operation for a digital quantum computer. For gate-based systems, since some qubit operations require two qubits, the quantum data plane must provide a programmable "wiring" network that enables two or more qubits to interact. Analog systems often require richer communication between the qubits, which must be supported by this layer. As discussed in Chapter 2, high qubit fidelity requires strong isolation from the environment, which has the effect of limiting connectivity—it may not be possible for every qubit to interact directly with every other qubit—so the computation needs to be mapped to the specific architectural constraints of this layer. These constraints mean that both the operation fidelity and connectivity are important metrics of the quantum data layer.[1]

Unlike a classical computer, where both the control plane and the data plane components use the same silicon technology and are integrated on the same device, control of the quantum data plane requires technology different from that of the qubits,[2] and is done externally by a separate control and measurement layer (described next). Control information for the qubits, which is analog in nature, must be sent to the correct qubit (or qubits). In some systems, this control information is transmitted electrically using wires, so these wires are part of the quantum data plane; in others, it is transmitted with optical or microwave radiation. Transmission must be implemented in a manner that has high specificity, so it affects only the desired qubit(s), without disrupting the other qubits in the system. This becomes increasingly difficult as the number of qubits grows; the number of qubits in a single module is therefore another important parameter of a quantum data layer.

Finding: The key properties that define the quality of a quantum data plane are the error rate of the single-qubit and two-qubit gates, the inter-qubit connectivity, qubit coherence times, and the number of qubits that may be contained within a single module.

5.1.2 Control and Measurement Plane

The control and measurement plane converts the control processor's digital signals, which indicates what quantum operations are to be performed, to the analog control signals needed to perform the operations on the qubits in the quantum data plane. It also converts the analog output of measurements of qubits in the data plane to classical binary data that the

---

[1] In some ways, the quantum data plane looks similar to a field programmable gate array, or FPGA. These are classical computing devices that contain a large number of flexible logic blocks. Each logic block can be configured—at program run time—to perform a logical function. In addition to these logic blocks, there is a configurable set of wires on the integrated circuit (IC), and one can configure the wires to interconnect the logic blocks to each other. This ability to program both the function of each logic block and their interconnection allows one to "program" the FPGA to implement the logic circuit needed to compute the desired result. Like an FPGA, "programming" of the quantum data plane also sets the function and the connections of the quantum computation.

[2] One potential qubit technology, semiconductor electrically gated qubits (see Section D.3.2) could be built using silicon, but even here it is not clear whether the processing for classical logic would be compatible with that required for qubit fabrication.

control processor can handle. The generation and transmission of control signals is challenging because of the analog nature of quantum gates; small errors in control signals, or irregularities in the physical design of the qubit, will affect the results of operations.[3] The errors associated with each gate operation accumulate as the machine runs.

Any imperfection in the isolation of these signals (so-called signal crosstalk) will cause small control signals to appear for qubits that should not otherwise be addressed during an operation, leading to small errors in their qubit state.[4] Proper shielding of the control signals is complicated by the fact that they must be fed through the apparatus which isolates the quantum date plane from its environment by vacuum, cooling, or both; this requirement constrains the type of isolation methods which are possible.

Fortunately, both qubit manufacturing errors and signal crosstalk errors are systematic, and change slowly with the mechanical configuration of the system. Effects of these slowly changing errors can be minimized by using control pulse shapes that reduce dependence of the qubit on these factors (see Section 3.2.1), and through periodic[5] system calibration, provided there is a mechanism to measure these errors and software to adjust the control signals to drive these errors to zero (system calibration). Since every control signal can potentially interact with every other control signal, the number of measurements and computation required to achieve this calibration more than doubles as the number of qubits in the system doubles.

The nature of a QC's control signals depends on the underlying qubit technology. For example, systems using trapped ion qubits usually rely upon microwave or optical signals (forms of electromagnetic radiation) transmitted through free space or waveguides and delivered to the location of the qubits. Superconducting qubit systems are controlled using microwave and low-frequency electrical signals, both of which are communicated through wires that run into a cooling apparatus (including a "dilution refrigerator" and a "cryostat") to reach the qubits inside the controlled environment.

Unlike classical gates, which have noise immunity and negligible error rates, quantum operations depend upon the precision with which control signals are delivered, and have nonnegligible error rates. Obtaining this

---

[3] Qubits that leverage basic atomic structure are not themselves subject to manufacturing variations. Instead, variations in the manufactured structures that hold these atoms, or in the manufactured systems generating the control signals, may lead to errors.

[4] It is worth noting that crosstalk can occur directly between the qubits themselves in the quantum data plane.

[5] The frequency of the calibration depends on the stability of both the quantum data plane and the control and measurement layer.

precision currently requires sophisticated generators built using classical technologies.

Since no quantum gate can be faster than the control pulse that implements it, even if the quantum system in principle allows ultrafast operation, the gate speed will be limited by the time required to construct and transmit an exquisitely precise control pulse. Fortunately, the speed of today's silicon technology is fast enough that gate speed is limited by the quantum data plane, and not the control and measurement plane. This gate speed is currently tens to hundreds of nanoseconds for superconducting qubits and one to a hundred microseconds for trapped ion qubits.

Finding: The speed of a quantum computer can never be faster than the time required to create the precise control signals needed to perform quantum operations.

5.1.3 Control Processor Plane and Host Processor

The control processor plane identifies and triggers the proper Hamiltonian or sequence of quantum gate operations and measurements (which are subsequently carried out by the control and measurement plane on the quantum data plane). These sequences execute the program, provided by the host processor, for implementing a quantum algorithm. Programs must be customized for the specific capabilities of the quantum layer by the software tool stack, as discussed in Chapter 6.

One of the most important and challenging tasks of the control processor plane will be to run the quantum error correction algorithm (if the QC is error corrected). Significant classical information processing is required to compute the quantum operations needed to correct errors based upon the measured syndrome results, and the time required for this processing may slow the operation of the quantum computer. This overhead is minimized if the error correction operations can be computed in a time comparable to that required for the quantum operations and measurements. Since this computational task grows with the size of the machine (the inputs and outputs of the function scale with the number of qubits, and the complexity scales with the "distance" of the error-correcting code), it is likely that this control processor plane will consist of multiple interconnected processing elements to handle the computational load.

Building a control processor plane for large quantum machines is challenging, and an active area of research. One approach splits the plane into two parts. The first part is simply a classical processor, which "runs" the quantum program. The second part is a scalable custom hardware block[6] that directly interfaces with the control and measurement plane, and combines the higher level "instructions" output by the main controller with the syndrome measurements to compute the next operations to be performed on the qubits. The challenge is in creating scalable custom hardware that is fast enough and can scale with machine size, and in creating the right high-level instruction abstraction.

The control processor plane operates at a low level of abstraction: it converts compiled code to commands for the control and measurement layer. As a result, a user will not interact with (or need to understand) the control processor plane directly. Rather, the user will interact with a host computer. This plane will attach to that computer and act to accelerate the execution of some applications. This type of architecture is widely used in today's computers, with "accelerators" for everything from graphics to machine learning to networking. Such accelerators generally have a high-bandwidth connection to the host processor, usually through shared access to part of the host processor's memory, which can be used to transfer both the program the control processor should run, and the data it should use during the run.

The host processor is a classical computer, running a conventional operating system with standard supporting libraries for its own operation. This computing system provides all of the software development tools and services users expect from a computer system. It will run the software development tools necessary to create applications to be run on the control processor, which are different from those used to control today's classical computers, as well as provide storage and networking services that a quantum application might require while running. Attaching a quantum processor to a classical computer allows it to utilize all of its features without needing to start entirely from scratch.

5.1.4 Qubit Technologies

After the discovery of Shor's algorithm in 1994, serious efforts were launched to find an adequate physical system in which to implement quantum logic operations. The rest of this chapter reviews the current candidate qubit technology choices upon which to base a quantum computer. For the two furthest developed quantum technologies, superconducting and trapped ion qubits, this discussion includes details of the qubit and control planes in use in prototypical computers at the time of publication of this report (2018), the current challenges that must be overcome for each technology, and an assessment of the prospects for scale-up to very

---

[6] This layer could be built using FPGAs initially, and move to a custom integrated circuit later, if additional performance is required.

large processor sizes in the long term. The review of other emerging technologies provides a sense of their current status, and potential advantages if they are developed further.

5.2 TRAPPED ION QUBITS

The first quantum logic gate was demonstrated in 1995 using trapped atomic ions [1], following a theoretical proposal earlier in the same year [2]. Since the original demonstration, technical advances in qubit control have enabled experimental demonstration of fully functional processors at small scale and implementation of a wide range of simple quantum algorithms.

Despite success in small-scale demonstrations, the task of constructing scalable and quantum computers considered viable by current computing industry standards out of trapped ions remains a significant challenge. Unlike the very large scale integration (VLSI) of transistors enabled by the integrated circuit (IC), building a quantum computer based upon trapped ion qubits requires integration of technologies from a wide range of domains, including vacuum, laser, and optical systems, radio frequency (RF) and microwave technology, and coherent electronic controllers [3-5]. A path to a viable quantum computer must address these integration challenges.

A trapped ion quantum data plane comprises the ions that serve as qubits and a trap that holds them in specific locations. The control and measurement plane includes a very precise laser (or microwave) source that can be directed at a specific ion to affect its quantum state, another laser to "cool" and enable measurement of the ions, and a set of photon detectors to "measure" the state of the ions by detecting the photons that they scatter. Appendix B provides a technical overview of current strategies for constructing a trapped ion quantum data plane and its associated control and measurement plane.

5.2.1 Current Trapped Ion Quantum "Computers"

Based on the high-fidelity component operations demonstrated to date, small-scale ion trap systems have been assembled where a universal set of quantum logic operations can be implemented on a 5-20 qubit system in a programmable manner [6-9], forming the basis of a general-purpose quantum computer. Not surprisingly, at 2-5 percent for two-qubit gates, the error rates of individual quantum logic operations in these fully functional 5-20 qubit systems lag behind the 10^{-2} to 10^{-3} range [10,11] for state-of-the-art demonstrations of two-qubit systems, pointing to the challenge of maintaining the high fidelity across all qubits as the system grows in size. Nonetheless, the versatility of these prototype systems has enabled a variety of quantum algorithms and tasks to be implemented on them. Fully programmable small-scale (three to seven qubit) trapped ion systems have been used to implement Grover's search algorithm [12,13], Shor's factoring algorithm [14], quantum Fourier transform [15,16], and others.

All of the prototype general-purpose trapped-ion quantum computer systems demonstrated to date consist of a chain of 5 to 20 static ions in a single potential well. In these machines, each single qubit gate operation takes 0.1-5 μs, and a multiqubit gate operation takes 50-3,000 μs depending on the nature of the gates used. Each ion in the chain interacts with every other ion in the chain due to the strong Coulomb interaction in a tight trap through motional degree of freedom that is shared among the ions. This interaction can be leveraged to realize quantum logic gates between nonadjacent ions, leading to dense connectivity among the qubits in a single ion chain. In one approach, a global entangling gate is applied to all qubits in the chain, where a subset of qubits are "hidden" from the others by changing their internal states, rendering them insensitive to the motion [17,18]. An alternative approach is to induce a two-qubit gate between an arbitrary pair of ions in the chain by illuminating specific ions with tightly focused and carefully tailored control signals, such that only the desired ions move—many control signals are used to make the force on all the other ions cancel out [19]. Using either approach, one can realize a general-purpose quantum processor with fully connected qubits [20], meaning that two-qubit gates may be implemented between arbitrary pairs of qubits in the system [21]; these capabilities are expected to scale to over 50 qubits in a relatively straightforward way [22].

5.2.2 Challenges and Opportunities for Creating a Scalable Ion Trap Quantum Computer

It is likely that some early, small-scale quantum computers (20-100 qubits) based on ion traps will become available by the early 2020s. Like current machines, these early demonstration systems are likely to consist of a single chain of ions and feature unique all-to-all connectivity among the qubits in the chain, efficiently implementing any quantum circuit with arbitrary circuit structures. However, many conceptual and technical challenges remain toward a creating a truly scalable, fault-tolerant ion trap quantum computer. Examples of such challenges include the difficulty of isolating individual ion motions as chain length increases, the number of ions one can individually address with gate laser beams, and measuring individual qubits. Further scaling of trapped ion quantum computers to well beyond the sizes necessary for demonstrating quantum supremacy toward implementing small instances of useful quantum algorithms will require strategies beyond the single ion chain approach.

A first strategy for scaling beyond a single chain is to trap multiple chains of ions in a single chip with the capability to separate, move or "shuttle," and remerge one or more ions from one chain to another [23]. Such shuttling requires a complex trap with multiple controllable electrodes. Because the quantum information is stored in the internal states of the ion, which have been shown to be unaffected by shuttling between chains in small experiments, this approach does not contribute to any detectable decoherence [24]. Recent adoption of semiconductor microfabrication techniques has enabled the design and construction of highly complex ion traps, which are now routinely used for sophisticated shuttling procedures. This technology could potentially be used to connect multiple ion chains on a single chip, enabling for an increase in scale—provided that the controllers necessary to manipulate these qubits can be integrated accordingly. Even if this ion shuttling is successful on a single chip, eventually the system will need to be scaled up further. Two approaches are currently being explored: photonic interconnections, and tiling chips.

A strategy for connecting multiple qubit subsystems into a much larger system is to use quantum communication channels. One viable approach involves preparing one of the ions in a subsystem in a particular excited state and inducing it to emit a photon in such a way that the quantum state of the photon (for example, its polarization or frequency) is entangled with the ion qubit [25,26]. Two identical setups are used in the two subsystems to generate one photon from each ion, and the two photons can be interfered on a 50/50 beamsplitter and detected on the output ports of the beamsplitter. When both output ports simultaneously record detection of a photon [27], it signals that the two ions that generated the photons have been prepared in a maximally entangled state [28,29]. This protocol entangles a pair of ion qubits across two chips, without the ion qubits ever directly interacting with each other. Although the protocol must be attempted many times until it succeeds, its successful execution is heralded by an unmistakable signature (both detectors registering photons), and can be used deterministically in ensuing computational tasks—for example, to execute a two-qubit gate acting across chips [30]. This protocol was indeed demonstrated first in trapped ions [31] followed by other physical platforms [32-34]. Although the success rate of generating cross-chip entangled pairs in the early experiments was very low due the inefficiency of collecting and detecting the emitted photons (one successful event every ~1,000 seconds), dramatic improvements in the generation rate have been accomplished over the last few years (one successful event every ~200 ms) [35]. Given the continued improvement of this technology, it might be possible that a cross-subsystem two-qubit gates could match the time scale of local two-qubit gates in a single chain (one event every ~100 μs) [36], making this a viable path to connecting ion trap chips using photonic networks. This approach opens up the possibility of using existing photonic networking technology, such as large optical cross-connect switches [37], to connect hundreds of ion trap subsystems into a network of modular, parallel quantum computers [38-40].

An alternative approach to the scaling beyond a single-ion trap chip is to tile all-electrical trap subsystems to create a system where ions from one ion trap chip can be transferred to another chip [41]. This shuttling across different integrated circuits requires careful alignment of shuttling channels and special preparation of the boundaries of these integrated circuits, which has not yet been demonstrated. In this proposal, all qubit gates are carried out by microwave fields and magnetic field gradients, free from the off-resonant spontaneous scattering and stability challenges associated with the use of laser beams [42]. While this integration approach remains entirely speculative at this point, this approach has the potential benefit of relying only on mature microwave technology and electrical control for the critical quantum logic gates, rather than using lasers and optics, which require much higher precision components.

For trapped ions, necessary technology developments toward scalable quantum computer systems include the ability to fabricate ion traps with higher levels of functionality, assemble stabilized laser systems with adequate control, deliver electromagnetic (EM) fields that drive the quantum gates (either microwave or optical) to the ions with sufficient levels of precision to affect only the qubit being targeted (preferably allowing multiple operations at a time), detect the qubit states in parallel without disturbing the data qubits, and program the control EM fields that manipulate the ion qubits so that the overall system achieves sufficient fidelity for the practical application needs. If these challenges are met, one will be able to take advantage of the strengths in trapped ions: some of the best performances of all physical systems in representing a single qubit, thanks to the fact that these qubits are fundamentally identical (as opposed to those which are manufactured), and the high fidelity of qubit operations at small experimental scales.

5.3 SUPERCONDUCTING QUBITS

Like current silicon integrated circuits, superconducting qubits are lithographically defined electronic circuits. When cooled to milli-Kelvin temperatures, they exhibit quantized energy levels (due to quantized states of electronic charge or magnetic flux, for example), and are thus sometimes called "artificial atoms" [43]. Their compatibility with microwave control electronics, ability to operate at nanosecond time scales, continually improving coherence times, and potential to leverage lithographic scaling, all converge to place superconducting qubits among the forefront of the qubit modalities being considered for both digital quantum computation and quantum annealing. Appendix C provides a technical overview of current strategies for constructing a superconductor quantum data plane and its associated control and measurement plane.

5.3.1 Current Superconducting Quantum "Computers"

In the context of digital quantum computation and quantum simulations, the present state-of-art for operational gate error rate is better than (below) 0.1 percent for single-qubit gates [44-46] and 1 percent for two-qubit gates [47], below the error threshold for the most lenient error detection protocols—for example, the surface code. Based on these developments, superconducting qubit circuits with around 10 qubits have been engineered to demonstrate prototype quantum algorithms [48,49] and quantum simulations [50,51], prototype quantum error detection [52-55], and quantum memories [56], and, as of 2018, cloud-based 5-, 16-, and 20-qubit circuits are available to users worldwide. However, the error rates are higher in these larger machines—for example, the 5-qubit machines available on the Web in 2018 have gate error rates of around 5 percent [57,58].

In the context of quantum annealing, commercial systems exist with over 2,000 qubits and integrated cryogenic control based on classical superconducting circuitry [59,60]. These are the largest qubit-based systems currently available, with two orders of magnitude (100 times) more qubits than current gate-based QCs. To achieve this scale machine required careful design trade-offs and significant engineering effort. The decision to integrate the control electronics with the qubits enabled D-Wave to rapidly scale the number of qubits in their system, but also results in the qubits being built in a more lossy material. They purposely traded off qubit fidelity for an easier scaling path. Thus, the coherence times of the qubits in these machines are over 3 orders of magnitude worse than those in current gate-based machines, although this is expected to be less of a limitation for quantum annealers than for gate-based machines.

Progress in gate-based machines has emphasized the optimization of qubit and gate fidelities, at sizes limited to on the order of tens of qubits. Since the first demonstration of a superconducting qubit in 1999, the qubit coherence time T_2 in gate-level machines has improved more than five orders-of-magnitude, standing at around 100 microseconds today. This remarkable improvement in coherence arose from reducing energy losses in the qubit through advances in materials science, fabrication engineering, and qubit design by groups worldwide.

5.3.2 Challenges and Opportunities for Creating a Scalable Quantum Computer

The current approach, using room temperature control and measurement planes, with multiple wires per qubit, should scale to around 1,000 physical qubits [61]. This section reviews the factors that cause this limit, and then discusses what is currently known about the path to even larger machines.

Reaching Many Hundreds of Qubits

Many factors will limit the size of machine that can be achieved by simply scaling up the number of qubits placed on a single integrated circuit. These include the following:

- *Maintaining qubit quality while scaling up the number of bits.* Superconducting qubits are lithographically scalable and compatible with semiconductor fabrication tools [62]. High-coherence qubits have been demonstrated on 200-mm wafers in a research foundry environment. In scaling to larger numbers of qubits, one needs to at least maintain qubit coherence and, ideally, increase it, as larger systems will likely aim to solve larger problems that require additional time, and higher fidelity enables more operations to be performed during the coherence time of the quantum processor. Of course, the fabrication variation that a number of qubits spans gets worse as the number of qubits increases, since a larger number of cells will include more improbable variations. The current approach to fabricating high-fidelity tunable qubits—shadow evaporation—will likely scale to the level of thousands of qubits, based on the process monitoring of device yield and variations currently being implemented at places like the Massachusetts Institute of Technology Lincoln Laboratory. Today's nominally identical qubits vary in frequency with a sigma of around 150 MHz, corresponding to a sigma in the Josephson junction critical current of 2-3 percent. While sufficient for scaling tunable qubits to the 1,000-qubit level, certain fixed-frequency qubit schemes will not be able to handle this larger variation.
- *Refrigeration, wiring, and packaging.* Present dilution refrigerator technology can handle up to several thousand DC wires and coaxial cables, which should support around 1,000 qubits. Achieving this level of wiring requires proper materials to reduce thermal loads, in particular from 300 K to the 3 K stage, and miniaturized coaxes and connectors. While the bandwidth required for control is generally limited to around 12 GHz for qubits being designed

today, controlling the out-of-band impedance out to higher frequencies can be important to minimize decoherence, and becomes more difficult as the physical size increases.

Building a large-scale quantum computer will require two dimensional (2D) arrays of qubits, and areal connection from the qubits to their housing, or "package," and from the package to the wires fed through the cryostat. This areal connection will need three-dimensional (3D) integration schemes using flip-chip bump-bonding and superconducting through-silicon vias, technologies that are being developed to connect high-coherence qubit chips with multilayer interconnect routing wafers [63,64].

- *Control and measurement.* As mentioned earlier, present designs require per qubit control signal generation. While in many current machines, these signals are generated by standard lab equipment, several companies now provide rack-mounted card designs that should scale to a few thousand qubits. Using rack-mounted electronics means that any time the next operation depends on a prior measurement, a common operation in error correction algorithms, there will be a delay in the machine's operation. Sending a signal down, getting a signal back, inferring the next signal to send, and triggering it to be sent takes 500-1,000 ns using current equipment, and limits the ultimate clock speed of the quantum computer. While this should be sufficient for 1,000 qubit circuits, reducing the clock period is advantageous, as it translates directly to lower error rates.

Scaling to Larger-Size Machines

First, qubit fidelities need to be improved to provide the lower error rates needed to support practical quantum error correction. Materials, fabrication and circuit-design advances will be key to achieving 10^{-3} to 10^{-4} qubit error rates. In addition, as the size of the computer increases to millions of qubits and beyond, advanced process monitoring, statistical process control, and new methods for reducing defects relevant to high-coherence devices will be required to assess and improve qubit yield. Just as fabrication tools have been specialized to target specific, advanced complementary metal-oxide semiconductor (CMOS) processes, it is likely that specialized tools that target specific qubit-fabrication processes will need to be developed to enhance yield and minimize fabrication-induced defects that cause decoherence.

Wafer real estate is another consideration for larger machines. Assuming qubit unit cells with repeat distance critical dimensions of 50 microns (state-of-the-art today) [65], a large integrated circuit of 20 mm by 20 mm could contain around 1,600 qubits. If one used an entire 300 mm wafer for one processor, the wafer could hold around 250,000 qubits. While that is sufficient for the near future, reducing the qubit unit cell critical dimension while retaining coherence and controllability will increase qubit density and enable larger numbers of qubits on a single 300 mm wafer.

Moving to wafer-size integrated circuits requires creating a new package. Today's high-coherence qubits operate in pristine microwave environments. The qubits are generally around 5 GHz, which corresponds to a free-space wavelength of around 60 mm. The wavelength is further reduced in the presence of dielectrics like the silicon wafer. Using the rule of thumb that a clean microwave environment requires dimensions less than one-quarter of a wavelength, it is clear that further research is needed before large high-quality packages can be built.

Controlling more than a thousand qubits will require a new strategy for the control and measurement plane. Instead of externally driving each control signal, some logic/control closer to the qubit will drive these signals, and a smaller number of external signals will be used to control this logic. This control logic will need to be introduced using either 3D integration to connect the qubit plane with this local control plane or fabricated monolithically (but must be done so without compromising qubit coherence and gate fidelity). Of course, this means that this logic will operate at very cold temperatures, either at tens of milli-Kelvins, or at 4 K. Operating at 4 K is much easier, since the capacity for heat dissipation is larger, and it saves on the wire count from room temperature to 4 K, but it still requires extensive control wiring to continue down to the base-temperature stage in the cryostat. While there are technologies that could operate at these temperatures, including cryogenic CMOS, single-flux quantum (SFQ), reciprocal quantum logic (RQL), and adiabatic quantum flux parametrons, significant research will be needed to be create these designs at scale, and then determine which approaches are able to create a local control and measurement layer that supports the needed high-fidelity qubit operations.

Even if one is able to scale to 300 mm wafers, a large quantum computer will need to use a number of these subsystems, and with high probability, the optimal size of the subsystem will be modules smaller than that. Thus, there will be a need to connect these subsystems to each other with some kind of quantum interconnect. There are two general approaches that are currently being pursued. One assumes that the interconnection between the modules is at milli-Kelvin temperatures, so one can use microwave photons to communicate. This involves creating guided channels for these photons, interconverting quantum information between a qubit and a microwave photon, and then converting the quantum information back from that photon to a second, distant qubit.

The other option is to couple the qubit state to a higher energy optical photon, which requires a high-fidelity microwave-to-optical conversion technique. This is an area of active research today.

5.4 OTHER TECHNOLOGIES

Since many technical challenges remain in scaling either trapped ion or superconducting quantum computers, a number of research groups are continuing to explore other approaches for creating qubits and quantum computers. These technologies are much less developed, and are still focused on creating single qubit and two qubit gates. Appendix D provides an introduction to these approaches, which is summarized in this section.

Photons have a number of properties that make them an attractive technology for quantum computers: they are quantum particles that interact weakly with their environment and with each other. This natural isolation from the environment makes them an obvious approach to quantum communication. This base communication utility, combined with excellent single-qubit gates with high fidelity means that many early quantum experiments were done using photons. One key challenge with photonic quantum computers is how to create robust two-qubit gates. Researchers are currently working on two approaches for this issue. In linear optics quantum computing, an effective strong interaction is created by a combination of single-photon operations and measurements, which can be used to implement a probabilistic two-qubit gate, which heralds when it was successful. A second approach uses small structures in semiconductor crystals for photon interaction, and can also be considered a type of semiconductor quantum computer. These structures can be naturally occurring, called "optically active defects," or man-made, which are often a structure called a "quantum dot."

Work on building small-scale linear photon computers has been successful, and there are a number of groups trying to scale up the size of these machines. One key scaling issue for these machines is the "size" of a photonic qubit. Because the photons used in photonic quantum computing typically have wavelengths that are around a micron, and because the photons move at the speed of light and are typically routed along one dimension of the optical chip, increasing the number of photons, and hence the number of qubits, to extremely large numbers in a photonic device is even more challenging than it is in systems with qubits that can be localized in space. However, arrays with many thousands of qubits are expected to be possible [66].

Neutral atoms are another approach for qubits that is very similar to trapped ions, but instead of using ionized atoms and exploiting their charge to hold the qubits in place, neutral atoms and laser tweezers are used. Like trapped ion qubits, optical and microwave pulses are used for qubit manipulation, with lasers also being used to cool the atoms before computation. In 2018, systems with 50 atoms have been demonstrated with relatively compact spacing between the atoms [67]. These systems have been used as analog quantum computers, where the interactions between qubits can be controlled by adjusting the spacing between the atoms. Building gate-based quantum computers using this technology requires creating high-quality two-qubit operations and isolating these operations from other neighboring qubits. As of mid-2018, entanglement error rates of 3 percent have been achieved in isolated two-qubit systems [68]. Scaling up a gate-based neutral atom system requires addressing many of the same issues that arise when scaling a trapped ion computer, since the control and measurement layers are the same. Its unique feature compared to trapped ions is its potential for building multidimensional arrays.

Semiconductor qubits can be divided into two types depending on whether they use photons or electrical signals to control qubits and their interactions. Optically gated semiconductor qubits typically use optically active defects or quantum dots that induce strong effective couplings between photons, while electrically gated semiconductor qubits use voltages applied to lithographically defined metal gates to confine and manipulate the electrons that form the qubits. While less developed than other quantum technologies, this approach is more similar to that used for current classical electronics, potentially enabling the large investments that have enabled the tremendous scalability of classical electronics to facilitate the scaling of quantum information processors. Scaling optically gated qubits requires improved uniformity and requires accommodation of the need to individually address optically each qubit. Electrically gated qubits are potentially very dense, but material issues have limited the quality of even single-qubit gates until recently [69]. While high density may enable a very large number of qubits to be integrated on the chip, it exacerbates the problem of building a control and measurement plane for these types of qubits: providing the needed wiring while avoiding interference and crosstalk between control signals will be extremely challenging.

The final approach to quantum computing discussed here uses topological qubits. In this system, operations on the physical qubits have extremely high fidelities because the qubit operations are protected by topological symmetry implemented at the microscopic level: error correction is done by the qubit itself. This will reduce and possibly eliminate the overhead of performing explicit quantum error correction. While this would be an amazing advance, topological qubits are the least developed technology platform. In mid-2018, there are many nontrivial steps that need to be done to demonstrate the existence of a topological qubit, including experimentally observing the basic structure that underlies these qubits. Once these structures are built and controlled in the lab, the error resilience properties of this approach might enable it to scale faster than the other approaches.

5.5 FUTURE OUTLOOK

Many qubit technologies have significantly improved over the past decade, leading to the small gate-based quantum computers available today. For all qubit technologies, the first major challenge is to lower qubit error rates in large systems while enabling measurements to be interspersed with qubit operations. As mentioned in Chapter 3, the surface code is currently the primary approach to error correction for systems with high error rates. Current systems are limited by two-qubit gate error rates, which is still above the surface code threshold for the larger systems available today; error rates of at least an order of magnitude better than threshold are required if quantum error correction is to be practical.

At ~1,000 physical qubits—used for both data qubits and syndrome measurement qubits—one can implement a distance ~16 quantum error correcting code for a single logical qubit. Assuming a physical-qubit error rate of 10^{-3} (an arbitrary but reasonable estimate, more than 10 times better than currently reported for 10 to 20 qubit machines), one can achieve a logical error rate of approximately 10^{-10}. Improving the physical error rate to 10^{-4} would decrease the logical error rate to 10^{-18}. This example illustrates the substantial win in overall logical error rate (from 10^{-10} to 10^{-18}, eight orders of magnitude) by a relatively modest improvement in physical qubit error rate (from 10^{-3} to 10^{-4}, only one order of magnitude). Clearly, improving physical qubit fidelity—through improvements to fabrication and control—is paramount to demonstrating logical qubits or even a machine with physical qubits that can cascade an interesting number of qubit operations before losing coherence.

The next challenge is to increase the number of qubits in the quantum computer. It seems clear that one will be able to build ICs with hundreds of superconductor qubits in the near future using procedures very similar to the methods used for today's 20-qubit ICs. In fact, by mid-2018 a number of companies have announced ICs that contained order of 50 qubits, but as of this writing there are no published results benchmarking the functionality or error rates of these systems. Unlike conventional silicon scaling, where creating the manufacturing process for the more complex integrated circuit set the pace of scaling, for quantum computing, scaling will be dictated by the degree of difficulty in obtaining low error rates with these larger qubit systems, a task that requires joint optimization of the IC, package, control and measurement plane, and the calibration method used.

Scaling trapped ion computing requires the design of new trap systems and the control and measurement plane optics/electronics for these new traps. The next generation are likely to use linear ion traps, which will scale to the order of 100 qubits. Further scaling will require another change to the trap design to enable shuttling of ions between different groups, which should also allow more flexible qubit measurements.

At some point in increasing the number of qubits in a quantum processor or chip, the scaling will become easier using a modular approach, where a number of chips are linked together to create a larger machine rather than creating a larger chip. A modular design will require the development of a fast, low error rate quantum interconnection between the modules; with photonic connections the most promising due to their speed and fidelity. While the component technologies and baseline protocols for realizing some of these integration strategies have already been demonstrated, system-scale demonstration with practical levels of performance remains a major challenge.

As a result of the challenges facing superconducting and trapped ion quantum data planes, it is not yet clear if or when either of these technologies can scale to the level needed for a large error corrected quantum computer. Thus, at this time, the viability of other, currently less-developed quantum data plane technologies cannot be ruled out, nor can the possibility that hybrid systems making use of multiple technologies might prevail.

5.6 NOTES

[1] C. Monroe, D.M. Meekhof, B.E. King, W.M. Itano, and D.J. Wineland, 1995, Demonstration of a fundamental quantum logic gate, *Physical Review Letters* 75:4714.
[2] J.I. Cirac and P. Zoller, 1995, Quantum computations with cold trapped ions, *Physical Review Letters* 74:4091.
[3] C. Monroe and J. Kim, 2013, Scaling the ion trap quantum processor, *Science* 339:1164-1169.
[4] K.R. Brown, J. Kim and C. Monroe, 2016, Co-designing a scalable quantum computer with trapped atomic ions, *npj Quantum Information* 2:16034.
[5] J. Kim, S. Crain, C. Fang, J. Joseph, and P. Maunz, 2017, "Enabling Trapped Ion Quantum Computing with MEMS Technology," pp. 1-2 in *2017 International Conference on Optical MEMS and Nanophotonics (OMN)*, https://ieeexplore.ieee.org.
[6] D. Hanneke, J.P. Home, J.D. Jost, J.M. Amini, D. Leibfried and D.J. Wineland, 2010, Realization of a programmable two-qubit quantum processor, *Nature Physics* 6:13.
[7] P. Schindler, D. Nigg, T. Monz, J. Barreiro, E. Martinez, S. Wang, S. Quint, M. Brandl, V. Nebendahl, C. Roos, M. Chwalla, M. Hennrich, and R. Blatt, 2013, A quantum information processor with trapped ions, *New Journal of Physics* 15:123012.
[8] S. Debnath, N.M. Linke, C. Figgatt, K.A. Landsman, K. Wright, and C. Monroe, 2016, Demonstration of a small programmable quantum computer with atomic qubits, *Nature* 536:63-66.

[9] N. Friis, O. Marty, C. Maier, C. Hempel, M. Holzapfel, P. Jurcevic, M. Plenio, M. Huber, C. Roos, R. Blatt, and B. Lanyon, 2017, "Observation of Entangled States of a Fully Controlled 20 Qubit System," arXiv:1711.11092.

[10] J.P. Gaebler, T.R. Tan, Y. Lin, Y. Wan, R. Bowler, A.C. Keith, S. Glancy, K. Coakley, E. Knill, D. Leibfried, and D.J. Wineland, 2016, High-fidelity universal gate set for $^9Be^+$ ion qubits, *Physical Review Letters* 117:060505.

[11] C.J. Ballance, T.P. Harty, N.M. Linke, M.A. Sepiol, and D.M. Lucas, 2016, High-fidelity quantum logic gates using trapped-ion hyperfine qubits, *Physical Review Letters* 117:060504.

[12] K.-A. Brickman, P.C. Haljan, P.J. Lee, M. Acton, L. Deslauriers, and C. Monroe, 2005, Implementation of Grover's quantum search algorithm in a scalable system, *Physical Review A* 72:050306(R).

[13] C. Figgatt, D. Maslov, K.A. Landsman, N.M. Linke, S. Debnath, and C. Monroe, 2017, Complete 3-qubit grover search on a programmable quantum computer, *Nature Communications* 8:1918.

[14] T. Monz, D. Nigg, E.A. Martinez, M.F. Brandl, P. Schindler, R. Rines, S.X. Wang, I.L. Chuang, and R. Blatt, 2016, Realization of a scalable Shor algorithm, *Science* 351:1068-1070.

[15] J. Chiaverini, J. Britton, D. Leibfried, E. Knill, M.D. Barrett, R.B. Blakestad, W.M. Itano, J.D. Jost, C. Langer, R. Ozeri, T. Schaetz, and D.J. Wineland, 2005, Implementation of the semiclassical quantum Fourier transform in a scalable system, *Science* 308:997-1000.

[16] A. Sørensen and K. Mølmer, 1999, Quantum computation with ions in a thermal motion, *Physical Review Letters* 82:1971.

[17] B.P. Lanyon, C. Hempel, D. Nigg, M. Müller, R. Gerritsma, F. Zähringer, P. Schindler, J.T. Barreiro, M. Rambach, G. Kirchmair, M. Hennrich, P. Zoller, R. Blatt, and C.F. Roos, 2011, Universal digital quantum simulation with trapped ions, *Science* 334:57-61.

[18] P.C. Haljan, K.-A. Brickman, L. Deslauriers, P.J. Lee, and C. Monroe, 2005, Spin-dependent forces on trapped ions for phase-stable quantum gates and entangled states of spin and motion, *Physical Review Letters* 94:153602.

[19] S.-L. Zhu, C. Monroe, and L.-M. Duan, 2006, Arbitrary-speed quantum gates within large ion crystals through minimum control of laser beams, *Europhyics Letters* 73(4):485.

[20] C.J. Ballance, T.P. Harty, N.M. Linke, M.A. Sepiol, and D.M. Lucas, 2016, High-fidelity quantum logic gates using trapped-ion hyperfine qubits, *Physical Review Letters* 117:060504.

[21] N.M. Linke, D. Maslov, M. Roetteler, S. Debnath, C. Figgatt, K.A. Landsman, K. Wright, and C. Monroe, 2017, Experimental comparison of two quantum computing architectures, *Proceedings of the National Academy of Sciences of the U.S.A.* 114:13.

[22] J. Zhang, G. Pagano, P.W. Hess, A. Kyprianidis, P. Becker, H.B. Kaplan, A.V. Gorshkov, Z.-X. Gong, and C. Monroe, 2017, Observation of a many-body dynamical phase transition with a 53-qubit quantum simulator, *Nature* 551:601-604.

[23] J. Chiaverini, B.R. Blakestad, J.W. Britton, J.D. Jost, C. Langer, D.G. Leibfried, R. Ozeri, and D.J. Wineland, 2005, Surface-electrode architecture for ion-trap quantum information processing, *Quantum Information and Computation* 5:419.

[24] J. Kim, S. Pau, Z. Ma, H.R. McLellan, J.V. Gates, A. Kornblit, R.E. Slusher, R.M. Jopson, I. Kang, and M. Dinu, 2005, System design for large-scale ion trap quantum information processor, *Quantum Information and Computation* 5:515.

[25] L.-M. Duan, B.B. Blinov, D.L. Moehring, and C. Monroe, 2004, Scalable trapped ion quantum computation with a probabilistic ion-photon mapping, *Quantum Information and Computation* 4:165-173.

[26] B.B. Blinov, D.L. Moehring, L.-M. Duan and C. Monroe, 2004, Observation of a entanglement between a single trapped atom and a single photon, *Nature* 428:153-157.

[27] D. Bouwmeester, P. Jian-Wei, K. Mattle, M. Eibl, H. Weinfurter, and A. Zeilinger, 1997, Experimental quantum teleportation, *Nature* 390:575-579.
[28] C. Simon and W.T.M. Irvine, 2003, Robust long-distance entanglement and a loophole-free bell test with ions and photons, *Physical Review Letters* 91:110405.
[29] L.-M. Duan, M.J. Madsen, D.L. Moehring, P. Maunz, R.N. Kohn Jr., and C. Monroe, 2006, Probabilistic quantum gates between remote atoms through interference of optical frequency qubits, *Physical Review A* 73:062324.
[30] D. Gottesman and I. Chuang, 1999, Quantum teleportation is a universal computational primitive, *Nature* 402:390-393.
[31] D.L. Moehring, P. Maunz, S. Olmschenk, K.C. Younge, D.N. Matsukevich, L.-M. Duan, and C. Monroe, 2007, Entanglement of a single-atom quantum bits at a distance, *Nature* 449:68-71.
[32] J. Hofmann, M. Krug, N. Ortegel, L. Gérard, M. Weber, W. Rosenfeld, and H. Weinfurter, 2012, Heralded entanglement between widely separated atoms, *Science* 337:72-75.
[33] H. Bernien, B. Hensen, W. Pfaff, G. Koolstra, M.S. Blok, L. Robledo, T.H. Taminiau, M. Markham, D.J. Twitchen, L. Childress, and R. Hanson, 2013, Heralded entanglement between solid-state qubits separated by 3 meters, *Nature* 497:86-90.
[34] A. Delteil, Z. Sun, W. Gao, E. Togan, S. Faelt and A. Imamoğlu, 2015, Generation of heralded entanglement between distant hole spins, *Nature Physics* 12:218-223.
[35] D. Hucul, I.V. Inlek, G. Vittorini, C. Crocker, S. Debnath, S.M. Clark, and C. Monroe, 2015, Modular entanglement of atomic qubits using photons and phonons, *Nature Physics* 11:37-42.
[36] T. Kim, P. Maunz, and J. Kim, 2011, Efficient collection of single photons emitted from a trapped ion into a single-mode fiber for scalable quantum-information processing, *Physical Review A* 84:063423.
[37] J. Kim, C.J. Nuzman, B. Kumar, D.F. Lieuwen, J.S. Kraus, A. Weiss, C.P. Lichtenwalner, et al., 2003, "1100 × 1100 port MEMS-based optical crossconnect with 4-dB maximum loss," *IEEE Photonics Technology Letters* 15:1537-1539.
[38] P. Schindler, D. Nigg, T. Monz, J.T. Barreiro, E. Martinez, S.X. Wang, S. Quint, et al., 2013, A quantum information processor with trapped ions, *New Journal of Physics* 15:123012.
[39] D. Hanneke, J.P. Home, J.D. Jost, J.M. Amini, D. Leibfried, and D.J. Wineland, 2010, Realization of a programmable two-qubit quantum processor, *Nature Physics* 6:13-16.
[40] C. Monroe, R. Raussendorf, A. Ruthven, K.R. Brown, P. Maunz, L.-M. Duan, and J. Kim, 2014, Large-scale modular quantum-computer architecture with atomic memory and photonic interconnects, *Physical Review A* 89:022317.
[41] B. Lekitsch, S. Weidt, A.G. Fowler, K. Mølmer, S.J. Devitt, C. Wunderlich, and W.K. Hensinger, 2017, Blueprint for a microwave trapped ion quantum computer, *Science Advances* 3:e1601540.
[42] C. Piltz, T. Sriarunothai, S.S. Ivanov, S. Wölk and C. Wunderlich, 2016, Versatile microwave-driven trapped ion spin system for quantum information processing, *Science Advances* 2:e1600093.
[43] W.D. Oliver and P.B. Welander, 2013, Materials in superconducting quantum bits, *MRS Bulletin* 38(10):816-825.
[44] S. Gustavsson, O. Zwier, J. Bylander, F. Yan, F. Yoshihara, Y. Nakamura, T.P. Orlando, and W.D. Oliver, 2013, Improving quantum gate fidelities by using a qubit to measure microwave pulse distortions, *Physical Review Letters* 110:0405012.
[45] R. Barends, J. Kelly, A. Megrant, A. Veitia, D. Sank, E. Jeffrey, T.C. White, et al., 2014, Logic gates at the surface code threshold: Supercomputing qubits poised for fault-tolerant quantum computing, *Nature* 508:500-503.
[46] S. Sheldon, E. Magesan, J. Chow, and J.M. Gambetta, 2016, Procedures for systematically turning up cross-talk in the cross-resonance gate, *Physical Review A* 93:060302.

[47] R. Barends, J. Kelly, A. Megrant, A. Veitia, D. Sank, E. Jeffrey, T.C. White, et al., 2014, Superconducting quantum circuits at the surface code threshold for fault tolerance, *Nature* 508(7497):500.
[48] L. DiCarlo, J.M. Chow, J.M. Gambetta, L.S. Bishop, B.R. Johnson, D.I. Schuster, J. Majer, A. Blais, L. Frunzio, S.M. Girvin, and R.J. Schoelkopf, 2009, Demonstration of two-qubit algorithms with a superconducting quantum processor, *Nature* 460:240-244.
[49] E. Lucero, R. Barends, Y. Chen, J. Kelly, M. Mariantoni, A. Megrant, P. O'Malley, et al., 2012, Computing prime factors with a Josephson phase qubit quantum processor, *Nature Physics* 8:719-723.
[50] P.J.J. O'Malley, R. Babbush, I.D. Kivlichan, J. Romero, J.R. McClean, R. Barends, J. Kelly, et al., 2016, Scalable quantum simulation of molecular energies, *Physical Review X* 6:031007.
[51] N.K. Langford, R. Sagastizabal, M. Kounalakis, C. Dickel, A. Bruno, F. Luthi, D.J. Thoen, A. Endo, and L. DiCarlo, 2017, Experimentally simulating the dynamics of quantum light and matter at deep-strong coupling, *Nature Communications* 8:1715.
[52] M.D. Reed, L. DiCarlo, S.E. Nigg, L. Sun, L. Frunzio, S.M. Girvin, and R.J. Schoelkopf, 2012, Realization for three-qubit quantum error correction with superconducting circuits, *Nature* 482:382-385.
[53] J. Kelly, R. Barends, A.G. Fowler, A. Megrant, E. Jeffrey, T. C. White, D. Sank, et al., 2015, State preservation by repetitive error detection in a superconducting quantum circuit, *Nature* 519:66-69.
[54] A.D. Córcoles, E. Magesan, S.J. Srinivasan, A.W. Cross, M. Steffen, J.M. Gambetta, and J.M. Chow, 2015, Demonstration of a quantum error detection code using a square lattice of four superconducting qubits, *Nature Communications* 6:6979.
[55] D. Ristè, S. Poletto, M.-Z. Huang, A. Bruno, V. Vesterinen, O.-P. Saira, and L. DiCarlo, 2015, Detecting bit-flip errors in a logical qubit using stabilizer measurements, *Nature Communications* 6:6983.
[56] N. Ofek, A. Petrenko, R. Heeres, P. Reinhold, Z. Leghtas, B. Vlastakis, Y. Liu, et al., 2016, Extending the lifetime of a quantum bit with error correction in superconducting circuits, *Nature* 536:441-445.
[57] IBM Q Team, 2018, "IBM Q 5 Yorktown Backend Specification V1.1.0," https://ibm.biz/qiskit-yorktown; IBM Q Team, 2018, "IBM Q 5 Tenerife backend specification V1.1.0," https://ibm.biz/qiskit-tenerife.
[58] Ibid.
[59] M.W. Johnson, M.H.S. Amin, S. Gildert, T. Lanting, F. Hamze, N. Dickson, R. Harris, et al., 2011, Quantum annealing with manufactured spins, *Nature* 473:194-198.
[60] D Wave, "Technology Information," http://dwavesys.com/resources/publications.
[61] John Martinis, private conversation.
[62] W.D. Oliver and P.B. Welander, 2013, Materials in superconducting qubits, *MRS Bulletin* 38:816.
[63] D. Rosenberg, D.K. Kim, R. Das, D. Yost, S. Gustavsson, D. Hover, P. Krantz, et al., 2017, 3D integrated superconducting qubits, *npj Quantum Information* 3:42.
[64] B. Foxen, J.Y. Mutus, E. Lucero, R. Graff, A. Megrant, Y. Chen, C. Quintana, et al., 2017, "Qubit Compatible Superconducting Interconnects," arXiv:1708.04270.
[65] J.M. Chow, J.M. Gambetta, A.D. Córcoles, S.T. Merkel, J.A. Smolin, C. Rigetti, S. Poletto, G.A. Keefe, M.B. Rothwell, J.R. Rozen, M.B. Ketchen, and M. Steffen, 2012, Universal quantum gate set approaching fault-tolerant thresholds with superconducting qubits, *Physical Review Letters* 109:060501.
[66] See, for example, J.W. Silverstone, D. Bonneau, J.L. O'Brien, and M.G. Thompson, 2016, Silicon quantum photonics, *IEEE Journal of Selected Topics in Quantum Electronics* 22:390-402;

T. Rudolph, 2017, Why I am optimistic about the silicon-photonic route to quantum computing?, *APL Photonics* 2:030901.

[67] H. Bernien, S. Schwartz, A. Keesling, H. Levine, A. Omran, H. Pichler, S. Choi, A.S. Zibrov, M. Endres, M. Greiner, V. Vuletić, and M.D. Lukin, 2017, "Probing Many-Body Dynamics on a 51-Atom Quantum Simulator," preprint arXiv:1707.04344.
[68] H. Levine, A. Keesling, A. Omran, H. Bernien, S. Schwartz, A.S. Zibrov, M. Endres, M. Greiner, V. Vuletić, and M.D. Lukin, 2018, "High-Fidelity Control and Entanglement of Rydberg Atom Qubits," preprint arXiv:1806.04682.
[69] J.J. Pla, K.Y. Tan, J.P. Dehollain, W.H. Lim, J.J. Morton, D.N. Jamieson, A.S. Dzurak, and A. Morello, 2012, A single-atom electron spin qubit in silicon, *Nature* 489:541-545.

6

Essential Software Components of a Scalable Quantum Computer

In addition to creating the hardware functionality to support quantum computing, a functional QC will also require extensive software components. This is analogous to the operation of classical computers, but new and different tools are required to support quantum operations, including programming languages that enable programmers to describe QC algorithms, compilers to analyze them and map them onto quantum hardware, and additional support to analyze, optimize, debug, and test programs for implementation on specific quantum hardware. Preliminary versions of some of these tools have been developed to support the QCs currently available on the web [1]. Ideally, these tools should be accessible to software developers without a background in quantum mechanics. They should offer abstractions that allow programmers to think at an algorithmic level with less concern for details like control pulse generation. Last, they should ideally enable programming of any quantum algorithm in a code that can translate to any target quantum architecture.

For the results described in Chapter 5, hardware controls and software implementation routines were deployed in an implementation-specific manner, with significant manual optimization. These approaches will not scale efficiently to large devices. Given the different, and emerging, approaches to building a quantum data plane, early-stage high-level software tools must be particularly flexible if they are to remain useful in the event of changes in hardware and algorithms. This requirement complicates the task of developing a complete software architecture for quantum computing. The rest of this chapter explores these issues in more detail, providing a look at the current state of progress in development of software tools for QC, and what needs to be accomplished to create a scalable QC.

The software ecosystem for any computer—classical or quantum—includes the programming languages and compilers used to map algorithms onto the machine, but also much more than that. Simulation and debugging tools are needed to debug the hardware and software (especially in situations where the hardware and software are being co-developed); optimization tools are required to help implement algorithms efficiently; and verification tools are needed to help work toward both software and hardware correctness.

For quantum computers, simulation tools, such as a so-called universal simulator, can provide a programmer with the ability to model each quantum operation and to track the quantum state that would results, along with its evolution in time. This capability is essential for debugging both programs and newly developed hardware. Optimization tools such as resource estimators would enable rapid estimation of the performance and qubit resources needed to perform different quantum algorithms. This enables a compiler to transform the desired computation into an efficient form, minimizing the number of qubits or qubit operations required for the hardware in question.

6.1 CHALLENGES AND OPPORTUNITIES

The QC software ecosystem is fundamental to QC systems design for several reasons. First, and most fundamentally, the compiler tool flows that map algorithms down to a QC hardware system are crucial for enabling its design and use. Even before the QC hardware is available, a compiler system coupled with resource estimators and simulation tools can be developed; these are critical for algorithm design and optimization. A good example of the power of this type of tool set can be found in the work by Reiher et al. on optimizing QC operations required to computationally model the biochemical process of nitrogen fixation [2]. By using feedback from resource estimators, and improved compiler optimizations, they were able to reduce the estimated run time of their quantum algorithm from a high-degree polynomial to a low-degree polynomial, bringing the expected time to solution using a quantum computer from billions of years down to hours or days.

This example shows how languages and compilers (the software "toolchain") can have a dramatic effect on the resources required to execute a quantum computation. Compilers—for both classical and quantum computing—perform many resource optimizations as they analyze and translate the algorithms to machine-executable code. Successful QC toolchain resource optimizations offer significant savings in terms of the number of qubits and the amount of time required to execute an algorithm, in turn helping accelerate the arrival of the QC versus classical "tipping point." In essence, high-performing synthesis and optimization offers the potential for implementing an algorithm in a much smaller QC system than would be required for an unoptimized version; while software development traditionally tends to come after hardware development, making good on the potential for concurrent hardware and software development could move forward the time quantum computing is practical by years.

Finally, digital noisy intermediate-scale quantum (NISQ) systems under current development are particularly sensitive to the quality and efficacy of the software ecosystem. By definition, NISQ systems are very resource constrained, with limited numbers of qubits and low gate fidelities. Therefore, making effective use of NISQ machines will require careful algorithm optimization, probably requiring nearly full stack information flow to identify tractable mappings from algorithms designed for these size devices to the specific NISQ implementation. In particular, information such as noise or error characteristics can usefully percolate up the stack to influence algorithm and mapping choices. Likewise, information about algorithm characteristics (e.g., parallelism) can usefully flow down the stack to inform mapping choices. Put another way, a digital NISQ may require communications between nearly every layer of the stack, meaning that there are fewer opportunities simplify the system design. These challenges will drive specific aspects of toolchain design—for example, limiting cross-layer abstraction or encouraging the use of libraries of "hand-tuned" modules.

Finding: To create a useful quantum computer, research and development on the software toolchain must be done concurrently with the hardware and algorithm development. In fact, insight gained from these tools will help drive research in algorithms, device technologies, and other areas, toward designs with the best chance for overall success.

Several challenges must be solved to create a complete QC software tool flow. Simulation, debugging, and validation are particularly problematic. The following sections describe these issues in more detail.

6.2 QUANTUM PROGRAMMING LANGUAGES

Algorithm design, including for QC algorithms, usually starts with a mathematical formulation of an approach for solving a problem. Programming and compilation are the nontrivial tasks of converting an algorithm's abstract mathematical description to an implementation that is executable on a physical computer. Programming languages support this process by offering syntax to support the natural expression of key concepts and operations. Programming QC systems requires very different concepts and operations than programming for classical computers, and as such requires new languages and a distinct set of tools. For example, designing a language that enables a programmer to exploit quantum interference in a quantum algorithm is a unique and nontrivial challenge.

There are several levels of abstraction in software and algorithms, so several layers of languages are required. At the highest level, a programming language should enable a user to easily and rapidly program an algorithm, while ideally shielding the programmer from detailed underlying hardware specifications. This abstraction of detail is helpful both because it can help mitigate the massive complexity of these systems and also because it can lead to more device-independent and portable software. This device independence can allow the same QC program to be recompiled to target different QC hardware implementations. Current prototype languages enable developers and programmers to interact with quantum hardware through a high-level language that is at least somewhat device independent.

At the lowest level, a language must be able to interact seamlessly with the hardware components and give a complete specification of the physical instructions necessary to execute a program at speed. While some low-level languages are used at present to program devices directly, the long-term vision and goal for quantum computing is to absorb such languages into automated tool flows; as in classical computers, the goal is to have lower-level QC device orchestration be automatically generated, and to abstract such low-level information away from the programmer.

Similar to early stages of a classical computing ecosystem, the current state of play in QC software includes many languages and tools, a number of them open-source efforts,[1] in development both commercially and academically. With the recent industry push toward larger quantum hardware prototypes (including availability on public clouds for broad use), there is an increased awareness of the need for full-stack QC software and hardware in order to encourage usage and nurture a developer community around quantum software and hardware. Thus, it is reasonable to expect that quantum programming languages and software ecosystems will receive considerable attention and may see significant changes in coming years.

---

[1] See, for example, https://github.com/markf94/os_quantum_software.

6.2.1 Programmer-Facing (High-Level) Programming Languages

An initial generation of QC programming languages has been developed, and continued attention is leading to the evolution of new languages and language constructs over time. From the nascent experiences so far, several programming language attributes seem likely to offer useful leverage in overall system design and success.

First, a high-level quantum programming language should strike a balance between abstraction and detail. On one hand, it should be capable of concisely expressing quantum algorithms and applications. On the other hand, it must allow the programmer to specify sufficient algorithmic detail to be used within the software tool flow that maps the quantum algorithm to the hardware-level primitive operations. High-level quantum programming languages are themselves domain-specific languages (DSLs), and in some cases there have been proposals for further specialization for given QC subdomains such as the variational quantum eigensolver, quantum approximate optimization algorithm, and others.

In some quantum programming languages, the approach is to describe an algorithm as a quantum circuit. Software toolchain systems then analyze this circuit in terms of both circuit width and circuit depth to optimize it for a particular quantum data plane. Somewhat in contrast to these approaches, other languages emphasize higher-level algorithm definition over circuit definition. To support good mappings to hardware despite this higher-level approach, some languages support extensive use of function libraries; these contain subroutines and high-level functions implemented as module mappings hand-tuned for particular hardware and are discussed in Section 6.2.3.

Programming languages fall generally into two categories: functional and imperative. QC programming languages of both types have been developed, and there is no consensus yet on whether one is better suited than the other for programming QC applications. Functional languages align well with more abstract or mathematical implementation of algorithms. This approach tends to lead to more compact—and, some programming language researchers argue, less error prone—codes. Examples of QC functional programming languages include Q#, Quipper, Quafl, and LIQuI|> ("Liquid"). Imperative languages, in contrast, allow direct modification of variables and are often viewed as supportive of the resource-efficient system design that QC systems, particularly NISQ systems, will need to be practical [3]. Examples of imperative QC languages are Scaffold [4] and ProjectQ [5].

Another design decision pertains to whether the language is "embedded" off a base language. Embedded languages are formally defined extensions of a base language, an approach that allows the language developer to use the base language's software stack to speed initial implementation. These languages are practically constructed through modest additions to the base language's compiler and related software, as opposed to writing an entire software ecosystem from scratch. To exploit commonality in this way, some current QC programming languages are embedded in widely used non-QC languages.[2] Others are not formally embedded but instead are very close in style to a non-QC base language.[3] Given the fast rate of change in QC hardware and systems design at present, a language that is either formally embedded or at least stylistically related to a widely used base language can allow compilers and other tools to be built quickly and modified more easily than "from-scratch" language design.

Another important design issue for QC programming languages is the language's approach to data typing. "Data typing" refers to programming language constructs that label the kind (or type) of data that a program or function expects, and allows the function to use the type of the data to determine how to perform a specific operation. All languages use some forms of data types. For example, in most programming languages, base data types are provided for integers, floating point numbers, characters, and other commonly used entities; the definition of addition is different for integers than it is for floating point numbers. Some more recent QC languages support a much richer data type system and have stronger type checking rules. These "strongly typed" languages yield even stricter guarantees on type safety that can be helpful in generating reliable software. In particular, compilers can perform type checking regarding whether the program being compiled manipulates variables of a particular data type correctly and abides by the corresponding rules when variables of one type are assigned to another variable. (By analogy, integer values may be assigned to a floating point variable without loss of precision, but an assignment of a floating point value to an integer variable would either be illegal or would result in a loss of precision depending on the language.)

Last, a discussion of programmer-facing software would not be complete without some mention of the user "command-line" interface. Because quantum computers are expected to be large, expensive, custom-built pieces of instrumentation in the near term, it is likely that such systems will be housed at a few designated locations, such as major data centers or manufacturers' facilities, and accessed by users through the Web over a cloud service.[4] Under these circumstances, various levels of

---

[2] This includes Quipper, Quafl, Quil, ProjectQ, and LIQuI |>.

[3] For example, the Scaffold language and ScaffCC toolchain are based on the C programming language. Scaffold uses a very widely used classical compiler infrastructure, LLVM (https://llvm.org/).

[4] Indeed, this is currently the case for D-Wave pilot systems installed at National Labs and with IBM's open superconducting qubit-based processors.

service can be provided to the users—for example, at an application level, as a programming environment, or at an application programming interface (API) level. The future user interface to QCs will continue to evolve, as the physical hardware, relevant applications, and the manufacturer, service provider, and user community all develop.

6.2.2 Control Processing (Low-Level) Languages

In addition to high-level programmer-facing languages for algorithm development, lower-level languages are also necessary in order to generate instructions for the control processor (Section 5.1.3) of a specific quantum data plane (Section 5.1.1). These languages correspond to the assembly language programming or "instruction set architecture" of classical computers. As such, they must be designed to express central aspects of QC execution, such as the fundamental low-level operations or "gates." They can also have constructs to express operation parallelism, qubit state motion, and control sequencing. They are sometimes referred to as a quantum intermediate representation (QIR).

For efficiency reasons, in the foreseeable future, lower-level QC programs and tools likely will need to be more hardware specific than the tools used with classical computers. Given the severe resource constraints facing quantum computers, compilation of quantum programs is likely to be tightly specialized to a particular program input—that is, compilation will likely need to be conducted before every task. For example, a QC running Shor's factoring algorithm would have a program compiled to factor a *specific* large number provided as a constant. Or a QC for chemistry simulations would have a program compiled to model a *specific* molecular structure. This is in contrast to classical computers where ample resources allow more generality. Classical computers compile programs such that they can be run with many different inputs: for example, a spreadsheet program accepts and calculates any numbers typed in by a user, rather than compiling a unique program for each new input. Until QC resource constraints relax considerably, a QC program compilation will much more closely resemble the tight optimization processes used in designing computer hardware (i.e., "hardware synthesis") than classical software compilation.

An early low-level language called QASM [6] provided very basic operational constructs, but was tied to the early QC practices of simple circuits expressed as linear sequences of gates. Subsequent variations of QASM have provided additional features to improve expressive power and scalability. For example, in conventional classical assembly code for classical computers, it would be common to have constructs for iteration (repeatedly executing a portion of code) and for subroutine calls (jumping to another module of code). Currently, some convergence is being seen on the OpenQASM [7] quantum assembly-level language, which combines elements of assembly languages and C with the original QASM constructs.

In the final phases of compilation, a program represented in a QIR like OpenQASM is translated into appropriate control instructions, producing code for the control processor. The control processor drives signals to the control and measurement plane. Languages and frameworks can help support the creation of the software for control generation and measurement equipment used in this plane. One example of this type of system is QcoDeS [8], a Python-based data acquisition framework and toolset to interact with physical devices. Other examples often correspond with particular hardware implementations; these include the OpenQASM backend for IBM Q, an open-source system called ARTIQ driven by the ion trap research community [9], and others.

Current NISQ systems are tightly resource constrained both in terms of circuit width (qubits) and depth (time steps or operation counts). This has placed a challenge on QC languages and compilers: mapping algorithms onto NISQ systems requires extensive, aggressive resource optimizations. This includes both algorithm-level resource reductions that are relatively hardware independent, and also lower-level optimizations that are more specific to a particular hardware instance or technology category. Some of the higher-level optimizations are applied using widely known transformations first developed for software compilers for classical computers, such as loop unrolling and constant propagation. Other high-level optimizations might be specific to QC, such as the QC gate operator selection discussed in Section 6.5.1.

Lower-level hardware-dependent optimizations more naturally focus on device specifics. These include optimizations to account for qubit layout and optimize for data communication. There are also approaches that optimize for very specific device characteristics including observed coherence intervals or device error rates [10]. As NISQ systems become more broadly available for public use, toolchains that are tightly tailored to real-machine characteristics are likely to be more widely used. Such tight tailoring in compiler tool flows can allow algorithms to most efficiently use the limited qubit counts available in the NISQ era.

6.2.3 Software Library Support

In classical computers, function libraries help programmers mitigate complexity by using prewritten subroutines for programs. In some cases, the library provides implementations for basic functions like fast Fourier transforms (FFTs) in order to ease programming and enable code reuse. In other cases, the library functions have been specifically tuned for a particular implementation, and thereby help programmers arrive at a more resource-efficient program than they otherwise would. Library approaches are similarly expected to be essential for efficient quantum computing.

One critical set of libraries arises from the need to evaluate commonly used functions within a quantum algorithm. Some quantum algorithms will require simple mathematical functions such as addition, or other, more complex functions such as modular arithmetic, implementation of block ciphers, and hash functions. A comprehensive set of library functions can save programmers time and help to reduce the likelihood of program errors. In addition, library functions can also be heavily tuned for specific implementations. This shields algorithm-level programmers from the burden of fully familiarizing themselves with hardware details while optimizing for circuit width or depth.

While optimized library functions are often a useful resource, it may be difficult for them to be fully optimized to each of the range of possible underlying hardware implementations. Programmers may find that their algorithm-level expression is—when compiled—more efficient than the library option. To address these trade-offs, there are QC libraries [11-13] that contain a number of options for how to construct the desired functionality—some hardware independent and others tailored for a particular implementation. The compiler tool flow can then use a resource estimate tool to choose the best option for the targeted hardware. Furthermore, if a given user's implementation remains superior to the library options, then in some cases (e.g., open-source scenarios) it too can be incorporated into the library for future use.

Creation and use of QC function libraries is a practical and effective approach to offering well-optimized solutions for commonly used functions, but their interplay with higher-level programming and compiling remains an area where further research and development are needed. Library development would benefit from further improvements in high-level compiler optimizations, to further support the compiler's ability to optimize the tradeoff between circuit depth and circuit width. Specific areas of need include better ways to perform ancilla management, and techniques to manage both "dirty" and "clean" ancilla qubits.[5] Another area of future research lies in being able to express and analyze what level of numerical precision is required in a quantum algorithm, and

---

[5] An "ancilla qubit" is a qubit used for scratch space during a quantum computation or circuit implementation. It is allocated temporarily and must be returned to either its identical starting state (if allocated in a nonzero state) or the clean zero state (if allocated in the zero state) when returned.

how to automatically determine such precisions within a compiler. Such precision analysis can be supportive of aggressive resource optimizations that reduce qubit or operator counts by doing the calculation only to the minimally required precision [14].

6.2.4 Algorithm Resource Analysis

A key to developing commercially or practically useful quantum applications and programs will be the ability to understand the cost and performance of that algorithm. Given the challenges of executing on real QC hardware or simulating QC systems at scale, other forms of early-stage resource estimation become especially critical. Fortunately, resource analysis is more tractable than QC simulation or real-machine execution because it needs to determine only the time and resources that would be required to compute the answer; it does not compute the answer itself. As such, it does not need to compute the full quantum state information, which is the intractable challenge in other approaches. Thus, resource estimation can be made efficient and scalable to very large qubit input sizes, and this allows one to analyze the performance of algorithms that are too large to simulate on a classical computer or run on current quantum computers. Resource estimators have been run for Shor's algorithm and other similarly scaled benchmarks, for up to hundreds of thousands of qubits and millions of quantum operations or execution timesteps [15].

The results of resource estimation analysis can be used by other software tools to guide optimization e orts, especially when mapping to the quantum data plane, and by programmers to identify realistic applications of quantum computers. This detailed analysis of the application is needed since the theoretical analysis gives only the asymptotic scaling of a quantum algorithm. On a particular QC system, the actual resource usage trade-offs may be heavily influenced by implementation choices such as qubit connectivity or communication approaches. Such implementation specifics can be accounted for by resource estimators, in order to get better understanding of what are promising design choices, rather than relying solely on asymptotic scaling estimates.

Resource analysis can be done at various abstraction levels in the compilation of the algorithm to the hardware, with varying trade-offs of detail versus accuracy. Each stage uses a model of the quantum hardware appropriate to the optimization issues at that stage. For example, one can analyze circuit width and depth after the algorithm has been mapped to a discrete set of single- and two-qubit operations to understand how best to minimize the *logical* resources necessary to run an application. Another level of analysis can be performed again after quantum error correction has been applied and the resulting code has been mapped to the actual

ESSENTIAL SOFTWARE COMPONENTS OF A SCALABLE QUANTUM COMPUTER   145

operations the hardware supports. This allows the estimate to account for QEC and communication overheads. Likewise, such estimates allow compiler analyses making use of the estimates to perform optimizations to reduce these overheads.

6.3 SIMULATION

Simulators serve a critical role in the development of quantum computers and their algorithms, and their implementation faces fundamental challenges in scalability and tractability. At the lowest level, a simulator can be used to simulate the operation of the native quantum hardware gates to provide the expected outputs of a quantum computer, and in turn can be used to help check the hardware. At the highest level, a simulator can track the logical algorithmic computation and the state of the logical qubits. Simulators can model the effect of noise for di erent hardware technologies. This helps algorithm designers to predict the e ects of noise on the performance of quantum algorithms before there are machines capable of running them. Such simulation capabilities will be particularly important for NISQ systems whose lack of QEC support means that noise effects will fundamentally impact algorithm performance and success.

The fundamental challenge of QC simulation is how quickly the state space scales. Since a gate operation can be implemented on a classical computer by a sparse matrix-vector multiplication, a simulation of a quantum computer is a sequence of matrix-vector multiplications. However, the size of the complex-valued wave function representing the state of a quantum computer with N qubits grows as 2^N. This means that QC hardware with just a single additional qubit has double the state space. Very quickly, the space becomes too large to be simulated tractably on even the largest classical supercomputer. Current supercomputers are capable of simulating on the order of 50-qubit systems.[6]

To work around the intractability of full-system QC simulation, QC simulators can be built to model subsets of quantum operations. For example, to evaluate the behavior of a particular QEC code, one may want to simulate just the relevant Clifford operations. (They do not constitute a "universal gate set," but they do comprise the gates of interest for certain

---

[6] While recent progress toward modeling larger systems has been reported, the exact number is currently up for debate, and depends upon the specifics of the method. See, for example, C. Neill, P. Roushan, K. Kechedzhi, S. Boixo, S.V. Isakov, V. Smelyanskiy, R. Barends, et al., 2018, A blueprint for demonstrating quantum supremacy with superconducting qubits, *Science* 360(6385):195-199; E. Pednault, J.A. Gunnels, G. Nannicini, L. Horesh, T. Magerlein, E. Solomonik, and R. Wisnieff, 2017, "Breaking the 49-Qubit Barrier in the Simulation of Quantum Circuits," arXiv:1710.05867; and J. Chen, F. Zhang, C. Huang, M. Newman, and Y. Shi, 2018, "Classical Simulation of Intermediate-Size Quantum Circuits," arXiv:1805.01450.

QEC approaches.) In this case, QC simulation is tractable [16] and error correction can be studied on upward of thousands of qubits. Simulation of the Toffoli, CNOT, and NOT gates is also efficient and enables studying and debugging large-scale arithmetic quantum circuits, for example. Another example is the simulation of Toffoli circuits, which contain only NOT (Pauli X), controlled-NOT, and doubly controlled-NOT (Toffoli) operations. Such circuits can be efficiently simulated on classical inputs.

For the universal gate scenarios that are most challenging to simulate, simulation speed can be improved by simulating some of the operations in the quantum algorithm at a higher level of abstraction [17]. For example, in a case in which the quantum program wants to execute the quantum Fourier transform, the simulator would invoke the fast Fourier transform on the wave function and evaluate that on the classical computer running the simulation. For a mathematical function such as modular addition, which is used in Shor's algorithm, the simulator again simply implements modular addition on each of the computational basis states rather than applying the sequence of quantum operations required for reversible modular addition. While creating these higher-level abstract functions is difficult in general, any existing options could be linked into the functional library. This approach is particularly useful for quantum algorithms that use "oracle functions," functions for which the quantum implementation is not known—in this case, the programmer can provide a classical implementation of the oracle function.

6.4 SPECIFICATION, VERIFICATION, AND DEBUGGING

The specification, verification, and debugging of quantum programs is an extremely difficult problem. First, the complexity of QC software and hardware makes their correct design extremely difficult. Second, the intractability of QC simulation limits the amount of predesign testing and simulation available to developers. Third, the nature of QC systems is that measurement collapses the state; therefore, conventional debugging methods based on measuring program variables during program execution would disrupt execution and so cannot be used.

At its heart, the verification problem asks the question is it possible for a classical client to verify the answer provided by a quantum computer? The difficulties in answering this question stem from fundamental principles of quantum mechanics and may seem inherently insurmountable: (1) direct simulation of quantum devices, even of moderate size, by classical computers is all but impossible, due to the exponential power of quantum systems, and (2) the laws of quantum mechanics severely limit the amount of information about the quantum state that can be accessed via measurement. Three avenues have been explored to answer this challenge. Each builds on results from the theory of interactive proof systems, exploring further the deep interaction of that theory with classical cryptography that has led to an amazing wealth of results over the past three decades.

In the first, the experimentalist or verifier is "slightly quantum," has the ability to manipulate a constant number of qubits, and has access to a quantum channel to the quantum computer [18,19]. The use of quantum authentication techniques helps keep the quantum computer honest. Security proofs for such protocols are extremely delicate and have only been obtained in recent years [20,21].

A second model considers a classical verifier interacting with multiple quantum devices sharing entanglement, and describes a scheme for efficiently characterizing the quantum devices, and verifying their answers [22-24]. In the context of quantum cryptography, this model, where the quantum devices are adversarial, has been studied under the name of device independence. Efficient protocols for certified random number generation in this have been obtained [25,26]. These have further led to protocols for fully device independent quantum key distribution [27-29].

A third model considers a classical verifier interacting with a single quantum device, where the verifier uses post-quantum cryptography to keep the device honest. Recent work shows how to carry out efficiently verifiable quantum supremacy based on trapdoor claw-free functions (which can be implemented based on learning with errors [LWE]) [30]. The paper also shows how to generate certifiable random numbers from a single quantum device. Recent work has shown how a classical client can use trapdoor claw-free functions to delegate a computation to a quantum computer in the cloud, without compromising the privacy of its data—a task known as "quantum fully homomorphic encryption" [31]. In a further development, it was shown [32] that an ingenious protocol based on trapdoor claw-free functions can be used to efficiently verify the output of a quantum computer.

As a result of the fact that measurement changes the system state, and provides limited information about that state, measuring the state of a quantum computer to better understand the source of errors is a complex task. Since each measurement returns only a single index of the overall quantum state, reconstructing the state itself requires repeatedly preparing and measuring it a large number of times to generate the probability distribution of quantum state being measured. This measurement method, called "quantum state tomography," provides an estimate of the underlying quantum state, but requires a large number of repeated preparations and measurements—for n qubits, 2^{2n} measurements are used to ensure adequate number of samples in each possible output state. If one is trying to debug a quantum circuit, then one needs to apply quantum process tomography, where quantum state tomography is performed on a number of different input sets, to characterize how the circuit transforms the quantum state of its input state to its output state. Process tomography represents a complete description of the errors during a circuit's operation, but it also requires an extremely large number of steps to implement.

Given the difficulty of developing quantum algorithms and tool flows, designers need methods to help validate both the initial algorithm and the low-level output that the compiler generates (to check the optimizations done in the compiler). QC developers will always be implementing some programs for QC machines before they have been built, making this task especially problematic. This situation will lead to programs that cannot be validated by direct execution.

There are several limited options for QC debugging today. For example, one can use classical or hybrid classical-quantum simulation to partially test an application, but this runs into the simulator limitations previously discussed in Section 6.3. Another option is to use programming language constructs such as data types or assertions to make errors easier to find. Assertions are inserted as lines into a program to state ("assert") some characteristic that should be true at that point in the execution. For example, a QC program might include assertions about the expected eigenstates or correlations at particular points in the algorithm progression. Compiler and run time analysis can then be used to check these types or assertions. However, since measurement of variables collapses their state, these assertion checks must either be limited to measurement of ancillary variables not central to the computation or must otherwise be structured such that their measurement ends the program at useful points.

Since full-state simulation is not practical for all but the smallest systems, users can use tools such as the resource estimators described in Section 6.2.3 to debug aspects of quantum programs. Tools also exist to test branches of the quantum program, subject to programmer specified expectations about branching probabilities or other statistics. In addition, QC tools can be integrated into conventional software development packages, to enable conventional software debugging strategies such as setting program breakpoints.

In general, however, the above techniques represent small and inadequate inroads into a largely unmapped space of challenges. The challenges of debugging QC systems—and more specifically the near-intractability of approaches like simulations or assertions—means that there remains a critical need to continue development of tools to verify and debug quantum software and hardware.

Finding: Development of methods to debug and analyze larger quantum systems and programs is a critical need in the development of large-scale quantum computers.

6.5 COMPILING FROM A HIGH-LEVEL PROGRAM TO HARDWARE

Classical computers manage the massive complexity of today's hardware and software systems (comprised of billions of transistors and lines of code, respectively) by layering many abstractions and tools. In contrast, QC systems, particularly near-term NISQ systems, will be too resource constrained to have that luxury. While the prior sections lay out categories of software, the stringent resource constraints have slowed the acceptance of well-defined abstraction layers, because the information-hiding aspect of traditional abstraction layers translates to higher circuit widths or depths in QC systems. Nonetheless, QC program compilation thus far typically follows stages somewhat similar to classical counterparts, as depicted in Figure 6.1 [33].

Figure 6.1 offers a general sketch of a compiler tool flow from high-level applications through compiler optimizations and down to the actual control pulses that create the quantum operations themselves. Given the unique requirements and operations of quantum algorithms, the programmer would use a domain specific language (DSL) created for quantum computing or perhaps even for algorithmic subdomains within QC. DSLs are programming languages designed with features specific to a particular problem domain. Programmers may also have access to libraries of useful routines written by others.

The first stage of the DSL compiler converts the program into a quantum intermediate representation (QIR) that represents the same program but in a lower-level form that is easier for the compiler to analyze and manipulate. This QIR then goes through a number of optimization passes to make it more efficient to run on the control processor and ultimately execute on the quantum computer. The final stages of this compiler map the qubits to physical locations on the quantum data plane, and then generate the sequence of operations that execute the desired quantum circuit on this data plane.

For QC compilers, appropriate layering approaches and abstractions are still being refined. For example, in classical computers, the instruction set architecture (ISA) forms a durable long-term abstraction of possible hardware targets. Namely, software can run on different implementations of the same ISA without recompiling. Current QC systems, in contrast, often expose details of the hardware all the way up to the programmer. The lack of abstractions is partly forced by extreme resource constraints, and partly due to simple conventions from early QC implementations

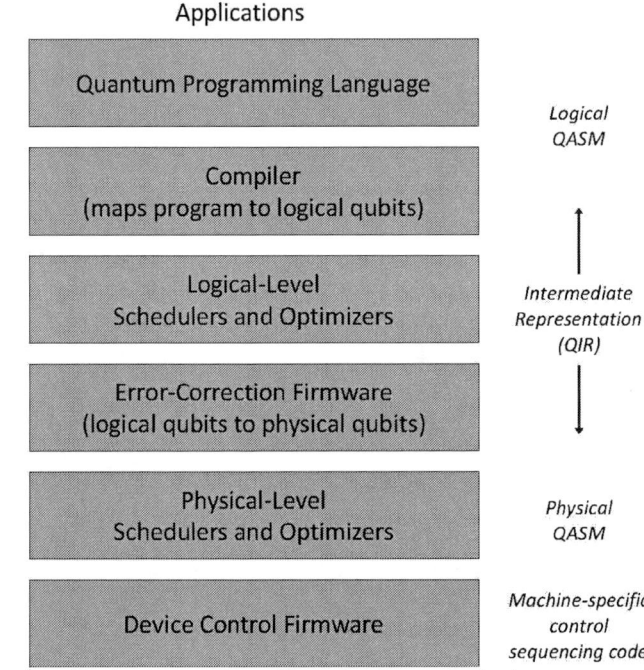

FIGURE 6.1 A generic tool flow for quantum programming. A quantum program is implemented in a domain-specific language (DSL) and then translated into hardware instructions after undergoing a series of compiler transformations and optimizations. A quantum intermediate representation (QIR) of the program can serve as a logical-level analog to conventional assembly code. For programs running on error-corrected qubits, the compiler would link in low-level QEC libraries into the code, transforming the logical qubit operations, to the physical operations on a number of qubits. The qubits of this "expanded" quantum program are then mapped onto a specific hardware implementation accounting for the specific gate operations and connectivity available. At the lowest level, the operations on physical qubits will be generated as instructions of the quantum control processor that orchestrate the specific control pulses (e.g., microwave or optical) required. For more detailed discussion of quantum computer software architectures, see F.T. Chong, D. Franklin, and M. Martonosi, 2017, Programming languages and compiler design for realistic quantum hardware, *Nature* 549(7671):180; and T. Häner, D.S. Steiger, K. Svore, and M. Troyer, 2018, A software methodology for compiling quantum programs, *Quantum Science and Technology* 3(2):020501.

that are expected to mature into more principled abstraction layers as QC implementations become more complex. Nonetheless, it is instructive to consider compilation as occurring in the illustrated phases. Some of the above steps have either already been discussed or are quite similar to compilation for classical computers, and need not be discussed further. The subsections that follow offer more details on two aspects of particular interest: gate synthesis and layout/QEC.

6.5.1 Gate Synthesis

One role of the physical-level (hardware-specific) compilation stage is to select and synthesize the particular gate functions needed for the computation. These gate functions are akin to the instruction set architecture or hardware functional units of a conventional computer. For example, multiqubit gates will be synthesized from one-qubit gates and a two-qubit gate specific to the qubit technology. Further hardware-specific rewriting rules are then applied, which include the decomposition of single-qubit operations into sequences of gates drawn from a technology-dependent set [34].

As mentioned earlier, *arbitrary* single-qubit rotations cannot be expressed exactly using a Clifford + T gate set; thus, these rotations must be decomposed (also called "synthesized") into a series of gate operations. Decomposition enables a general circuit expressed in arbitrary unitaries to be synthesized into an approximate circuit composed of a sequence of elementary gates, where the gates are drawn from a given universal, discrete set. The typical universal gate set employed is the Clifford + T gate set; however, other gates are also possible (e.g., Clifford and Toffoli, V basis gate set, etc.). Choice of a particular universal gate set is driven by hardware considerations as well as requirements for fault tolerance and quantum error correction. In general, state-of-the-art synthesis methods [35-40] have been developed that enable a quantum single-qubit rotation to be synthesized in roughly $log(1/\varepsilon)$ gates, where ε is the accuracy of the sequence. This means that the number of required gates grows slowly with increased accuracy.

6.5.2 Quantum Error Correction

Given the high error rates of quantum gates, once quantum error correction can be deployed, one of the key jobs of the tool flow is to map the needed logical qubits into a set of the physical qubits, and the logical qubit operations into operations on the physical qubits. Until qubit gate error probabilities fall precipitously, the fault-tolerant architectures adopted will have complex structures (both in terms of the number of physical qubits and the sequence of gate operations among them necessary to accomplish fault tolerance). These quantum computers will therefore benefit from being designed with the fault-tolerance architecture for the system in mind. As described in Chapter 3, feasible architectures include surface codes implemented on a two-dimensional (2D) array of qubits with nearest neighbor gates [41,42] and concatenated Calderbank-Shor-Steane (CSS) codes implemented on a densely connected quantum register with modules connected in a network [43,44]. Many alternative fault-tolerant architectures are being actively investigated and developed in order to identify architectures requiring fewer resources and better error correction properties.

Given the large number of qubits and operations required for error correction, it is essential that the error correction operations be accomplished as efficiently as possible. Since these operations will be created by the software tool chain, achieving this efficiency requires that the tool chain be tightly configured for the hardware it is targeting.

6.6 SUMMARY

The software tools needed to create and debug quantum programs are as essential to all scales of quantum computer as the underlying quantum data plane. While good progress has been made in this area, a number of challenging problems remain to be solved before a practical machine could become operational. One challenge is in simulation—both higher-level algorithmic simulation and lower-level physics simulation. A typical computer design cycle often involves simulating designs that have not yet been built using current-generation already-built systems. They allow us to estimate run time performance and hardware resource requirements, and they allow some degree of correctness testing. Both types of simulation are important for planning and debugging next-stage QC hardware and software systems designs, and both represent fundamental challenges. At the algorithm level, the state-space of QC systems is so large that even simulating the QC algorithmic behavior of around 60 or more qubits cannot be done in reasonable time or space on today's classical machines. The same capability to represent complex state spaces that makes QC compellingly attractive also makes it fundamentally difficult or intractable to simulate on classical hardware.

Lower-level simulations accounting for noise and other environmental and hardware specifications have even more limited performance, because the detail they attempt to account for can be vastly beyond the abilities of classical computers to represent. As a result, the QC community is developing methods in which smaller quantum systems may be used to simulate specific aspects of larger ones, analogous to the so-called "bootstrapping methods" employed in the classical computer hardware design community where a current-generation machine is used to simulate newly proposed next-generation machines to be built. In addition, approximate simulations of the full system can have value for early design assessments and may be performed on high-end classical machines.

Debugging and verification of quantum programs are also major challenges. Most classical computers provide programmers the ability to stop execution at an arbitrary point in the program, and examine the machine state—that is, the values of program variables and other items stored in memory. Programmers can determine whether the state is correct or not, and if not, find the program bug. In contrast, a QC program has an exponentially large state-space that is collapsed by physical qubit measurements, and QC execution cannot be restarted after a mid-run measurement. Thus, design of debugging and verification techniques for quantum programs is an essential and fundamentally challenging requirement to enable progress in QC development.

While QC simulation and debugging are truly grand challenge research endeavors, other aspects of the software toolchain such as languages and compilers have seen greater progress, but also remain important.

The NISQ era may prove to be one of significant change in software compilation and tools. In particular, the ability to rapidly develop and test quantum programs on real hardware will be critical in developing a deeper understanding of the power of quantum computers for concrete applications, as well as enabling fast feedback and progress in hardware development. Coordinating the advancement of software techniques in addition to hardware ones will help spur progress for the field overall.

6.7 NOTES

[1] For example, QISKit and OpenQASM from IBM (https://www.qiskit.org/) and Forest from Rigetti (https://www.rigetti.com/forest).
[2] M. Reiher, N. Wiebe, K.M. Svore, D. Wecker, and M. Troyer, 2017, Elucidating reaction mechanisms on quantum computers, *Proceedings of the National Academy of Sciences of the U.S.A.* 201619152.
[3] F.T. Chong, D. Franklin, and M. Martonosi, 2017, Programming languages and compiler design for realistic quantum hardware, *Nature* 549(7671):180.
[4] A. Javadi-Abhari, S. Patil, D. Kudrow, J. Heckey, Al. Lvov, F.T. Chong, and M. Martonosi, 2014, "ScaffCC: A Framework for Compilation and Analysis of Quantum Computing Programs," in *Proceedings of the 11th ACM Conference on Computing Frontiers*, http://dx.doi.org/10.1145/2597917.2597939.
[5] ProjectQ can be found at https://github.com/ProjectQ-Framework/ProjectQ.
[6] A.W. Cross, unpublished, https://www.media.mit.edu/quanta/quanta-web/projects/qasm-tools/.
[7] A.W. Cross, L.S. Bishop, J.A. Smolin, and J.M. Gambetta, 2017, "Open Quantum Assembly Language," arXiv:1707.03429.
[8] QCoDeS has recently been released and is available at http://qcodes.github.io/

Qcodes/.
[9] The latest version of the ARTIQ is available at https://github.com/m-labs/artiq.
[10] IBM Q Experience Device, https://quantumexperience.ng.bluemix.net/qx/devices.
[11] M. Soeken, M. Roetteler, N. Wiebe, and G. De Micheli, 2016, "Design Automation and Design Space Exploration for Quantum Computers," arXiv:1612.00631v1.
[12] A. Parent, M. Roetteler, and K.M. Svore, 2015, "Reversible Circuit Compilation with Space Constraints," arXiv:1510.00377v1.
[13] P.M. Soeken, T. Häner, and M. Roetteler, 2018, "Programming Quantum Computers Using Design Automation," arXiv:1803.01022v1.
[14] M. Roetteler and K.M. Svore, 2018, Quantum computing: Codebreaking and Beyond, *IEEE Security and Privacy* 16(5):22-36.
[15] Microsoft's Quantum Development Kit found at https://www.microsoft.com/en-us/quantum/development-kit; ScaffCC found at https://github.com/epiqc/ScaffCC.
[16] S. Aaronson and D. Gottesman, 2004, Improved simulation of stabilizer circuits, *Physical Review A* 70:052328.
[17] T. Häner, D.S. Steiger, K.M. Svore, and M. Troyer, 2018, A software methodology for compiling quantum programs, *Quantum Science and Technology* 3:020501.
[18] D. Aharonov, M. Ben-Or, E. Eban, and U. Mahadev, 2017, "Interactive Proofs for Quantum Computations," preprint arXiv:1704.04487.
[19] A. Broadbent, J. Fitzsimons, and E. Kashefi, 2009, "Universal Blind Quantum Computation," pp. 517-526 in *50th Annual IEEE Symposium on Foundations of Computer Science 2009*.
[20] J.F. Fitzsimons, and E. Kashefi, 2017, Unconditionally verifiable blind quantum computation, *Physical Review A* 96(1):012303.
[21] D. Aharonov, M. Ben-Or, E. Eban, and U. Mahadev, 2017, "Interactive Proofs for Quantum Computations," preprint arXiv:1704.04487.
[22] B.W. Reichardt, F. Unger, and U. Vazirani, 2012, "A Classical Leash for a Quantum System: Command of Quantum Systems via Rigidity of CHSH Games," preprint arXiv:1209.0448.
[23] B.W. Reichardt, F. Unger, and U. Vazirani, 2013, Classical command of quantum systems, *Nature* 496(7446):456.
[24] A. Natarajan and T. Vidick, 2017, "A Quantum Linearity Test for Robustly Verifying Entanglement," pp. 1003-1015 in *Proceedings of the 49th Annual ACM SIGACT Symposium on Theory of Computing*.
[25] S. Pironio, A. Acín, S. Massar, A. Boyer de La Giroday, D.N. Matsukevich, P. Maunz, S. Olmschenk, et al., 2010, Random numbers certified by Bell's theorem, *Nature* 464(7291):1021.
[26] U. Vazirani and T. Vidick, 2012, "Certifiable Quantum Dice: Or, True Random Number Generation Secure Against Quantum Adversaries," pp. 61-76 in *Proceedings of the Forty-Fourth Annual ACM Symposium on Theory of Computing*.
[27] U. Vazirani and T. Vidick, 2014, Fully device-independent quantum key distribution, *Physical Review Letters* 113(14):140501.
[28] C.A. Miller and Y. Shi, 2016, Robust protocols for securely expanding randomness and distributing keys using untrusted quantum devices, *Journal of the ACM (JACM)* 63(4):33.
[29] R. Arnon-Friedman, R. Renner, and T. Vidick, 2016, "Simple and Tight Device-Independent Security Proofs," preprint arXiv:1607.01797.
[30] Z. Brakerski, P. Christiano, U. Mahadev, U. Vazirani, and T. Vidick, 2018, "A Cryptographic Test of Quantumness and Certifiable Randomness from a Single Quantum Device," in *Proceedings of the 59th Annual Symposium on the Foundations of Computer Science*.
[31] U. Mahadev, 2018, "Classical Homomorphic Encryption for Quantum Circuits," Pro-

ceedings of the 59th Annual Symposium on the Foundations of Computer Science.
[32] U. Mahadev, 2018, "Classical Verification of Quantum Computations," *Proceedings of the 59th Annual Symposium on the Foundations of Computer Science*.
[33] F.T. Chong, D. Franklin, and M. Martonosi, 2017, Programming languages and compiler design for realistic quantum hardware, *Nature* 549(7671):180.
[34] T. Häner, D.S. Steiger, K.Svore, and M. Troyer, 2018, A software methodology for compiling quantum programs, *Quantum Science and Technology* 3(2):020501.
[35] V. Kliuchnikov, A. Bocharov, M. Roetteler, and J. Yard, 2015, "A Framework for Approximating Qubit Unitaries," arXiv:1510.03888v1.
[36] V. Kliuchnikov and J. Yard, 2015, "A Framework for Exact Synthesis," arXiv:1504.04350v1.
[37] V. Kliuchnikov, D. Maslov, and M. Mosca, 2012, "Practical Approximation of Single-Qubit Unitaries by Single-Qubit Quantum Clifford and T Circuits," arXiv:1212.6964.
[38] N.J. Ross and P. Selinger, 2014, "Optimal Ancilla-Free Clifford+T Approximation of z-Rotations," arXiv:1403.2975v3.
[39] A. Bocharov, M. Roetteler, and K.M. Svore, 2014, "Efficient Synthesis of Probabilistic Quantum Circuits with Fallback," arXiv:1409.3552v2.
[40] A. Bocharov, Y. Gurevich, and K.M. Svore, 2013, "Efficient Decomposition of Single-Qubit Gates into V Basis Circuits," arXiv:1303.1411v1.
[41] R. Raussendorf and J. Harrington, 2007, Fault-tolerant quantum computation with high threshold in two dimensions, *Physical Review Letters* 98:190504.
[42] A.G. Fowler, M. Mariantoni, J.M. Martinis, and A.N. Cleland, 2012, Surface codes: Towards practical large-scale quantum computation, *Physical Review A* 86:032324.
[43] C. Monroe, R. Raussendorf, A. Ruthven, K.R. Brown, P. Maunz, L.-M. Duan, and J. Kim, 2014, Large-scale modular quantum-computer architecture with atomic memory and photonic interconnects, *Physical Review A* 89:022317.
[44] M. Ahsan, R. Van Meter, and J. Kim, 2015, Designing a million-qubit quantum computer using resource performance simulator, *ACM Journal on Emerging Technologies in Computing Systems* 12:39.

7

Feasibility and Time Frames of Quantum Computing

A large-scale, fault-tolerant, gate-based quantum computer capable of carrying out tasks of practical interest has not yet been achieved in the open science enterprise. While a few researchers [1] have argued that practical quantum computing is fundamentally impossible, the committee did not find any fundamental reason that such a system could not be built—provided the current understanding of quantum physics is accurate. Yet significant work remains, and many open questions need to be tackled to achieve the goal of building a scalable quantum computer, both at the foundational research and device engineering levels. This chapter assesses the progress (as of mid-2018) and possible future pathways toward a universal, fault-tolerant quantum computer, provides a framework for assessing progress in the future, and enumerates key milestones along these paths. It ends by examining some ramifications of research and development in this area.

7.1 THE CURRENT STATE OF PROGRESS

Small demonstration gate-based quantum computing systems (on the order of tens of qubits) have been achieved, with significant variation in qubit quality; however, device size increases are being announced with increasing frequency. Significant efforts are under way to construct noisy intermediate-scale quantum (NISQ) systems—with on the order of hundreds of higher-quality qubits that, while not fault tolerant, are robust enough to conduct some computations before decohering [2].

A scalable, fully error-corrected machine (which can be thought of using the abstraction of logical qubits) capable of a larger number of operations appears to be far off. While researchers have successfully engineered individual qubits with high fidelities, it has been much more challenging to achieve this for all qubits in a large device. The average error rate of qubits in today's larger devices would need to be reduced by a factor of 10 to 100 before a computation could be robust enough to support error correction at scale, and at this error rate, the number of physical qubits that these devices hold would need to increase by at least a factor of 10^5 in order to create a useful number of effective logical qubits. The improvements required to enable logical computation are significant, so much so that any predictions of time frames for achieving these requirements based upon extrapolation would exhibit significant uncertainty.

In the course of gathering data for this study, the committee heard from several individuals with experience directing different kinds of large-scale engineering efforts.[1] Each described the minimum time frame for funding, developing, building, and demonstrating a complex system as being approximately 8 to 10 years from the time at which a concrete system design plan is finalized [3]. As of mid-2018, there have been no publicly announced design plans for building a large-scale, fault-tolerant quantum computer, although it is possible that such designs exist outside the public domain; the committee had no access to classified or proprietary information.

Key Finding 1: Given the current state of quantum computing and recent rates of progress, it is highly unexpected that a quantum computer that can compromise RSA 2048 or comparable discrete logarithm-based public key cryptosystems will be built within the next decade.

Given the long time horizon for achieving a scalable quantum computer, rather than attempting to predict exactly when a certain kind of system will be built—a task fraught with unknowns—this chapter proposes a framework for assessing progress. It presents a few scaling metrics for

---

[1] These included the U.S. Department of Energy's Excascale Computing project, the commercial development of DRAM and 3DNAND technologies, and current efforts to build the world's largest Tokamak (fusion reactor) at the International Thermonuclear Experimental Reactor site in France. While very different projects, all project directors noted their empirical observations of similar time frames for completing very large engineering projects. To provide context for this estimate of 8 to 10 years, the committee notes that even the Manhattan Project, arguably one of history's most ambitious and resource-intensive science and engineering projects (with an estimated cost of $22 billion, adjusted to 2016 inflation levels, and an all-hands-on-deck approach to manpower, with 130,000 dedicated staff) took 6 years from its inception in 1939 to successful demonstration in the Trinity Test of 1945.

tracking growth of quantum computers—which could be extrapolated to predict near-term trends—and a collection of key milestones and known challenges that must be overcome along the path to a scalable, fault-tolerant quantum computer.

7.1.1 Creating a Virtuous Cycle

As pointed out in Chapter 1, progress in any field that requires significant engineering effort is very strongly related to the strength of the research and development effort on which it depends, which, in turn, depends on available funding. This is clearly the case in quantum computing, where increased public and private sector investment have enabled much of the recent progress. Recently, the private sector has demonstrated significant engagement in quantum computing (QC) research and development (R&D), as has been broadly reported in various media [4]. However, the current investments in quantum computing are largely speculative—while there are potentially marketable near-term applications of qubits for quantum sensing and metrology, the objective of R&D on quantum computing systems is to build technology that will create a new market. A virtuous cycle, similar to that of the semiconductor industry, has not yet begun for quantum computing technologies. As a technology, quantum computing is still in early stages.[2]

The current enthusiasm for quantum computing could lead to a virtuous cycle of progress, but only if a near-term application emerges for the technologies under development—or if a major, disruptive breakthrough is made which enables the development of more sophisticated machines. Reaching these milestones would likely yield financial returns and stimulate companies to dedicate even more resources to their R&D in quantum computing, which would further increase the likelihood that the technology will scale to larger machines. In this scenario, one is likely to see sustained growth in the capacity of quantum processors over time.

However, it is also possible that even with steady progress in QC R&D, the first commercially useful application of a quantum computer will require a very large number of physical qubits—orders of magnitude larger than currently demonstrated or expected in the near term. In this case, government or other organizations with long time horizons can continue to fund this area, but this funding is less likely to grow rapidly, leading to a Moore's law-type of development curve. It is also possible

---

[2] In fact, QC has been on Gartner's list of emerging technologies 11 times between 2000 and 2017, each time listed in the earliest stage in the hype cycle, and each time with the categorization that commercialization is more than 10 years away; see https://www.gartner.com/smarterwithgartner/the-cios-guide-to-quantum-computing/.

that in the absence of near-term commercial applications, funding levels could potentially flatten or decline. This situation is common for startup technologies; surviving this phenomenon is referred to as crossing the "valley of death" [5,6]. In severe cases, funding dries up, leading to the departure of talent from industry and academia, and leaves behind a field where little progress can be made in an area for a long time in the future, since the field has a bad reputation. Avoiding this scenario requires some funding to continue even if commercial interest wanes.

Key Finding 2: If near-term quantum computers are not commercially successful, government funding may be essential to prevent a significant decline in quantum computing research and development.

As the virtuous cycle that fueled Moore's law shows, successful outcomes are critical, not only to fund future development but also to bring in the talent needed to make future development successful. Of course, the definition of a successful outcome varies among stakeholders. There is a core group of people for whom advances in the theory and practice of quantum science is all the success they need. Others, including those groups funded through companies or the venture capital (VC) community, are interested in some combination of scientific progress, changing the world, and financial rewards. For the latter group, commercial success will be required. Given the large number of technical challenges that need to be resolved before a large, error-corrected quantum computer can be built, a vibrant ecosystem that can be sustained over a long period of time will be critical to support quantum computing and enable it to reach its full potential.

7.1.2 Criticality of Applications for a Near-Term Quantum Computer

In the committee's assessment, the most critical period for the development of quantum computing will begin around the early 2020s, when current and planned funding efforts are likely to require renewal. The best machines that are likely to have been achieved by that time are NISQ computers. If commercially attractive applications for these machines emerge within a reasonable period of time after their introduction, private-market investors might begin to see revenues from the companies they have invested in, and government program managers will begin to see results with important scientific, commercial, and mission applications emerging from their programs. This utility would support arguments in favor of further investments in quantum computing, including reinvestment of the capital these early successes bring in. In addition, the ability of working quantum computers to solve problems of real-world interest will create demand for expert staff capable of deploying them for that purpose, and training staff in academic and other programs who can drive progress in the future. This training will be facilitated by the availability of NISQ computers to program and improve. Commercial applications for a NISQ computer—that is, some application that will create sufficient market interest to generate a return on investment—will thus be a major step in starting a virtuous cycle, where success leads to increased funding and talent, which enables improvements in quantum computing capacity, which in turn enables further success.

NISQ computers are likely to have up to hundreds of physical (not error-corrected) qubits, and, as described in Chapter 3, while there are promising research directions, there are at present no known algorithms or applications that could make effective use of this class of machine. Thus, formulating an R&D program with the aim of developing commercial applications for near-term quantum computing is critical to the health of the field. Such a program would include the following:

1. Identification of algorithms with modest problem size and limited gate depth that show quantum speedup, in application domains where algorithms for classical computers are unlikely to improve much.
2. Identification of algorithms for which hybrid classical-quantum techniques using modest-size quantum subsystems can provide significant speedup.
3. Identification of problem domains in which the best algorithms on classical computers are currently running up against inherent scale limits of classical computation, and for which modest increases in problem size can bring economically significant increases in solution impact.

Key Finding 3: Research and development into practical commercial applications of noisy intermediate-scale quantum (NISQ) computers is an issue of immediate urgency for the field. The results of this work will have a profound impact on the rate of development of large-scale quantum computers and on the size and robustness of a commercial market for quantum computers.

Even in the case where near-term quantum computers have sufficient economic impact to bootstrap a virtuous cycle of investment, there are many steps between a machine with hundreds of physical qubits and a large-scale, error-corrected quantum computer, and these steps will likely require significant time and effort. To provide insights into how to monitor the transition between these types of machine, the next section proposes two strategies for tracking and assessing progress.

7.2 A FRAMEWORK FOR ASSESSING PROGRESS IN QUANTUM COMPUTING

Given the difficulty of predicting future inventions or unforeseen problems, long-term technology forecasting is usually inaccurate. Typically, technological progress is predicted by extrapolating future trends from past performance data using some quantifiable metric of progress. Existing data on past trends can be used to create short-term forecasts, which can be adjusted as new advances are documented to update future predictions. This method works when there are stable metrics that are good surrogates for progress in a technology. While this method does not work well for all fields, it has been successful in several areas, including silicon computer chips (for which the metric is either the number of transistors per computer chip, or the cost per transistor) and gene sequencing (for which the metric is cost per base pair sequenced), for which progress proceeded at an exponential rate for many years.

For quantum computing, an obvious metric to track is the number of physical qubits operating in a system. Since creating a scalable quantum computer that can implement Shor's algorithm requires improvements by many orders of magnitude in both qubit error rates and number of physical qubits, reaching this number in any reasonable time period requires a collective ability of the R&D community to improve qubit quantity per device exponentially over time. However, simply scaling the number of qubits is not enough, as they must also be capable of gate operations with very low error rates. Ultimately, error-corrected logical qubits will be required, and the number of physical qubits needed to create one logical qubit for a given QECC depends strongly on the error rate of basic qubit operations, as discussed in Chapter 3.

7.2.1 How to Track Physical and Logical Qubit Scaling

One can separate progress in quantum computing hardware into two regimes, each with its own metric: the first tracks progress of machines in which physical qubits are used directly without quantum error correction, and the second tracks progress toward systems where quantum error correction is effective.[3] The first metric (referred to as "Metric 1") is the time

---

[3] As previously mentioned, qubit connectivity is also an important parameter that changes the overhead for carrying out a computation on a device; however, it is not as important as qubit number and error rate, and its importance depends upon the specific context of a given system's overall design. Connectivity is thus not included in the metric proposed here.

required to double the number of physical qubits in a system, where the average fidelity of all the qubits (and single and two-qubit gates) is held constant. Tracking the size and doubling times for systems at different average physical qubit gate error rates, for example, 5 percent, 1 percent, and 0.1 percent, provides a method to extrapolate progress in both qubit quality and quantity.[4] Since the committee is interested in the error rates that will occur when the operations are used in a computation carried out in a real device, it notes that randomized benchmark testing (RBM), is an effective method of determining this error rate. This method will ensure that the reported error rates account for all system-level errors, including crosstalk.[5]

Even though several companies have announced superconducting chips comprised of more than 50 qubits [7], as of mid-2018, no concrete numbers on error rates for gate operations have been published for these chips; the largest superconducting QC with a reported error rate is IBM's 20 qubit system. Their system's average two-qubit gate error rate is around 5 percent [8]. During the early stages of QC, growth will initially be seen at the higher gate error-rate levels that will preclude achieving error-free operations using QEC; however, over time, this growth will move into higher quality qubit systems with lower error rates such that fully error corrected operation is possible. Tracking the growth of physical qubits at constant average gate error rate will provide a way to estimate the arrival time of future machines, which is useful, especially if NISQ computers become commercially viable.

The second metric (referred to as "Metric 2") comes into play once QC technology has improved to the point where early quantum computers can run error-correcting codes and improve the fidelity of qubit operations. At this point, it makes sense to start tracking the effective number of logical qubits[6] on a given machine, and the time needed to

---

[4] Other metrics have been proposed—and new metrics may be proposed in the future—but most are based on these parameters. For example, the metric of quantum volume (https://ibm.biz/BdYjtN) combines qubit number and effective error rate to create a single number. Quantum computer performance metrics are an active area of research. The committee has chosen metric 1 for a simple and informative approach now.

[5] Unfortunately, this metric has not been published for many of the current machines. Thus, while the committee recommends that RBM be used in determining metric 1, the examples used to illustrate determination of metric 1 in this chapter often use the average two-qubit error rate of the machine as a placeholder. This data should be updated when RBM data is available.

[6] The number of physical qubits needed to create a logical qubit depends on the error rate of the physical qubits, and the required error rate of the logical qubits, as was described in Section 3.2. This required error rate of the logical qubits depends on the logical depth of the computation. For this metric, one would choose a large but constant logical depth—for example, 10^{12}—and use that to track technology scaling.

double this number. To estimate the effective number of logical qubits in a small machine with error correction, one can extrapolate the number of physical qubits required to reach a target logical gate error rate (e.g., <10^{-12}) from the measured error rates using different numbers of physical qubits. For concatenated codes, this comes from the number of levels of concatenation needed, and for surface codes, it is the size (distance) of required code, as described in Chapter 3. The number of logical qubits is simply the size (that is, the number of physical qubits) of the QC that was fabricated divided by the calculated number required to create a logical qubit; in the near-term, the value of this metric will be less than one.[7] One way to envision this metric is shown in Figure 7.1, which plots the effective error probability (or infidelity) of the two-qubit gate operation (which is in practice typically worse than that of the single-qubit operation) for physical qubits along the *x*-axis and the number of physical qubits along

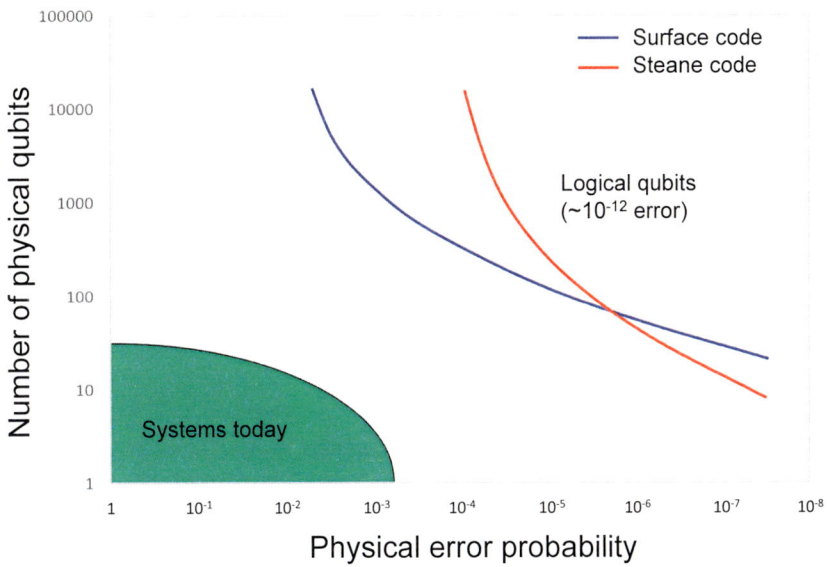

FIGURE 7.1 Qubit error probability fidelity versus number of physical qubits for existing QCs and the resource requirements for realizing a logical qubit with error probability of 10^{-12}. Different lines correspond to the requirements of specific QECs (surface code and concatenated Steane code shown here). SOURCE: Data for logical qubit curves from A. Javadi-Abhari, Ph.D. thesis, Princeton University, 2017.

---

[7] It should be noted that this calculation does not account for the cost of implementing a universal gate set; it only tracks the number of physical qubits needed to hold the logical qubit state. For example, performing T gates on logical qubits under the surface code requires many more physical qubits than other operations.

the y-axis, with the goal of achieving a high-performance logical qubit protected by QECC. The different lines show the requirements for achieving logical error probabilities of 10^{-12} for two different QEC codes. The results of running QEC will allow one to extract the overall qubit quality for this machine. The number of logical qubits is the ratio between the fabricated number of qubits and the smallest size shown in Figure 7.1 for a logical qubit using qubits with the measured physical error rate.

Tracking the number of logical qubits has clear advantages over tracking the number of physical qubits in predicting timing of future error-corrected quantum computers. This metric assumes the construction of error-corrected logical qubits with a target gate error rate, and naturally reflects progress resulting from improvements in the physical qubit quality or QEC schemes which decrease the physical qubit overhead and lead to more logical qubits for a given number of physical qubits. Thus, the number of logical qubits can serve as a single representative metric to track scaling of quantum computers. This also means that the scaling rates for physical and logical qubits are likely to be different; the doubling time for logical qubits should be faster than physical qubits if qubit quality and QEC performance continue to improve with time. While physical qubit scaling is important for near term applications, it is the scaling trend for logical qubits that will determine when a large-scale, fault-tolerant quantum computer will be built.

Key Finding 4: Given the information available to the committee, it is still too early to be able to predict the time horizon for a scalable quantum computer. Instead, progress can be tracked in the near term by monitoring the scaling rate of physical qubits at *constant average gate error rate*, as evaluated using randomized benchmarking, and in the long term by monitoring the effective number of logical (error-corrected) qubits that a system represents.

As Chapter 5 discusses, while superconducting and trapped-ion qubits are at present the most promising approaches for creating the quantum data plane, other technologies such as topological qubits have advantages that might in the future allow them to scale at a faster rate and overtake the current leaders. As a result, it makes sense to track both the scaling rate of the best QC of any technology and the scaling rates of the different approaches to better predict future technology crossover points.

7.2.2 Current Status of Qubit Technologies

The characteristics of the various technologies that can be used to implement qubits have already been discussed in detail in the body of this report.

Of the technologies that the report discusses, only two, superconducting and trapped ion qubits, have achieved sufficient quality and integration to try to extract preliminary qubit scaling laws, but even for these, the historical data is limited. Figure 7.2 plots the number of qubits versus time, using rainbow colors to group machines with different error rates, with red points having highest and purple points the lowest error rate. Historically, it has taken more than 2 years for the number of qubits to double, if one holds the error rate constant. After 2016, superconducting qubit systems might have started a faster scaling path, doubling the number of qubits every year. If this scaling continues, one should see a 40-50 qubit system with average error rates of less than 5 percent in 2019. The ability to extract trends with which to make future predictions will improve as the number of data points increases, most likely within the next few years.

Figure 7.3 plots these same data points, but now with error rate on the y-axis, and representing the machine size by color. This data clearly shows the steady decrease in error rate for two-qubit systems, halving roughly every 1.5 to 2 years. Larger qubit systems have higher error rates, with the current 20-qubit systems at error rates that are 10 times higher than two-qubit systems (a shift of 7 years).

It is again worth noting the limited number of data points that can be plotted in this way, in part because those building prototypical QC devices do not necessarily report comparable data. More data points—and, more importantly for Metric 1, consistent reporting on the effective error rate using RBM on one-qubit and two-qubit gates within a device—would make it easier to examine these trends and compare devices.

For the rest of this chapter, machine milestones mapping progress in QC will be measured in the number of doublings in qubit number, or halving of the error rate required from the current state-of-the-art functioning QC system, which is assumed to be the order of 2^4 physical qubits in mid-2018, with 5 percent error rates.

The performance of a quantum computer depends on the number and quality of its qubits, which can be tracked by the metrics defined in this section, and the speed and connectivity of its gates. As with classical computers, different quantum computers will operate at different clock rates, exploit different levels of quantum gate parallelism, and support different primitive gate operations. Machines that can run any application will support a universal set of primitive operations, of which there are many different possible sets. The efficiency of an application's execution will depend on the set of operations that the quantum data plane supports, and the ability of the software compilation system to optimize the application for that quantum machine.

To help track the quality of the software system and the underlying operations provided by the quantum data layer, it will be useful to

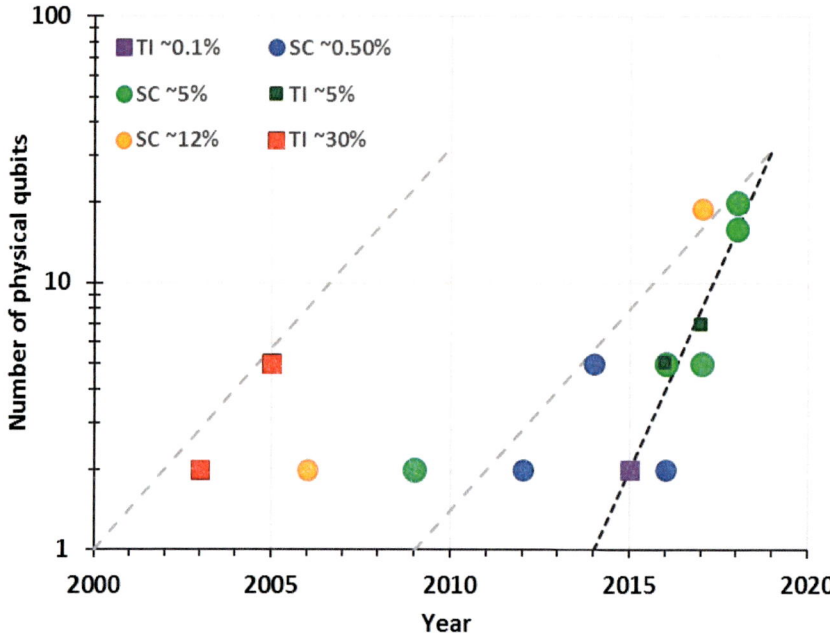

FIGURE 7.2 The number of qubits in superconductor (SC) and trapped ion (TI) quantum computers versus year; note the logarithmic scaling of the vertical axis. Data for trapped ions are shown as squares and for superconducting machines are shown as circles. Approximate average reported two-qubit gate error rates are indicated by color; points with the same color have similar error rates. The dashed gray lines show how the number of qubits would grow if they double every two years starting with one qubit in 2000 and 2009, respectively; the dashed black line indicates a doubling every year beginning with one qubit in 2014. Recent superconductor growth has been close to doubling every year. If this rate continued, 50 qubit machines with less than 5 percent error rates would be reported in 2019. SOURCE: Plotted data obtained from multiple sources. Data points were obtained from H. Häffner, W. Hänsel, C.F. Roos, J. Benhelm, D. Chek-al-kar, M. Chwalla, T. Körber, et al., 2005, Scalable multiparticle entanglement of trapped ions, *Nature* 438:643-646, https://quantumoptics.at/images/publications/papers/nature05_haeffner.pdf; D. Leibfried, B. DeMarco, V. Meyer, D. Lucas, M. Barrett, J. Britton, W.M. Itano, B. Jelenković, C. Langer, T. Rosenband, and D.J. Wineland, 2003, Experimental demonstration of a robust, high-fidelity geometric two ion-qubit phase gate, *Nature* 422:412-415, https://ws680.nist.gov/publication/get_pdf.cfm?pub_id=104991; F. Schmidt-Kaler, H. Häffner, M. Riebe, S. Gulde, G.P.T. Lancaster, T. Deuschle, C. Becher, C.F. Roos, J. Eschner, and R. Blatt, 2003, Realization of the Cirac-Zoller controlled-NOT quantum gate, *Nature* 422:408-411, https://quantumoptics.at/images/publications/papers/nature03_fsk.pdf; M. Steffen, M. Ansmann, R.C. Bialczak, N. Katz, E. Lucero, R. McDermott, M. Neeley,

(*caption continues*)

(FIGURE 7.2 *Continued*)
E.M. Weig, A.N. Cleland, and J.M. Martinis, 2006, Measurement of the entanglement of two superconducting qubits via state tomography, *Science*, 313:1423-1425; L. DiCarlo, J.M. Chow, J.M. Gambetta, L.S. Bishop, B.R. Johnson, D.I. Schuster, J. Majer, A. Blais, L. Frunzio, S.M. Girvin, and R.J. Schoelkopf, 2009, Demonstration of two-qubit algorithms with a superconducting quantum processor, *Nature* 460:240-244; J.M. Chow, J.M. Gambetta, A.D. Córcoles, S.T. Merkel, J.A. Smolin, C. Rigetti, S. Poletto, G.A. Keefe, M.B. Rothwell, J.R. Rozen, M.B. Ketchen, and M. Steffen, 2012, Universal quantum gate set approaching fault-tolerant thresholds with superconducting qubits, *Physical Review Letters* 109:060501; S. Sheldon, E. Magesan, J.M. Chow, and J.M. Gambetta, 2016, Procedure for systematically tuning up cross-talk in the cross-resonance gate, *Physical Review A* 93:060302(R); J.P. Gaebler, T.R. Tan, Y. Lin, Y. Wan, R. Bowler, A.C. Keith, S. Glancy, K. Coakley, E. Knill, D. Leibfried, and D.J. Wineland, 2016, High-fidelity universal gate set for $^9Be^+$ ion qubits, *Physical Review Letters* 117:060505; C.J. Ballance, T.P. Harty, N.M. Linke, M.A. Sepiol, and D.M. Lucas, 2016, High-fidelity quantum logic gates using trapped-ion hyperfine qubits, *Physical Review Letters* 117:060504, https://journals.aps.org/prl/pdf/10.1103/PhysRevLett.117.060504; S. Debnath, N.M. Linke, C. Figgatt, K.A. Landsman, K. Wright, and C. Monroe, 2016, Demonstration of a small programmable quantum computer with atomic qubits, *Nature* 536:63-66, http://www.pnas.org/content/114/13/3305.full; and IBM Q Experience, https://quantumexperience.ng.bluemix.net/qx/devices.

standardize a set of simple benchmark applications[8] that can be used to measure both the performance and the fidelity of computers of any size. However, because many primitive operations may be required to complete a particular task,[9] the speed or quality of a single primitive may not be a reasonable measure of the system's overall performance. Instead, benchmarking of application performance will enable a more useful comparison between machines with different fundamental operations.

The benchmark applications would need to be periodically updated as the power and complexity of quantum computers improves. Such a set of evolving benchmarks is analogous to the Standard Performance Evaluation Corporation benchmark application suite [9] that has been used to compare classical computer performance for many decades. This

---

[8] These applications could include different quantum error-correcting codes, variational eigensolvers, and "classic" quantum algorithms, and should be able to run on different-size "data sets" to enable then to be able to measure different-size quantum computers.

[9] For example, many of the superconducting data planes support only nearest neighbor communication, which means that two-input gates must use adjacent qubits. Thus, a two-input gate requiring distant qubits would need to be broken into a number of steps to move information to two adjacent qubits before the operation can be completed. Similarly, some qubit rotations need to be decomposed into a number of operations to approximate a desired rotation.

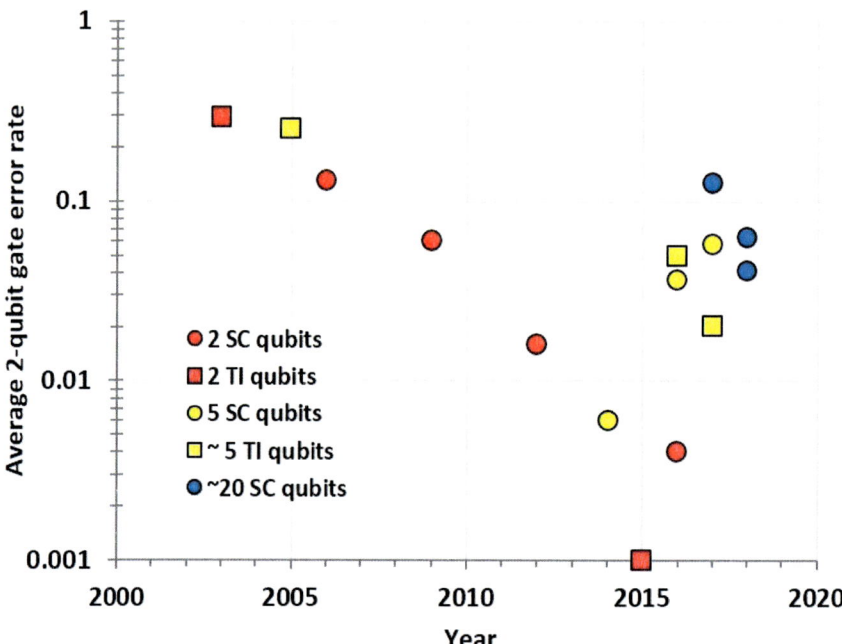

FIGURE 7.3 The average error rate of two-qubit gates for trapped ion and superconductor quantum computers. Trapped ion points are shown as squares, and superconducting machine points are shown as circles. The color of the point indicates the size of the quantum computer. The error rates of two-qubit machines have decreased by roughly a factor of two every 1.5 (trapped ion) to 2 (superconducting) years. Large machines (around 20 qubits) have error rates that match two-qubit machines that are 7 to 8 years older. Not enough data exist on these larger machines to estimate how rapidly their error rates will improve. SOURCE: Same data as in Figure 7.2.

was originally a simple set of commonly used programs and has changed over time to more accurately represent the compute loads of current applications. Given the modest computing ability of near-term quantum computers, it seems clear that at first these applications would be relatively simple, containing a set of common primitive routines, including quantum error correction, which can be scaled for different-size machines.

Key Finding 5: The state of the field would be much easier to monitor if the research community adopted clear reporting conventions to enable comparison between devices and translation into metrics such as those proposed in this report. A set of benchmarking applications that enable comparison between different machines would help drive improvements in the efficiency of quantum software and the architecture of the underlying quantum hardware.

7.3 MILESTONES AND TIME ESTIMATES

A large-scale, fully error corrected quantum computer is expected to require logical (error corrected) qubits in a design that can scale to many thousands, and a software infrastructure that can efficiently help programmers use this machine to solve their problems. This capability will likely be reached incrementally via a series of progressively more complex computers. These systems comprise a set of milestones that can be used to track progress in quantum computing, and in turn depend on progress in hardware, software and algorithms. As the previous section made clear, early work on algorithms is essential to help drive a growing quantum ecosystem, and work on hardware is needed to increase the number of physical qubits and improve qubit fidelity. Software and QEC improvements will also help by reducing the number of physical qubits needed for each application. These milestone computers are illustrated in Figure 7.4, and the main technical challenges that must be overcome to create them are described in the following sections.

7.3.1 Small (Tens of Qubits) Computer (Milestone G1)

The first benchmark machine is the class of digital (gate-based) quantum computers containing around 2^4 qubits with average gate error rate better than 5 percent, which first became available in 2017. At the time of this writing, the largest operational gate-based quantum computer is a 20-qubit system from IBM Q [10] with an average two-qubit gate error rate of about 5 percent. Systems with similar approach are also available from other university groups and commercial vendors [11]. In these systems, the control plane and control processor are all placed at room temperature with the control signals flowing through a cryostat to the quantum plane. Ion-trap QCs exist at a similar scale. Papers on a 7-qubit system from the University of Maryland with two-qubit error rate of 1-2 percent [12], and a 20-qubit system from Innsbruck [13] were published in 2017. The results from Innsbruck are not based on a conventional quantum gate-based approach,[10] so it is hard to extract gate error rates, but the results do indicate scaling progress in trapped ion machines.

---

[10] Instead of two-qubit gates, they use a "global" gate that entangles all the qubits in the chain, with the option of pulling some qubits out of the gate (any qubit combination can be "pulled" from this gate). They also have individually addressed single-qubit gates. While in principle these operations provide a complete gate set, characterizing an error rate is problematic.

7.3.2 Gate-Based Quantum Supremacy (Milestone G2a)

The next benchmark system is a quantum computer that demonstrates quantum supremacy—that is, one that can complete some task (which may or may not be of practical interest) that no existing classical computer can. Current projections from the literature indicate that this would require a machine with more than 50 qubits, and average gate error rate around 0.1 percent. However, this is necessarily a moving target, as improvements continue to be made in the approaches for classical computers that the quantum computers are trying to outperform. For a rough estimate of the limit of a classical computer, researchers have benchmarked the size of the largest quantum computer that a classical computer can simulate. Improvements in classical algorithms for simulating a quantum computer have recently been reported, and such progress may raise the bar somewhat, but not by orders of magnitude [14].[11]

This class of machine represents two generations (about a factor of 4) of scaling from machines available in 2017, and a decrease in average gate error rate of at least an order of magnitude. Several companies are actively trying to design and demonstrate quantum processors that achieve this goal, and some have already announced superconducting chips that surpass the threshold number of qubits identified. However, as of the time of this writing, none have demonstrated quantum supremacy or even published results from a working system using these quantum data planes [15].

Growing the number of qubits to meet this milestone does not require any new fabrication technology. The manufacturing process for both superconducting and trapped ion qubit arrays can easily accommodate the incorporation of additional qubits into the quantum data plane of a device. The challenge is to maintain or improve the quality of the qubits and qubit operations as the number of qubits and associated control signals scale. This challenge arises from two factors. First, since each manufactured qubit (or, in the case of trapped ions, the electrodes and optical coupling that contain or drive the qubits) is a little different than its neighbors, as the number of qubits increases, the expected variance in qubits also increases. Second, these additional qubits require additional control signals, increasing the potential for crosstalk noise. Thus, the main challenge is to mitigate these added "noise" sources through careful design and calibration. This problem will get harder as the system size increases, and the quality of calibration will likely define the qubit

---

[11] For example, researchers have taken advantage of the limitations of the machines being simulated to reduce the problem space for the classical algorithm. See E. Pednault, J.A. Gunnels, G. Nannicini, L. Horesh, T. Magerlein, E. Solomonik, and R. Wisnieff, 2017, "Breaking the 49-Qubit Barrier in the Simulation of Quantum Circuits," arXiv: 1710.05867v1.

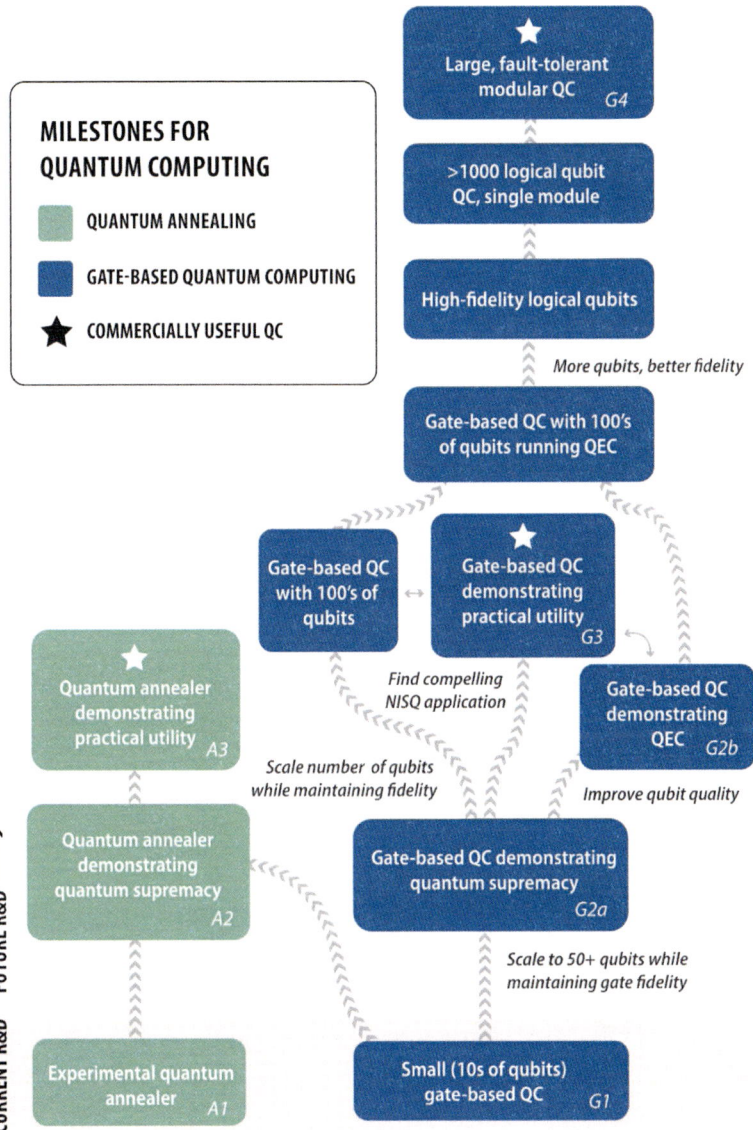

FIGURE 7.4 An illustration of potential milestones of progress in quantum computing. The arrangement of milestones corresponds to the order in which the committee thinks they are likely to be achieved; however, it is possible that some will not be achieved, or that they will not be achieved in the order indicated.

fidelity of the resulting system and determine when quantum supremacy will be achieved. As noted in Chapter 3, several companies are trying to demonstrate quantum supremacy in 2018.

Achieving quantum supremacy requires a task which is difficult to perform on a classical computer but easy to compute on the quantum data plane. Since there is no need for this task to be useful, the number of possible tasks is quite large. Candidate applications have already been identified, as discussed in Chapter 3, so the development of benchmark applications for this specific purpose are unlikely to delay the time frame for achieving this milestone.

7.3.3 Annealer-Based Quantum Supremacy (Milestone A2)

While Chapters 5 and 6 focused on gate-based quantum computing, as Chapter 3 showed, quantum computing need not be gate based. D-Wave has been producing and selling superconducting qubit-based quantum annealers since 2011. While this family of systems has generated much interest and produced papers that show performance gains for specific applications, recent results [16] have shown that algorithms for classical computers can usually be optimized to the specifics of the given problem, enabling classical systems to outperform the quantum annealer. It is unclear whether these results are indicative of limitations in the current D-Wave architecture (how the qubits are connected) and qubit fidelity, or are more fundamental to quantum annealing. It follows that a key benchmark of progress is a quantum annealer that can demonstrate quantum supremacy.

Reaching this milestone is more challenging than simply scaling the number and improving the fidelity of qubits: the desired problems to be solved must be matched to the annealer's architecture. This makes it challenging to estimate the time frame within which this milestone will likely be met. Since theoretical analysis of these problems is difficult, designers must test different problems and architectures in order to find an appropriate problem to attack. Even if a problem is found for which a quantum speedup is apparent, there is no way to rule out the possibility that a better classical computing approach will be found for the same class of problem. All initial D-Wave speedups were negated by demonstration of a better classical approach. In one instance of a specific synthetic benchmark problem, D-Wave's performance roughly matched that of the best classical approach [17], but the use of faster classical CPUs or GPUs leads to outperformance of the annealer. Given the challenge associated with formally demonstrating supremacy on a quantum annealer, if this milestone is not met by the early 2020s, researchers may choose instead to direct their efforts toward the better-defined problem of building a quantum annealer that can perform a useful task—an attribute that is more straightforward to identify, and may nonetheless lead to quantum supremacy.

7.3.4 Running QEC Successfully at Scale (Milestone G2b)

While both trapped ion and superconducting qubits have demonstrated qubit gate error rates below the threshold required for error correction, these gate error-rate performances have not yet been demonstrated in systems with tens of qubits, nor are these early machines able to measure individual qubits in the middle of a computation. Thus, creation of a machine that successfully runs QEC, yielding one or more logical qubits of better error rates than possible with physical qubits, is an important milestone. It will demonstrate not only one's ability to create a system where the worst gate of the system still has an error rate below the threshold for error correction, but also that QEC codes are effective at correcting the types of errors that occur on the quantum data plane used in that machine. These machines will also provide opportunities for software and algorithm designers to further optimize the codes for the types of errors that occur.

This milestone may occur around the time gate-based quantum supremacy is demonstrated, since machines of that scale are expected to be large enough, and have low enough error rates, to employ QEC. The time order of these events will depend on the exact error rates needed to achieve quantum supremacy, compared to the QEC requirement that the effective error rate determined by RBM testing is much less than 1 percent [18].

As discussed at the beginning of this chapter, this milestone is also important because, once it is surpassed, the scaling rate for subsequent machines can be tracked in terms of the number of logical qubits, rather than the number of physical qubits and their error rates. In the committee's assessment, machines of this scale are likely to be produced in academia or the private sector by the early 2020s.

The engineering process for scaling the number of logical qubits will likely proceed via two related efforts. The first will take the current best qubit design and focus on scaling the number of physical qubits in the system while maintaining or decreasing qubit error rates. The challenging aspect of this task is to scale the control layer to provide sufficient control bandwidth and isolation between the growing number of control signals and the quantum data plane, and to create the methodology for calibrating these increasingly complex systems. Addressing these challenges will drive learning about system design and scaling issues.

The other effort will explore ways of changing the qubit or system design to decrease its error rates, and will focus on smaller systems to ease analysis. Successful approaches for decreasing error rates can then be transferred to the larger system designs. For example, decoherence-free subspaces and noiseless subsystem-based approaches to error mitigation could help to improve on qubit and gate error rates. Another promising approach may be to consider systems with inherent error correction as these technologies emerge or improve, such as topological qubits based on non-Abelian anyons, described in Chapter 5. While achieving quality improvement through QEC shows that building a logical qubit is possible, the overhead of QEC is strongly dependent on the error rates of the physical system, as shown earlier in Figure 7.1. Improvement in both areas is required in order to achieve an error-corrected quantum computer that can scale to thousands of logical qubits.

7.3.5 Commercially Useful Quantum Computer (Milestones A3 and G3)

As mentioned earlier in this chapter, recent progress and the likelihood of demonstrating quantum supremacy in the next few years will probably create enough interest to drive quantum computing investment and scaling into the early 2020s. Further investment will be required for improvements to continue through the end of the 2020s, and this investment will likely depend upon some demonstration of commercial utility—that is, upon demonstration that quantum computers can perform some tasks of commercial interest significantly more efficiently than classical computers. Thus, the next major milestone is creation of a quantum computer that generates a commercial demand, to help launch a virtuous cycle for quantum computation.

This successful machine could be either gate based or an analog quantum computer. As Chapter 3 described, both machines use the same basic quantum components—qubits and methods for these qubits to interact—so increasing resources toward building any type of computer would likely have spillover effects for the entire quantum computing ecosystem.

Many groups are working hard to address this issue, by providing Web-based access to existing quantum computers to enable a larger group of people to explore different applications, creating better software development environments, and exploring physics and chemistry problems that seem well matched to these early machines. If digital quantum computers advance at an aggressive rate of doubling qubits every year, they will likely have hundreds of physical qubits in roughly five years, which still may be not be enough to support one full logical qubit. Therefore, a useful application would most likely need to be found for a NISQ computer in order to stimulate a virtuous cycle. The timing of this milestone again depends not only on device scaling but also on finding an application that can run on a NISQ computer; thus, the time frame is more difficult to project.

7.3.6 Large Modular Quantum Computer (Milestone G4)

At some point, the current approaches to scaling the number of qubits, discussed in Chapter 5, will reach practical limits. For superconducting qubits in gate-based machines, this will likely manifest as a practical inability to manage the control lines required to operate a device above a certain size threshold—in particular, to pass them through the cryostat within which the device is contained. Superconducting qubit-based annealers have already addressed this issue through the integration of the control and qubit planes, albeit with a trade-off in qubit fidelity; some of these engineering strategies could potentially inform those for gate-based systems. For trapped ions, this is likely to manifest as the complexity in the optical systems used to deliver the control signals, or the practical challenge to control the motional degree of freedom for the ions as the size of the ion crystal grows. These limits are likely to be reached for both superconducting and trapped-ion gate-based technologies when the number of physical qubits grows to around 1,000, or six doublings from now. Similar limitations arise for all large engineered systems. As a result, many complex systems use a modular design approach: the final system is created by connecting a number of separate, often identical modules, each in turn often built by assembling a set of even smaller modules. This approach, which is shown in Figure 7.5, enables the number of qubits in a computer to scale by increasing the number of quantum data plane modules it contains.

There are a large number of system issues that would need to be solved before these large-scale machines could be realized. First, owing

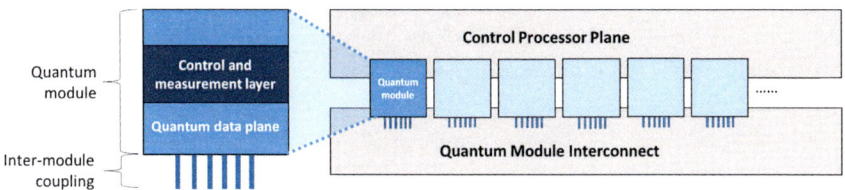

FIGURE 7.5 Schematic of a modular design approach to a large-scale, fault-tolerant quantum computer. The diagram represents device abstractions and is not intended to imply any particular physical device layout, which will depend on the specific technology and implementation. Each quantum module consists of its own data plane and control and measurement layer and intersects with the control processor plane.

to space constraints, it is likely that the control and measurement layer will need to be integrated into a quantum module, as has been done in large quantum annealers to achieve cold control electronics (at the cost of increased noise). Thought must also be given to strategies for debugging and repairing individual modules, since in a large machine some modules are likely to break; for systems that run at very cold temperatures, a faulty module would require warming, repair, and recooling—a time- and energy-intensive process that would disrupt the entire machine. In addition to these module- and system-level challenges, two key interconnection challenges must be addressed to enable this type of modular design. The first is creating a robust mechanism for coupling quantum states contained in different modules at low error rates, since gate operations must be supported between qubits in different modules. The second is to create an interconnection architecture and module size that maximizes the overall performance while minimizing the cost of building the machine, since these module connections are difficult to create with sufficiently low error rates. Since the dominant algorithm that will be run on any error-corrected quantum computer is QEC, efficient execution of QEC is expected to drive many of these design trade-offs. *Last, it is highly likely that such systems will be large and energy intensive.* Needless to say, it is too early to anticipate how these challenges might be overcome, as other near-term challenges remain the immediate bottleneck to progress.

7.3.7 Milestone Summary

The time to create a large fault-tolerant quantum computer that can run Shor's algorithm to break RSA 2048, run advanced quantum chemistry computations, or carry out other practical applications likely is more than a decade away. These machines require roughly 16 doublings of the number of physical qubits, and 9 halvings of qubit error rates. The qubit metrics and quantum computing milestones introduced in this chapter can be used to help track progress toward this goal. As more experimental data becomes available, the extracted metrics will allow for short-term predictions about the number and error rates of future machines, and later, the number of logical qubits they will contain. The milestones are useful for tracking some of the larger issues that affect this rate of progress, since they represent some of the larger hurdles that need to be crossed to create a large fault tolerant quantum computer. Table 7.1 summarizes the milestone machines, the advances they required, and information on timing.

TABLE 7.1 Key Milestones along the Path to a Large-Scale, Universal, Fault-Tolerant Quantum Computer

Milestone	Technical Advances Required	Expected Time Frames
A1—Experimental quantum annealer	N/A	Systems of this type already exist.
G1—Small (tens of qubits) computer	N/A	Systems of this scale already exist.
G2a—Gate-based quantum computer that demonstrates quantum supremacy	• Create order of 100 qubit systems (scale up G1 machines by about 4×). • Decrease average error rate to better than 0.5% (10× better than G1 machines). • Find a task that it can compute but that is difficult for a classical computer. • Verify accuracy of result, and to see if better approaches for classical computers are developed.	There are active efforts to create these machines in 2018. The community expects these machines to exist by the early 2020s, but their exact timing is uncertain. The timing depends on both hardware progress and the ability of classic hardware to simulate these machines.
A2—Quantum annealer that demonstrates quantum supremacy	• Identify benchmark problems suited to the system architecture. • Carry out a benchmark task that no classical computer can. • If that benchmark is new, encourage better algorithms for classical computers to demonstrate supremacy over the best classical approach. • Verify accuracy of result	Unknown.

continued

TABLE 7.1 Continued

Milestone	Technical Advances Required	Expected Time Frames
G2b—Implementation of QEC for improved qubit quality	• Use the same physical hardware as G2a, perhaps with lower error rate. • Create the software/control processor/control and measurement layer that can implement QEC in real time. • Use information gain from the measurements to improve QEC operation. • Demonstrate error-corrected qubits.	Similar timing to G2a machines. Might be available earlier, if simulation techniques on classical machines continue to improve.
A3/G3—Commercially useful quantum computer	• Identify useful task that a NISQ computer can carry out more efficiently than a classical computer. • Hone the corresponding quantum algorithm for efficiency on the physical device being used.	Funding of QC will likely be impacted if this milestone is not available in mid- to late 2020s. The actual timing depends on the application, which is currently unknown.
G4—Large (>1,000 qubits), fault-tolerant, modular quantum computer	• Develop a modular construction approach that overcomes the physical barriers of many-qubit systems. • Establish mechanisms for intermodule communication and coupling.	Timing unknown, since current research is focused on achieving robust internal logic rather than on linking modules.

7.4 QUANTUM COMPUTING R&D

Regardless of the exact time frame or prospects of a scalable QC, there are many compelling reasons to invest in quantum computing R&D, and this investment is becoming increasingly global. QC is one element (perhaps the most complex) of a larger field of quantum technology. Since the different areas in quantum technology share common hardware components, analysis methods, and algorithms, and advances in one field may often be leveraged in another, funding for all quantum technology is often lumped together. Quantum technology generally includes quantum sensing, quantum communication, and quantum computing. This section examines the funding for research in this area, and the benefits from this research.

7.4.1 The Global Research Landscape

Publicly funded U.S. R&D efforts in quantum information science and technology are largely comprised of basic research programs and proof-of-concept demonstrations of engineered quantum devices.[12] Recent initiatives launched by the National Science Foundation (NSF) and the Department of Energy (DOE) add to the growing framework of research funded by the National Institute of Standards and Technology (NIST), the Intelligence Advanced Research Projects Activity (IARPA), and the Department of Defense (DOD). The latter agency's efforts include the Air Force Office of Scientific Research (AFOSR), the Office of Naval Research (ONR), the Army Research Office (ARO), and the Defense Advanced Research Projects Agency (DARPA). There are now major efforts in quantum computing at several national laboratories and nonprofit organizations in the United States [19]. These publicly funded efforts are being amplified by growing interest from industry in quantum engineering and technology, including significant efforts at major publicly traded companies [20]. A number of startup companies, funded by private capital, have been created and are growing in this space [21].

While U.S. R&D in quantum science and technology are substantial, the true scale of such efforts is global. A 2015 report from McKinsey corporation placed global nonclassified investment in R&D in quantum technology at €1.5 billion ($US1.8 billion), distributed as indicated in Figure 7.6.

This large international funding is likely to grow as a result of a number of several noteworthy non-U.S. national-level programs and

---

[12] The funding efforts described in this section are for quantum information science and technology, which is broader than QC; the data is aggregated such that levels for QC in particular cannot be extracted.

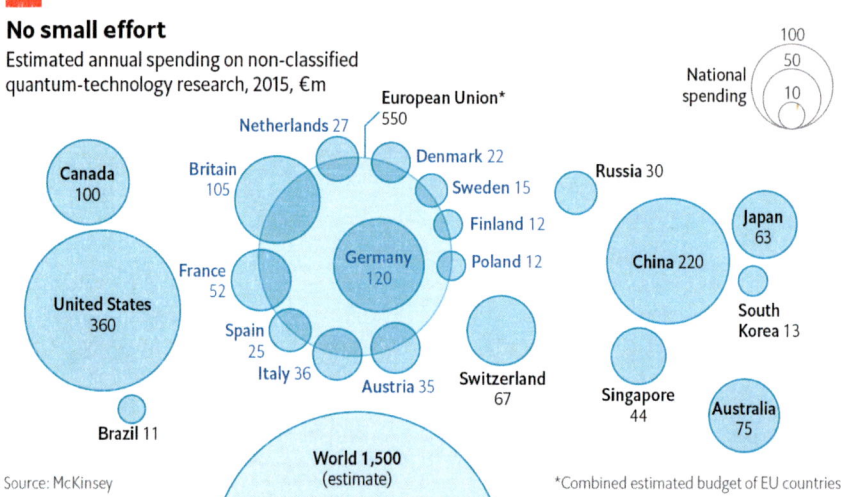

FIGURE 7.6 Estimated annual spending as of 2015 on nonclassified quantum technology research by nation, in millions of euros. Estimated investment levels due to more recently announced national R&D initiatives (as of mid-2018) are provided in Table 7.2. SOURCE: Data from McKinsey, as reported by *The Economist*. Reprinted with permission of *The Economist*, from "Here, There, and Everywhere: Quantum Computing Is Beginning to Come into Its Own," March 9, 2017; permission conveyed through Copyright Clearance Center, Inc.

initiatives in quantum information science and technology (QIST) that have been announced recently, which may reshape the research landscape in years to come. These initiatives, summarized in Table 7.2, and described in Appendix E, illustrate the commitment of the corresponding governments to leadership in QIST writ large. In general, they span a range of subfields, and are not focused on quantum computing exclusively. As of the time of this writing, the United States had released a *National Strategic Overview for Quantum Information Science*, emphasizing a science-first approach to R&D, building a future workforce, deepening engagement with industry, providing critical infrastructure, maintaining national security and economic growth, and advancing international cooperation [22]. Several pieces of legislation for a national quantum initiative have been introduced and advanced in the U.S. Senate and House of Representatives.

TABLE 7.2 Publicly Announced National and International Initiatives in Quantum Science and Technology Research and Development, as of Mid-2018

Nation(s)	Initiative	Year Announced	Investment, Time Frame	Scope
United Kingdom	UK National Quantum Technologies Program	2013	£270 million (US$358 million) over 5 years, beginning in 2014	Sensors and metrology, quantum enhanced imaging (QuantIC), networked quantum information technologies (NQIT), quantum communications technologies
European Union	Quantum Technologies Flagship	2016	€1 billion (US$1.1 billion) over 10 years; preparations under way; launch expected 2018	Quantum communication, metrology and sensing, simulation, computing, and fundamental science
Australia	Australian Centre for Quantum Computation and Communication Technology	2017	$33.7 million (US$25.11 million) over seven years	Quantum communication, optical quantum computation, silicon quantum computation, and quantum resources and integration
Sweden	Wallenberg Center for Quantum Technology	2017	SEK 1 billion (US$110 million)	Quantum computers, quantum simulators, quantum communication, quantum sensors; sponsored by industry and private foundation
China	National Laboratory for Quantum Information Science	2017	76 billion Yuan (US$11.4 billion); construction over 2.5 years	Centralized quantum research facility

7.4.2 Importance of Quantum Computing R&D

The potential for building a quantum computer that could efficiently perform tasks that would take lifetimes on a classical computer—even if far off, and even though not certain to be possible—is a highly compelling prospect. Beyond potential practical applications, the pursuit of quantum computing requires harnessing and controlling the quantum world to an as yet unprecedented degree to create state spaces that humans have never had access to before, the so-called "entanglement frontier." This work requires extensive engineering to create, control, and operate low-noise entangled quantum systems, but it also pushes at the boundaries of what we have known to be possible.

As QCs mature, they will be a direct test of the theoretical predictions of how they work, and of what kind of quantum control is fundamentally possible. For example, the quantum supremacy experiment is a fundamental test of the theory of quantum mechanics in the limit of highly complex systems. It is likely that observations and experiments on the performance of quantum computers throughout the course of QC R&D will help to elucidate the profound underpinnings of quantum theory and feed back into development and refinement of quantum theory writ large, potentially leading to unexpected discoveries.

More fundamentally, development of elements of the theories of quantum information and quantum computation have already begun to affect other areas of physics. For example, the theory of quantum error correction, which must be implemented in order to achieve fault-tolerant QCs, has proven essential to the study of quantum gravity and black holes [23]. Furthermore, quantum information theory and quantum complexity theory are directly applicable to—and have become essential for—quantum many-body physics, the study of the dynamics of systems of a large-number of quantum particles [24]. Advances in this field are critical for a precise understanding of most physical systems.

Advances in QC theory and devices will require contributions from many fields beyond physics, including mathematics, computer science, materials science, chemistry, and multiple areas of engineering. Integrating the knowledge required to build and make use of QCs will require collaboration across traditional disciplinary boundaries; this cross-fertilization of ideas and perspectives could generate new ideas and reveal additional open questions, stimulating new areas of research.

In particular, work on the design of quantum algorithms (required to make use of a quantum computer) can help to advance foundational theories of computation. To date, there are numerous examples of quantum computing research results leading directly to advances in classical computing via several mechanisms. First, approaches used for developing quantum algorithms have in some cases turned out to be translatable to classical algorithms, yielding improved classical methods [25-27].[13] Second, quantum algorithms research has yielded new fundamental proofs, answering previously open questions in computer science [28-31].[14] Last, progress in quantum computing can be a unique source of motivation for classical algorithm researchers; discovery of efficient quantum algorithms has spurred the development of new classical approaches that are even more efficient and would not otherwise have been pursued [32-35].[15] Fundamental research in quantum computing is thus expected to continue to spur progress and inform strategies in classical computing, such as for assessing the safety of cryptosystems, elucidating the boundaries of physical computation, or advancing methods for computational science.

Progress in technology has always gone hand-in-hand with foundational research, as the creation of new cutting-edge tools and methods provides scientists access to regimes previously not accessible, leading to new discoveries. For example, consider how advances in cooling technologies led to the discovery of superconductivity; the engineering of high-end optical interferometers at LIGO enabled the observation of gravitational waves; the engineering of higher-performance particle accelerators enabled the discovery of quarks and leptons. Thus, QC R&D could lead to technologies—whether component technologies or QCs themselves—that similarly enable new discoveries or advances in a host of scientific disciplines, such as physics, chemistry, biochemistry, and materials science. These in turn enable future advances in technology. As with all foundational science and engineering, the future impacts of this work are not easily predictable, but they could potentially offer transformational change and significant economic benefits.

---

[13] See, for example, quantum-inspired improvements in classical machine learning (Wiebe et al., 2015) and optimization algorithms (Zintchenko et al., 2015).

[14] For example, the quantum approximate optimization algorithm (QAOA), while no more efficient than classical approaches, has a performance guarantee for a certain type of problem that researchers were able to prove formally—something never achieved previously for any approach to this type of problem (Farhi et al., 2014). In another instance, properties of quantum computers were critical to proving the power of certain types of classical computers (Aaronson, 2005). In a third example, an argument based upon quantum computing was used to prove for the first time that a classical coding algorithm called a "two-query locally decodable code" cannot be carried out efficiently (Kerenidis et al., 2004).

[15] For example, the discovery of an efficient quantum algorithm for a linear algebra problem called MaxE3Lin2 (Farhi et al., 2014) spurred computer scientists to develop multiple new, more efficient classical approaches to the same problem (Barak et al., 2015; Hastad, 2015). These results in turn spurred improvement of the quantum approach, although the classical approaches remain more efficient. In another example, an undergraduate student discovered a classical algorithm whose performance matched that of an important quantum algorithm, providing exponential speedup over all previous classical approaches. (Hartnett, 2018).

Key Finding 6: Quantum computing is valuable for driving foundational research that will help advance humanity's understanding of the universe. As with all foundational scientific research, discoveries in this field could lead to transformative new knowledge and applications.

In addition to its strength as a foundational research area, quantum computing R&D is a key driver of progress in the field of quantum information science (QIS) more broadly, and closely related to progress in other areas of quantum technology. The same types of qubits currently being explored for applications in quantum computing are being used to build precision clocks, magnetometers, and inertial sensors—applications that are likely to be achievable in the near term. Quantum communication, important both for intra- and intermodule communication in a quantum computer, is also a vibrant research field of its own; recent advances include entanglement distribution between remote qubit nodes mediated by photons, some over macroscopic distances for fundamental scientific tests, and others for establishing quantum connections between multiple quantum computers.

Work toward larger-scale quantum computers will require improvements in methods for quantum control and measurement, which will also likely have benefits for other quantum technologies. For example, advanced quantum-limited parametric amplifiers in the microwave domain, developed recently for measuring superconducting qubits in QC systems, are used to achieve unprecedented levels of sensitivity for measuring nonclassical states of microwave fields (such as squeezed states), which have been explored extensively for achieving sensitivities beyond the standard limit in sensing and metrology [36,37]. In fact, results from quantum computing and quantum information science have already led to techniques of value for other quantum technologies, such as quantum logic spectroscopy [38] and magnetometry [39].

Key Finding 7: Although the feasibility of a large-scale quantum computer is not yet certain, the benefits of the effort to develop a practical QC are likely to be large, and they may continue to spill over to other nearer-term applications of quantum information technology, such as qubit-based sensing.

Quantum computing research has clear implications for national security. Even if the probability of creating a working quantum computer was low, given the interest and progress in this area, it seems likely this technology will be developed further by some nation-states. Thus, all nations must plan for a future of increased QC capability. The threat to current asymmetric cryptography is obvious and is driving efforts toward transitioning to post-quantum cryptography as described in Chapter 4.

Any entity in possession of a large-scale, practical quantum computer could break today's asymmetric cryptosystems and obtain a significant signals intelligence advantage. While deploying post-quantum cryptography in government and civilian systems may help protect subsequent communications, it will not protect communications or data that have already been intercepted or exfiltrated by an adversary. Access to prequantum encrypted data in the post-quantum world could be of significant benefit to intelligence operations, although its value would very likely decrease as the time horizon to building a large-scale QC increases. Furthermore, new quantum algorithms or implementations could lead to new cryptanalytic techniques; as with cybersecurity in general, post-quantum resilience will require ongoing security research.

But the national security implications transcend these issues. A larger, strategic question is about future economic and technological leadership. Quantum computing, like few other foundational research areas, has a chance of causing dramatic changes in a number of different industries. The reason is simple: advances in classical computers have made computation an essential part of almost every industry. This dependence means that any advances in computing could have widespread impact that is hard to match. While it is not certain when or whether such changes will be enabled, it is nonetheless of strategic importance for the United States to be prepared to take advantage of these advances when they occur and use them to drive the future in a responsible way. This capability requires strong local research communities at the cutting edge of the field, to engage across disciplinary and institutional boundaries and to capitalize on advances in the field, regardless of where they originate. Thus, building and maintaining strong QC research groups is essential for this goal.

Key Finding 8: While the United States has historically played a leading role in developing quantum technologies, quantum information science and technology is now a global field. Given the large resource commitment several non-U.S. nations have recently made, continued U.S. support is critical if the United States wants to maintain its leadership position.

7.4.3 An Open Ecosystem

Historically, the unclassified quantum computing community has been collaborative, with results openly shared. Recently, several user communities have formed to share prototypical gate-based and annealing machines, including through remote or cloud access. For example, the USC-Lockheed-Martin Quantum Computing Center was the first shared user facility, established in 2011 with a 128-qubit D-Wave One System, which currently operates a D-Wave 2X system. Another shared user facility, for a 512-qubit D-Wave Two quantum annealing system, was established at the Ames Research Center in 2013,[16] and another was formed by the Quantum Institute at Los Alamos National Laboratory for a D-Wave 2X quantum annealing system.[17] On the digital QC front, both Rigetti and IBM provide Web access to their gate-based computers. Anyone (e.g., students, researchers, members of the public) interested in implementing quantum logic on an actual device may create an account and remotely experiment with one of these systems, under the condition that the results of their experimentation also be made available to others to help advance the state of knowledge about and strategies for programming this hardware. Dozens of research papers have already emerged as a result of these collaborations [40].

Open research and development in quantum computing is not limited to hardware. Many software systems to support quantum computing are being developed and licensed using an open source model, where users are free to use and help improve the code [41]. There are a number of emerging quantum software development platforms pursuing an open source environment.[18] Support for open quantum computing R&D has helped to build a community and ecosystem of collaborators worldwide, the results and advances of which can build upon each other. If this continues, this ecosystem will enable discoveries in quantum science and engineering—and potentially in other areas of physics, mathematics, and computation—advancing progress in foundational science and expanding humanity's understanding of the building blocks of the physical world.

At the same time, the field of quantum computing is becoming increasingly globally competitive. As described in the previous section, several countries have announced large research initiatives or programs to support this work, including China, the UK, the EU, and Australia, and many are aiming to become leaders in this technology. This increased competition among nation-states or private sector entities for leadership in quantum computing could drive the field to be less open in publishing

---

[16] This is a collaboration between Google, the USRA, and NASA Advanced Computing Division, currently in use to study machine learning applications.

[17] The machine is called "Ising." One of the aims of the facility is to develop an open network for the exchange of ideas, connecting users to enable collaboration and exploration of a range of applications of the system.

[18] For example, Microsoft released the Quantum Development Kit and corresponding language Q# under an open source license to encourage broad developer usage and advancement in quantum algorithms and libraries. Other open source quantum software packages include ProjectQ developed at ETH Zurich, Quipper at Dalhousie University, and QISKit developed at IBM.

and sharing research results. While it is reasonable for companies to desire to retain some intellectual property, and thus not publish all results openly, reducing the open flow of ideas can have a dampening effect on progress in development of practical technologies and human capital.[19]

Key Finding 9: An open ecosystem that enables cross-pollination of ideas and groups will accelerate rapid technology advancement.

7.5 TARGETING A SUCCESSFUL FUTURE

Quantum computing provides an exciting potential future, but to make this future happen, a number of challenges will need to be addressed. This section looks at the most important ramifications of the potential ability to create a large fault-tolerant quantum computer and will end with a list of the key challenges to achieve this goal.

7.5.1 Cybersecurity Implications of Building a Quantum Computer

The main risk arising from the construction of a large general-purpose quantum computer is the collapse of the public-key cryptographic infrastructure that underpins much of the security of today's electronic and information infrastructure. Defeating 2048-bit RSA encryption using the best known classical computing techniques on the best available hardware is utterly infeasible, as the task would require quadrillions of years [42]. On the other hand, a general-purpose quantum computer with around 2,500 logical qubits could potentially perform this task in no more than a few hours.[20] As mentioned in Chapter 4, there are protocols for classical machines currently believed to be resistant to such attack—however, they are not widely deployed; and any stored data or communications encrypted with nonresilient protocols will be subject to compromise by any adversary with a sufficiently large quantum computer. As Chapter 4 explained, deploying a new protocol is relatively easy but replacing an old one is very hard, since it can be embedded in every computer, tablet, cell phone, automobile, Wi-Fi access point, TV cable box, and DVD player (as well as hundreds of other kinds of devices, some quite small and

---

[19] While it is difficult to provide evidence of cases where the lack of dissemination of research results caused a technology to fail, there are cases that illustrate the contrapositive. For example, consider the wealth of applications developed by the thriving open-source software community, or the rapid development of the Internet after the launch of NSFNet (the original backbone of the civilian Internet) and subsequent commercial investments.

[20] See estimates in Table 4.1.

inexpensive). Since this process can take decades, it needs to be started well before the threat becomes available.

Key Finding 10: Even if a quantum computer that can decrypt current cryptographic ciphers is more than a decade off, the hazard of such a machine is high enough—and the time frame for transitioning to a new security protocol is sufficiently long and uncertain—that prioritization of the development, standardization, and deployment of post-quantum cryptography is critical for minimizing the chance of a potential security and privacy disaster.

7.5.2 Future Outlook for Quantum Computing

Our understanding of the science and engineering of quantum systems has improved dramatically over the past two decades, and with this understanding has come an improved ability to control the quantum phenomena that underlie quantum computing. However, significant work remains before a quantum computer with practical utility can be built. In the committee's assessment, the key technical advances needed are:

- Decreased qubit error rates to better than 10^{-3} in many-qubit systems to enable QEC.
- Interleaved qubit measurements and operations.
- Scaling the number of qubits per processor while maintaining/improving qubit error rate.
- Development of methods to simulate, verify, and debug quantum programs.
- Creating more algorithms that can solve problems of interest, particularly at lower qubit counts or shallow circuit depths to make use of NISQ computers.
- Refining or developing QECCs that require low overhead; the problem is not just the number of physical qubits per logical qubit, but to find approaches that reduce the large overheads involved with implementing some operations on logical qubits (for example, T-gates or other non-Clifford gates in a surface code) take a very large number of qubits and steps to implement.
- Identifying additional foundational algorithms that provide algorithmic speedup compared to classical approaches.
- Establishing intermodule quantum processor input and output (I/O).

While the committee expects that progress will be made, it is difficult to predict how and how soon this future will unfold: it might grow slowly and incrementally, or in bursts from unexpected innovation, analogous to the rapid improvement in gene sequencing that resulted from building "short read" machines. The research community's ability to do this work in turn depends on the state of the overall quantum computing ecosystem, which will depend upon the following factors:

- Interest and funding levels in the private sector, which may in turn depend on
  - Achievement of commercial benchmarks, especially the development of a useful near-term application for noisy intermediate-scale quantum computers that sustain private-sector investments in the field; and
  - Progress in the field of quantum computing algorithms and the presence of marketable applications for QC devices of any scale.
- Availability of a sufficient level of government investment in quantum technology and quantum computing R&D, especially under the scenario that private-sector funding collapses.
- Availability of a multidisciplinary pipeline of scientists and engineers with exposure to systems thinking to drive the R&D enterprise.
- The openness of collaboration and exchange of ideas within the research community.

Over time, the state of progress in meeting the open technical challenges and the above nontechnical factors may be assessed while monitoring the status of the two doubling metrics defined earlier in this chapter. Regardless of when—or whether—the milestones identified in this chapter are achieved, continued R&D in quantum computing and quantum technologies promise to expand the boundaries of humanity's scientific knowledge and will almost certainly lead to interesting new scientific discoveries. Even a negative result—such as proof that quantum supremacy cannot be achieved or that today's description of quantum mechanics is incomplete or inaccurate—would help elucidate the limitations of quantum information technology and computing more generally, and would in itself be a groundbreaking discovery. As with all foundational scientific research, the results yet to be gleaned could transform our understanding of the universe.

7.6 NOTES

[1] See, for example, G. Kalai, 2011, "How Quantum Computers Fail: Quantum Codes, Correlations in Physical Systems, and Noise Accumulation," preprint arXiv:1106.0485.

[2] J. Preskill, 2018, "Quantum Computing in the NISQ Era and Beyond," preprint arXiv:1801.00862.

[3] Remarks from John Shalf, Gary Bronner, and Norbert Holtkamp, respectively, at the third open meeting of the Committee on Technical Assessment of the Feasibility and Implications of Quantum Computing.

[4] See, for example, A. Gregg, 2018, "Lockheed Martin Adds $100 Million to Its Technology Investment Fund," *The Washington Post*, https://www.washingtonpost.com/business/economy/lockheed-martin-adds-100-million-to-its-technology-investment-fund/2018/06/10/0955e4ec-6a9e-11e8-bea7-c8eb28bc52b1_story.html;

M. Dery, 2018, "IBM Backs Australian Startup to Boost Quantum Computing Network," *Create Digital*, https://www.createdigital.org.au/ibm-startup-quantum-computing-network/;

J. Tan, 2018, "IBM Sees Quantum Computing Going Mainstream Within Five Years," *CNBC*, https://www.cnbc.com/2018/03/30/ibm-sees-quantum-computing-going-mainstream-within-five-years.html;

R. Waters, 2018, "Microsoft and Google Prepare for Big Leaps in Quantum Computing," *Financial Times*, https://www.ft.com/content/4b40be6c-0181-11e8-9650-9c0ad-2d7c5b5;

R. Chirgwin, 2017, "Google, Volkswagen Spin Up Quantum Computing Partnership," *The Register*, https://www.theregister.co.uk/2017/11/08/google_vw_spin_up_quantum_computing_partnership/;

G. Nott, 2017, "Microsoft Forges Multi-Year, Multi-Million Dollar Quantum Deal with University of Sydney," *CIO*, https://www.cio.com.au/article/625233/microsoft-forges-multi-year-multi-million-dollar-quantum-computing-partnership-sydney-university/;

J. Vanian, 2017, "IBM Adds JPMorgan Chase, Barclays, Samsung to Quantum Computing Project," *Fortune*, http://fortune.com/2017/12/14/ibm-jpmorgan-chase-barclays-others-quantum-computing/;

J. Nicas, 2017, "How Google's Quantum Computer Could Change the World," *Wall Street Journal*, https://www.wsj.com/articles/how-googles-quantum-computer-could-change-the-world-1508158847;

Z. Thomas, 2016, "Quantum Computing: Game Changer or Security Threat?," *BBC News*, https://www.bbc.com/news/business-35886456;

N. Ungerleider, 2014, "IBM's $3 Billion Investment in Synthetic Brains and Quantum Computing, *Fast Company*, https://www.fastcompany.com/3032872/ibms-3-billion-investment-in-synthetic-brains-and-quantum-computing.

[5] Committee on Science, U.S. House of Representatives, 105th Congress, 1998, "Unlocking Our Future: Toward a New National Science Policy," Committee Print 105, http://www.gpo.gov/fdsys/pkg/GPO-CPRT-105hprt105-b/content-detail.html.

[6] L.M. Branscomb and P.E. Auerswald, 2002, "Between Invention and Innovation—An Analysis of Funding for Early-Stage Technology Development," NIST GCR 02-841, prepared for Economic Assessment Office Advanced Technology Program, National Institute of Standards and Technology, Gaithersburg, Md.

[7] See, for example, Intel Corporation, 2018, "2018 CES: Intel Advances Quantum and Neuromorphic Computing Research," *Intel Newsroom*, https://newsroom.intel.com/news/intel-advances-quantum-neuromorphic-computing-research/;

Intel Corporation, 2017, "IBM Announces Advances to IBM Quantum Systems and Ecosystems," *IBM*, https://www-03.ibm.com/press/us/en/pressrelease/53374.wss;

J. Kelly, 2018, "A Preview of Bristlecone, Google's New Quantum Processor," *Google AI Blog*, https://ai.googleblog.com/2018/03/a-preview-of-bristlecone-googles-new.html.

[8] Current performance profiles for IBM's two cloud-accessible 20-qubit devices are published online: https://quantumexperience.ng.bluemix.net/qx/devices.

[9] See Standard Performance Evaluation Corporation, https://www.spec.org/.

[10] See, for example, B. Jones, 2017, "20-Qubit IBM Q Quantum Computer Could Double Its Predecessor's Processing Power," *Digital Trends*, https://www.digitaltrends.com/computing/ibm-q-20-qubits-quantum-computing/;

S.K. Moore, 2017, "Intel Accelerates Its Quantum Computing Efforts With 17-Qubit Chip," *IEEE Spectrum*, https://spectrum.ieee.org/tech-talk/computing/hardware/intel-accelerates-its-quantum-computing-efforts-with-17qubit-chip.

[11] See, for example, Rigetti, "Forest SDK," http://www.rigetti.com/forest.

[12] N.M. Linke, S. Johri, C. Figgatt, K.A. Landsman, A.Y. Matsuura, and C. Monroe, 2017, "Measuring the Renyi Entropy of a Two-Site Fermi-Hubbard Model on a Trapped Ion Quantum Computer," arXiv:1712.08581.

[13] N. Friis, O. Marty, C. Maier, C. Hempel, M. Holzapfel, P. Jurcevic, M.B. Plenio, M. Huber, C. Roos, R. Blatt, and B. Lanyon, 2018, "Observation of Entangled States of a Fully Controlled 20-Qubit System," https://arxiv.org/pdf/1711.11092.pdf.

[14] T. Simonite, 2018, "Google, Alibaba Spar Over Timeline For 'Quantum Supremacy,'" *Wired*, https://www.wired.com/story/google-alibaba-spar-over-timeline-for-quantum-supremacy/.

[15] See, for example, J. Kahn, 2017, "Google's 'Quantum Supremacy' Moment May Not Mean What You Think," *Bloomberg*, https://www.bloomberg.com/news/articles/2017-10-26/google-s-quantum-supremacy-moment-may-not-mean-what-you-think;

P. Ball, 2018, "The Era of Quantum Computing Is Here. Outlook: Cloudy," *Quanta Magazine*, https://www.quantamagazine.org/the-era-of-quantum-computing-is-here-outlook-cloudy-20180124/.

[16] T.F. Rønnow, Z. Wang, J. Job, S. Boixo, S.V. Isakov, D. Wecker, J.M. Martinis, D.A. Lidar, and M. Troyer, 2014, Defining and detecting quantum speedup, *Science* 345(6195):420-424.

[17] In this case, D-Wave demonstrated a constant speedup for an abstract problem optimized to the machine. See S. Mandrà and H.G. Katzgraber, 2017, "A Deceptive Step Towards Quantum Speedup Detection," arXiv:1711.01368.

[18] A.G. Fowler, M. Mariantoni, J.M. Martinis, and A.N. Cleland, 2012, "Surface Codes: Towards Partical Large-Scale Quantum Computation," https://arxiv.org/ftp/arxiv/papers/1208/1208.0928.pdf.

[19] Quantum Computing Report, "Government/Non-Profit," https://quantumcomputingreport.com/players/governmentnon-profit/.

[20] Quantum Computing Report, "Public Companies," https://quantumcomputingreport.com/players/public-companies/.

[21] Quantum Computing Report, "Private/Startup Companies," https://quantumcomputingreport.com/players/privatestartup/.

[22] Office of Science and Technology Policy, 2018, *National Strategic Overview for Quantum Information Science*, https://www.whitehouse.gov/wp-content/uploads/2018/09/National-Strategic-Overview-for-Quantum-Information-Science.pdf.

[23] D. Harlow, 2018, "TASI Lectures on the Emergence of Bulk Physics in AdS/CFT," arXiv:1802.01040.

[24] G.K.L. Chan, A. Keselman, N. Nakatani, Z. Li, and S.R. White, 2016, Matrix product operators, matrix product states, and ab initio density matrix renormalization group algorithms, *Journal of Chemical Physics* 145(1):014102.

[25] N. Wiebe, A. Kapoor, C. Granade, and K.M. Svore, 2015, "Quantum Inspired Training for Boltzmann Machines," preprint arXiv:1507.02642.
[26] I. Zintchenko, M.B. Hastings, and M.Troyer, 2015, From local to global ground states in Ising spin glasses, *Physical Review B* 91(2):024201.
[27] G.K.L. Chan, A. Keselman, N. Nakatani, Z. Li, and S.R. White, 2016, Matrix product operators, matrix product states, and ab initio density matrix renormalization group algorithms, *Journal of Chemical Physics* 145(1):014102.
[28] E. Farhi, J. Goldstone, and S. Gutmann, 2014, "A Quantum Approximate Optimization Algorithm," preprint arXiv:1411.4028.
[29] S. Aaronson, 2005, Quantum computing, postselection, and probabilistic polynomial-time, *Proceedings of the Royal Society of London A* 461(2063):3473-3482.
[30] I. Kerenidis and R. De Wolf, 2004, Exponential lower bound for 2-query locally decodable codes via a quantum argument, *Journal of Computer and System Sciences* 69(3):395-420.
[31] S. Aaronson, 2006, Lower bounds for local search by quantum arguments, *SIAM Journal on Computing* 35(4):804-824.
[32] E. Farhi, J. Goldstone, and S. Gutmann, 2014, "A Quantum Approximate Optimization Algorithm Applied to a Bounded Occurrence Constraint Problem," preprint arXiv:1412.6062.
[33] B. Barak, A. Moitra, R. O'Donnell, P. Raghavendra, O. Regev, D. Steurer, L. Trevisan, A. Vijayaraghavan, D. Witmer, and J. Wright, 2015, "Beating the Random Assignment on Constraint Satisfaction Problems of Bounded Degree," preprint arXiv:1505.03424.
[34] J. Hastad, 2015, *Improved Bounds for Bounded Occurrence Constraint Satisfaction*, Royal Institute of Technology, Stockholm, Sweden.
[35] K. Hartnett, 2018, "Major Quantum Computing Advance Made Obsolete By Teenager," *Quanta Magazine*, https://www.quantamagazine.org/teenager-finds-classical-alternative-to-quantum-recommendation-algorithm-20180731/.
[36] C. Macklin, K. O'Brien, D. Hover, M.E. Schwartz, V. Bolkhovsky, X. Zhang, W.D. Oliver, and I. Siddiqi, 2015, A near-quantum-limited Josephson traveling-wave parametric amplifier, *Science* 350(6258):307-310.
[37] A. Roy and M. Devoret, 2018, Quantum-limited parametric amplification with Josephson circuits in the regime of pump depletion, *Physical Review B* 98(4):045405.
[38] P.O. Schmidt, T. Rosenband, C. Langer, W.M. Itano, J.C. Bergquist, and D.J. Wineland, 2005, Spectroscopy using quantum logic, *Science* 309:749-752.
[39] J.R. Maze, P.L. Stanwix, J.S. Hodges, S. Hong, J.M. Taylor, P. Cappellaro, L. Jiang, et al., 2008, Nanoscale magnetic sensing with an individual electronic spin in diamond, *Nature* 455(7213):644.
[40] B. Sutor, 2018, "First IBM Q Hub in Asia to Spur Academic, Commercial Quantum Ecosystem," *IBM News Room*, http://newsroom.ibm.com/IBM-research?item=30486.
[41] Quantum Computing Report, "Tools," https://quantumcomputingreport.com/resources/tools/.
[42] digicert, "Check our Numbers," https://www.digicert.com/TimeTravel/math.htm.

Appendixes

A

Statement of Task

A study will provide an independent assessment of the feasibility and implications of creating a functional quantum computer capable of addressing real-world problems including but not limited to deployment of Shor's algorithm. The study will examine hardware and software requirements, quantum algorithms, drivers of advances in quantum computing and quantum devices, benchmarks associated with relevant use cases, the time and resources required, and how to assess the probability of success. The committee will consider:

1. What are the technical risks associated with developing a quantum computer, and what are realistic timelines to achieve a functionally useful machine? Who are the primary players capable of producing and using a quantum computer?
2. What are the implications of having a quantum computer, for example on signals intelligence, communications, banking, and commerce?
3. What is the future of public key cryptography? What are the prospects and time scales for developing and deploying quantum-resistant encryption?
4. What are the costs and benefits from a national security perspective of quantum computing, under various assumptions of time, cost, non-U.S. development, alternative technologies, etc.?

In its report, the committee will provide an assessment of prospects and implications but make no recommendations.

B

Trapped Ion Quantum Computers

This appendix reviews the technology used to create the quantum data plane and the control and measurement plan for trapped ion quantum computers. Since individual ions serve as qubits, the qubits themselves do not face the challenges of manufacturing defects; this approach has the potential of low error rate gate operations.

B.1 ION TRAPS

Atomic ions are trapped in space using electromagnetic fields. A point charge (an ion) cannot be stably trapped in free space using a static, or constant, electric field only, so either a combination of electric and magnetic fields (Penning trap) [1] or a time-dependent electric field (Paul trap) [2] must be used to trap arrays of atomic ions. These traps are operated in a vacuum to avoid interactions with background molecules in the environment.

Most trapped ion quantum computing systems use a Paul trap, where a radio frequency (RF) signal is applied to two electrodes arranged in parallel to ground electrodes, to form a quadrupole RF field (Figure B.1b). At the quadrupole "null"—where the RF field vanishes—atomic ions feel a trapping potential, which typically takes the shape of a line (Figure B.1a). Other electrodes carrying direct current (DC) fields can be used to create a nonuniform trapping field profile along the length of this line, which further confine and fine-tune the location of the trapped atomic chain [3]. Traditionally, these trap structures were constructed by machining and

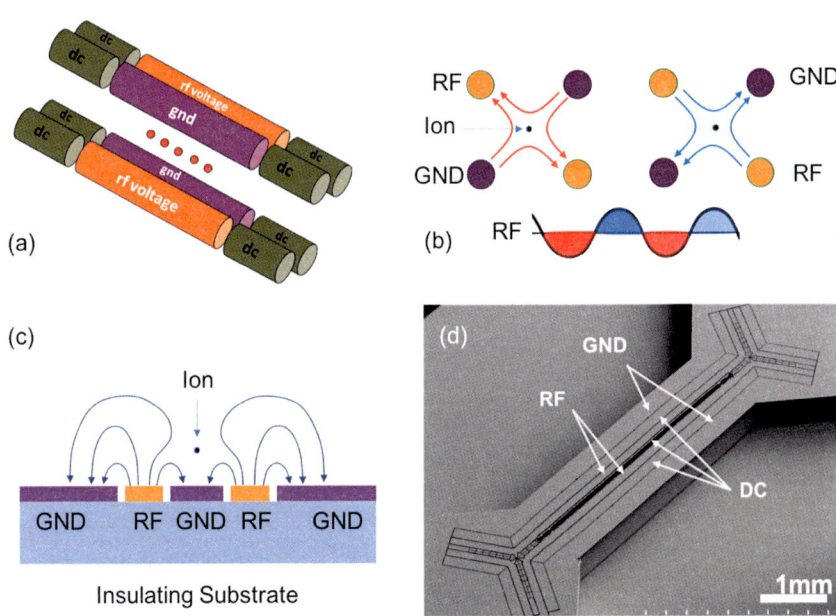

FIGURE B.1 Operating principle of RF Paul trap. (a) An example of a traditional RF Paul trap using four rods. Two rods in the diagonal serve as RF grounds, while an RF voltage is applied to the remaining two. This geometry creates a quadrupole electric field profile in the plane perpendicular to the axis of the rods and forms a one-dimensional (1D) linear trapping potential, where a chain of ions can be readily trapped. (b) During the negative cycle of the RF voltage (red arrows), the positively charged ion is pushed away from the ground electrodes toward the RF electrodes, while during the positive cycle of the RF voltage (blue arrows), the ions are pushed in the opposite direction. If the frequency of the RF voltage is much higher than the natural motional frequency of the ion (called the "secular frequency"), then the ions feel confining potential where the electric field forms a quadrupole null ("zero-field region"). (c) A linear trapping potential can be created by electrodes fabricated on a planar surface of a substrate. The cross-sectional view of the electric field forms the quadrupole null, and a linear trap is formed above the surface of the trap. (d) An example of a microfabricated surface trap, designed to provide adequate optical access to the ions trapped above the surface of the trapping electrodes. SOURCE: (a) Image from D. Hayes, Ph.D. thesis, University of Maryland, 2012. (c) Image courtesy of Sandia National Laboratories, 2015.

assembling metal parts, similar to quadrupole ion mass spectrometers. New designs map the electrodes of a Paul trap onto a planar geometry [4] and use semiconductor microfabrication technologies, much like those used for classical computing hardware, to construct the trap structures (Figure B.1c) [5,6]. The adoption of microfabrication technologies could enable the creation of more complex trap structures and new mechanisms for manipulating the trapped ions—for example, shuttling across junctions [7-10]—which, as will be shown later, is critical for scaling up the number of qubits in these systems (Figure B.1d). These microfabricated traps have also accelerated the development of advanced features of the ion traps by integrating various optical [11-13] and microwave components [14-16]. Microfabricated ion traps within which high-performance qubit manipulations are routinely carried out, made by various academic institutions, government laboratories, and industry foundries today, have been adopted by research groups around the world.

B.2 QUBIT CONTROL AND MEASUREMENT

Once ions are held within a trap inside a vacuum chamber, they are laser-cooled to near the ground state of motion in order to remove random variations that can affect their multiqubit operations. It is important to note that the motion of the ions does not directly impact the qubit stored in the internal states of the atomic ions. Subsequently, electromagnetic radiation is used to operate on the qubit state. There are two main types of trapped ion qubits, defined by the physical states used to represent the qubit states: "optical qubits" and "hyperfine qubits."

An optical qubit (Figure B.2a) makes use of the ground electronic state and a metastable excited electronic state of an ion, for which the energy difference between these levels is equal to the energy of a photon from the right "color" optical laser, the "qubit laser." Optical qubits can be prepared and detected with efficiencies better than 99.9 percent, with coherence times in the range of 1 to 30 seconds. A significant technical challenge in the operation of optical qubits is maintaining control of the qubit laser to enable precise and coherent control of the qubits. This requires stabilization of (1) the laser's output frequency over the time frame of qubit coherence (to approximately one part in 10^{14} or 10^{15}), and (2) the overall optical path lengths that the laser beam traverses to within a fraction of the optical wavelength over the duration of the quantum computation (or, that of quantum error correction that can recover from the phase errors). This optical frequency precision is just achievable in 2018 with state-of-the art laser sources.

A hyperfine qubit (Figure B.2b) uses a different pair of energy states that are called "hyperfine" levels of the ground electronic state of an

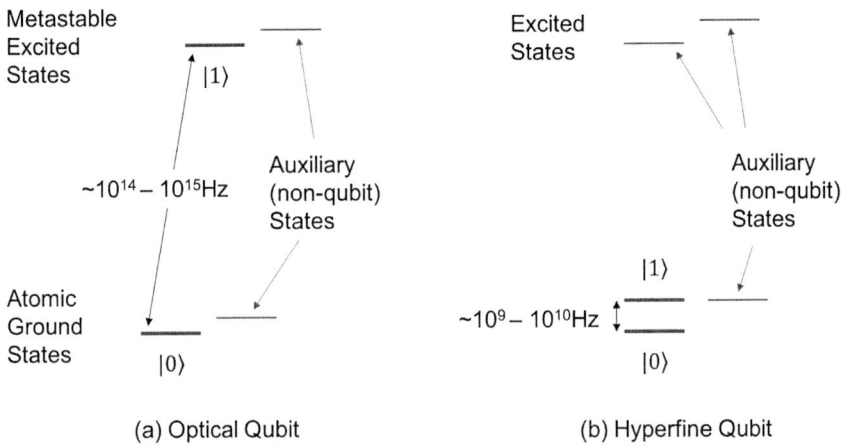

FIGURE B.2 Qubits in an atomic ion. (a) An optical qubit consists of one of the atomic ground states and one of the metastable excited states, separated by ~10^{14} to 10^{15} Hz. (b) A hyperfine qubit consists of two of the ground states, separated by ~10^9 to 10^{10} Hz. Usually some excited states are used to support qubit manipulation operations. In both cases, there are other (auxiliary) states in the ground, excited, and metastable excited states than those chosen to represent the qubit.

atomic ion with nonzero nuclear spin. The magnetic field can often be designed such that the energy separation between the two qubit states (typically corresponding to the microwave frequency range of 1 to 20 gigahertz [GHz]) is insensitive to the changes in the magnetic field to first order, which lead to long coherence times (1 to 1,000 seconds) [17-19]. Coherent control of hyperfine qubits also requires precise experimental control of the radiation—in this case, either microwave frequencies and phases, or the frequency difference of two laser fields that correspond to the qubit frequency. However, this is much more manageable at microwave than at optical frequencies [20-22].

Qubit measurement is carried out by "state-dependent fluorescence," where the ion is illuminated with a laser beam that causes only one of the two possible output states to scatter photons repeatedly, which can be measured with an optical detector. The presence or absence of scattered photons indicates which state the qubit is in. High-fidelity qubit state preparation and detection have been demonstrated for both optical (with error rates, or probabilities, of ~10^{-4})[23] and hyperfine qubits (with error rates of ~10^{-3}) [24,25]. While reliable measurement is possible, as of 2018, the process affects other qubits in the region where the qubit is being measured, and can leave the measured qubit in an excited state. So current systems measure all qubits at the same time, and they need to be "cooled" before being used again.

Single-qubit gate operations are carried out by driving the atomic states with resonant optical (for optical qubits) or microwave (for hyperfine qubits) fields. Hyperfine qubits can also be driven by a pair of laser beams whose frequency difference is precisely tuned to the qubit microwave frequency, via a process called "Raman transition" [26]. Hyperfine qubits driven by microwave fields have reached single qubit gate error rates (defined as the probability that applying a gate yields an incorrect state) in the 10^{-4} to 10^{-6} range, limited purely by the inherent coherence time of the qubit rather than any systematic errors in the control fields [27-29]. The key to achieving these error rates is to carefully shape the amplitude of the microwave pulse so that small errors in the pulse width or amplitude cancel out to first order [30-32]. Reaching similar limits with optical control signals had been hampered by the difficulty of stabilizing the laser field experienced by the qubits; ultraviolet (UV) laser beam outputs often used to drive gates can be distorted by mechanical, thermal, and air-density fluctuations in the laser beam path. The availability of single-mode optical fibers that can withstand high levels of UV optical power [33] has led to dramatic increases in the fidelity of microwave qubits using two Raman lasers in recent years. As experimental techniques for controlling systematic errors in the gate-driving optical fields continue to improve, single-qubit gates are reaching error rates of 10^{-4} to 10^{-5} [34,35].

To create two-qubit gates, these systems make use of charge interactions between trapped ions. Using either optical or microwave fields, one can excite an ion to oscillate in space such that it induces another ion to move as well. By carefully tuning the frequency of the driving fields, one can arrange the external control field to "push" the ions only if the targeted ion is in a specific qubit state; this mechanism is often called the "state-dependent force." As long as the excited motion remains fully coherent, it can serve as a "quantum bus" that mediates interaction between the qubits and realizes a two-qubit gate, analogous to an interconnect bus connecting different parts of the chip in an integrated circuit. Novel gate schemes have been developed to make such interactions robust against the exact details of the motion [36-38]. The error rates of the two-qubit gates (characterized by the probability of resulting in the wrong output state) have reached the 10^{-2} to 10^{-3} range using both optical [39,40] and microwave fields [41]. The mechanisms that limit this fidelity are known, and researchers continue to work to improve the quality of this operation.

B.3 CONTROL AND MEASUREMENT PLANE

The control system for a trapped ion quantum computer is made of four main subsystems: (1) the RF and DC voltages that operate the trap; (2) the continuous wave (CW) lasers used for "incoherent" operations such as cooling or reading out qubits; (3) the "coherent qubit control system" responsible for enacting coherent quantum logic gates; and (4) the photon detectors used for measuring the qubit states.

The basic operation of a Paul trap requires an RF source, typically in the frequency range of 20-200 MHz, with voltage amplitudes in the 30-400 V range. The DC voltages in the range of 0-30 V are used to define the trapping potential in the axial direction. In modern microfabricated traps, up to a hundred or more DC electrodes are used, requiring as many voltage sources to control them. Programmable multichannel digital-to-analog converters (DACs) are used to control these traps, which are capable of supporting several chains of ions, splitting and merging actions of ion chains, and physically shuttling ions between different regions of the trap.

The CW lasers are a set of lasers whose frequency is stabilized (typically to one part in 10^9) to the energy required for qubit transitions. These laser sources typically go through several optical modulators that are used to control the frequency and the amplitude of laser beams applied to the ions. The modulated CW laser beams are used to cool the ions to close to their motional ground state in the trap, to initialize the qubit state (by optical pumping), and for the readout of the qubit by inducing one of the qubit states to scatter photons. Frequency stabilization of these lasers to an absolute frequency reference is routinely accomplished using standard frequency locking setups.

The coherent qubit control system drives all the quantum logic gates in the system, and often dictates the performance of the quantum circuit execution in the quantum processor. The implementation of the coherent control system varies depending on the qubits used: for optical qubits, this tends to be an "ultra-stable frequency" CW laser (typically stabilized to one part in 10^{13} to 10^{15}), and for hyperfine qubits, it is often two laser beams with the difference frequency locked to the energy difference between the two qubit levels. One also needs a delivery system that can direct these laser beams to the target ions to operate the logic gates. The coherent control is often carried out by modulating these lasers with optical modulators, driven by programmable RF sources. There have been recent proposals where the coherent qubit control can be performed entirely using microwave sources, rather than lasers. Designing and constructing a high-quality coherent qubit control system is a challenging task that will determine the performance of the trapped ion quantum computer, such as individual gate error rates and the ability to run complex circuits.

The detection system often consists of imaging optics that collect photons scattered from the ions, and photon-counting detectors (such as photomultiplier tubes) capable of measuring the collected photons. The detected photons (counts, arrival time, etc.) can be used to reliably determine the state of the qubits.

B.4 NOTES

[1] H. Dehmelt, 1988, A single particle forever floating at rest in free space: New value for electron radius, *Physica Scripta* T22:102-110.

[2] W. Paul, 1990, Electromagnetic traps for charged and neutral particles, *Review of Modern Physics* 62:531.

[3] D.J. Wineland, C. Monroe, W.M. Itano, D. Leibfried, B.E. King, and D.M. Meekhof, 1998, Experimental issues in coherent quantum-state manipulation of trapped atomic ions, *Journal of Research of the National Institute of Standards and Technology* 103:259-328.

[4] J. Chiaverini, B.R. Blakestad, J.W. Britton, J.D. Jost, C. Langer, D.G. Leibfried, R. Ozeri, and D.J. Wineland, 2005, Surface-electrode architecture for ion-trap quantum information processing, *Quantum Information and Computation* 5:419-439.

[5] J. Kim, S. Pau, Z. Ma, H. R. McLellan, J. V. Gates, A. Kornblit, R. E. Slusher, R. M. Jopson, I. Kang, and M. Dinu, 2005, System design for large-scale ion trap quantum information processor, *Quantum Information and Computation* 5:515.

[6] D. Stick, W.K. Hensinger, S. Olmschenk, M.J. Madsen, K. Schwab, and C. Monroe, 2006, Ion trap in a semiconductor chip, *Nature Physics* 2:36-39.

[7] D. Kielpinski, C. Monroe, and D.J. Wineland, 2002, Architecture for a large-scale ion-trap quantum computer, *Nature* 417:709-711.

[8] R.B. Blakestad, C. Ospelkaus, A.P. VanDevender, J.H. Wesenberg, M.J. Biercuk, D. Leibfried, and D.J. Wineland, 2011, Near-ground-state transport of trapped-ion qubits through a multidimensional array, *Physical Review A* 84:032314.

[9] D.L. Moehring, C. Highstrete, D. Stick, K.M. Fortier, R. Haltli, C. Tigges, and M.G. Blain, 2011, Design, fabrication and experimental demonstration of junction surface ion traps, *New Journal of Physics* 13:075018.

[10] K. Wright, J.M. Amini, D.L. Faircloth, C. Volin, S.C. Doret, H. Hayden, C.-S. Pai, D.W. Landgren, D. Denison, T. Killian, R.E. Slusher, and A.W. Harter, 2013, Reliable transport through a microfabricated X-junction surface-electrode ion trap, *New Journal of Physics* 15:033004.

[11] A.P. VanDevender, Y. Colombe, J. Amini, D. Leibfried, and D.J. Wineland, 2010, Efficient fiber optic detection of trapped ion fluorescence, *Physical Review Letters* 105:023001.

[12] J.T. Merrill, C. Volin, D. Landgren, J.M. Amini, K. Wright, S.C. Doret, C.-S. Pai, H. Hayden, T. Killian, D. Faircloth, K.R. Brown, A.W. Harter, and R.E. Slusher, 2011, Demonstration of integrated microscale optics in surface-electrode ion traps, *New Journal of Physics* 13:103005.

[13] M. Ghadimi, V. Blūms, B.G. Norton, P.M. Fisher, S.C. Connell, J.M. Amini, C. Volin, H. Hayden, C.-S. Pai, D. Kielpinski, M. Lobino, and E.W. Streed, 2017, Scalable ion-photon quantum interface based on integrated diffractive mirrors, *npj Quantum Information* 3:4.

[14] C. Ospelkaus, U. Warring, Y. Colombe, K.R. Brown, J.M. Amini, D. Leibfried, and D.J. Wineland, 2011, Microwave quantum logic gates for trapped ions, *Nature* 476:181.

[15] D.T.C. Allcock, T.P. Harty, C.J. Ballance, B.C. Keitch, N.M. Linke, D.N. Stacey, and D.M. Lucas, 2013, A microfabricated ion trap with integrated microwave circuitry, *Applied Physics Letters* 102:044103.

[16] C.M. Shappert, J.T. Merrill, K.R. Brown, J.M. Amini, C. Volin, S.C. Doret, H. Hayden, C.-S. Pai, K.R. Brown, and A.W. Harter, 2013, Spatially uniform single-qubit gate operations with near-field microwaves and composite pulse compensation, *New Journal of Physics* 15:083053.

[17] P.T.H. Fisk, M.J. Sellars, M.A. Lawn, and C. Coles, 1997, Accurate measurement of the 12.6 GHz 'clock' transition in trapped ^{171}Yb$^+$ ions, *IEEE Transactions on Ultrasonics, Ferroelectrics, and Frequency Control* 44:344-354.

[18] C. Langer, R. Ozeri, J.D. Jost, J. Chiaverini, B. DeMarco, A. Ben-Kish, R.B. Blakestad, et al., 2005, Long-lived qubit memory using atomic ions, *Physical Review Letters* 95:060502.

[19] T. P. Harty, D.T.C. Allcock, C.J. Ballance, L. Guidoni, H.A. Janacek, N.M. Linke, D.N. Stacey, and D.M. Lucas, 2014, High-fidelity preparation, gates, memory, and readout of a trapped-ion quantum bit, *Physical Review Letters* 113:220501.

[20] H. Dehmelt, 1988, A single particle forever floating at rest in free space: New value for electron radius, *Physica Scripta* T22:102-110.

[21] S. Olmschenk, K.C. Younge, D.L. Moehring, D.N. Matsukevich, P. Maunz, and C. Monroe, 2007, Manipulation and detection of a trapped Yb+ hyperfine qubit, *Physical Review A* 76:052314.

[22] T.P. Harty, D.T.C. Allcock, C.J. Ballance, L. Guidoni, H.A. Janacek, N.M. Linke, D.N. Stacey, and D.M. Lucas, 2014, High-fidelity preparation, gates, memory, and readout of a trapped-ion quantum bit, *Physical Review Letters* 113:220501.

[23] A.H. Myerson, D.J. Szwer, S. C. Webster, D.T.C. Allcock, M. J. Curtis, G. Imreh, J.A. Sherman, D.N. Stacey, A.M. Steane, and D.M. Lucas, 2008, High-fidelity readout of trapped-ion qubits, *Physical Review Letters* 100:200502.

[24] T.P. Harty, D.T.C. Allcock, C.J. Ballance, L. Guidoni, H.A. Janacek, N.M. Linke, D.N. Stacey, and D.M. Lucas, 2014, High-fidelity preparation, gates, memory, and readout of a trapped-ion quantum bit, *Physical Review Letters* 113:220501.

[25] R. Noek, G. Vrijsen, D. Gaultney, E. Mount, T. Kim, P. Maunz, and J. Kim, 2013, High speed, high fidelity detection of an atomic hyperfine qubit, *Optics Letters* 38:4735-4738.

[26] D.J. Wineland, C. Monroe, W.M. Itano, B.E. King, D. Leibfried, D.M. Meekhof, C. Myatt, and C. Wood, 1998, Experimental primer on the trapped ion quantum computer, *Fortschritte der Physik* 46:363-390.

[27] K.R. Brown, A.C. Wilson, Y. Colombe, C. Ospelkaus, A.M. Meier, E. Knill, D. Leibfried, and D J. Wineland, 2011, Single-qubit-gate error below 10-4 in a trapped ion, *Physical Review A* 84:030303.

[28] T.P. Harty, D.T.C. Allcock, C.J. Ballance, L. Guidoni, H.A. Janacek, N.M. Linke, D.N. Stacey, and D.M. Lucas, 2014, High-fidelity preparation, gates, memory, and readout of a trapped-ion quantum bit, *Physical Review Letters* 113:220501.

[29] R. Blume-Kohout, J.K. Gamble, E. Nielsen, K. Rudinger, J. Mizrahi, K. Fortier, and P. Maunz, 2017, Demonstration of qubit operations below a rigorous fault tolerance threshold with gate set tomography, *Nature Communications* 8:4485.

[30] S. Wimperis, 1994, Broadband, narrowband, and passband composite pulses for use in advanced NMR experiments, *Journal of Magnetic Resonance A* 109:221-231.

[31] K.R. Brown, A.W. Harrow, and I.L. Chuang, 2004, Arbitrarily accurate composite pulse sequences, *Physical Review A* 70:052318.

[32] G.H. Low, T.J. Yoder, and I.L. Chuang, 2014, Optimal arbitrarily accurate composite pulse sequences, *Physical Review A* 89:022341.

[33] Y. Colombe, D.H. Slichter, A.C. Wilson, D. Leibfried, and D.J. Wineland, 2014, Single-mode optical fiber for high-power, low-loss UV transmission, *Optics Express* 22:19783-19793.

[34] T.P. Harty, D.T.C. Allcock, C.J. Ballance, L. Guidoni, H.A. Janacek, N.M. Linke, D.N. Stacey, and D.M. Lucas, 2014, High-fidelity preparation, gates, memory, and readout of a trapped-ion quantum bit, *Physical Review Letters* 113:220501.

[35] E. Mount, C. Kabytayev, S. Crain, R. Harper, S.-Y. Baek, G. Vrijsen, S.T. Flammia, K.R. Brown, P. Maunz, and J. Kim, 2015, Error compensation of single-qubit gates in a surface-electrode ion trap using composite pulses, *Physical Review A* 92:060301.

[36] A. Sørensen and K. Mølmer, 1999, Quantum computation with ions in a thermal motion, *Physical Review Letters* 82:1971.

[37] D. Leibfried, B. DeMarco, V. Meyer, D. Lucas, M. Barrett, J. Britton, W.M. Itano, B. Jelenkovic, C. Langer, T. Rosenband, and D.J. Wineland, 2003, Experimental demonstration of a robust, high-fidelity geometric two ion-qubit phase gate, *Nature* 422:412-415.

[38] P.C. Haljan, K.-A. Brickman, L. Deslauriers, P.J. Lee, and C. Monroe, 2005, Spin-dependent forces on trapped ions for phase-stable quantum gates and entangled states of spin and motion, *Physical Review Letters* 94:153602.

[39] J.P. Gaebler, T.R. Tan, Y. Lin, Y. Wan, R. Bowler, A.C. Keith, S. Glancy, K. Coakley, E. Knill, D. Leibfried, and D.J. Wineland, 2016, High-fidelity universal gate set for ^{9}Be$^+$ ion qubits, *Physical Review Letters* 117:060505.

[40] C.J. Ballance, T.P. Harty, N.M. Linke, M.A. Sepiol, and D.M. Lucas, 2016, High-fidelity quantum logic gates using trapped-ion hyperfine qubits, *Physical Review Letters* 117:060504.

[41] T.P. Harty, M.A. Sepiol, D.T.C. Allcock, C.J. Ballance, J.E. Tarlton, and D.M. Lucas, 2016, High-fidelity trapped-ion quantum logic using near-field microwaves, *Physical Review Letters* 117:140501.

C

Superconducting Quantum Computers

This appendix reviews the technology used to create the quantum data plane and the control and measurement plan for superconducting qubits. In this design, a superconducting resonator is coupled with a nonlinear inductor to form an artificial atom, and these "atoms" are used as the qubits for the computer.

C.1 FABRICATION

Low loss requires superconductors: a unique class of materials that exhibit no electrical resistance at zero frequency (that is, for direct currents) when cooled to below a critical temperature, T_c. Qubits for digital quantum computing and quantum simulation are most commonly fabricated from aluminum wiring (T_c = 1.2 K) and aluminum-amorphous aluminum oxide-aluminum (Al-AlOx-Al) Josephson junctions on either silicon or sapphire substrates. While superconducting qubits can be fabricated using the same design tools and fabrication equipment used to build silicon chips, the premium placed on high coherence necessitates that the specific fabrication steps be modified to eliminate defects that create losses. As a result, the highest-coherence qubits fabricated today—with coherence times of around 100 microseconds—are generally very simple devices, using a single layer of metal, rather than the complex processes of 10 metal layers used with the digital silicon or superconducting logic devices in today's classical computers.

In contrast, commercial quantum annealing computers that feature in excess of 2,000 superconducting qubits are fabricated using a more complex technology. This technology uses niobium wiring (T_c = 9.2 K) and niobium-amorphous aluminum oxide-niobium (Nb/AlOx/Nb) Josephson junctions [1,2] in a process that supports up to eight metal layers. This more complex fabrication process enables the qubits and superconducting control electronics to be integrated together in a single niobium fabrication process (an instance of "monolithic integration"). However, due to the fabrication complexity, additional processing steps, and the need for an interwiring layer of dielectric materials like silicon dioxide or silicon nitride that cause loss, qubits made in multilayer niobium processes generally have low coherence times, typically in the 10-100 nanosecond range [3].

C.2 QUBIT DESIGN

Like a trapped ion qubit, a superconducting qubit can exist in a series of quantized energy states; the two lowest states can be accessed selectively to realize the qubit. Rather than using an atom, this design uses a simple inductor and capacitor circuit, which also has quantized energy at low temperatures. To make the energy difference between its levels distinct, a nonlinear inductive element, the Josephson junction (JJ) is added to the circuit. With a JJ, the difference between the ground state and the first excited state may be uniquely addressed by a frequency f_{01}. This means that the microwave radiation, typically designed to be around 5 GHz, can be used to cause transitions between these two states without accessing the higher-excited states. Thus, this structure can be used as a qubit: a two-level quantum system.

There are a number of ways the inductor, capacitor, and JJ can be arranged to create a qubit, and how the qubits are connected to each other to enable two-qubit operations. These differences trade off between simpler control and better isolation and control of qubit operations, as follows:

- *Fixed-frequency versus tunable qubits.* Frequency-tunable qubits can be calibrated and corrected for qubit frequency variations that arise from variations in the fabrication process or as a result of device aging. An advantage is that one microwave tone can control multiple qubits, a savings in hardware. Gaining this advantage requires an additional control signal to adjust the frequency and adds an additional path for noise to enter the qubit. The two most common qubits in use today for digital superconducting quantum computing are the "transmon qubit," [4-7] which comes

in single-junction nontunable and two-junction tunable forms, and the "flux qubit" [8-11]. Both transmon designs are being used in leading edge efforts.
- *Static versus tunable coupling.* Static coupling between qubits—for example, by using a capacitor or an inductor to mediate interaction—is an "always-on" coupling that is fixed by design. The coupling is turned "on" by bringing two qubits into resonance, and it is turned off by detuning the qubits. Yet even in the off state, there still is a small residual coupling. This tuning can be further reduced by adding a third object—either another coupler qubit or a resonator—between the two qubits. The two qubits are then coupled by adjusting the qubits and the resonator to the proper frequency.

In addition to the qubits, the circuits include a simple mechanism to couple the qubit to its 5 GHz microwave control signal and to a superconducting resonator, typically designed to operate at around 7-8 GHz, which reads out the qubit state using the circuit quantum electrodynamics architecture [12].

C.3 REFRIGERATION

Superconducting qubits require milli-Kelvin (mK) temperatures to operate. For digital quantum computing, the qubit operation frequency is typically around 5 GHz, which corresponds to a thermal energy of approximately 250 mK; the qubit must thus be operated at much lower temperatures in order to avoid unwanted thermal excitation of the excited state. This is achieved using commercial ^{3}He/^{4}He dilution refrigerators, which are capable of cooling to sub-10 mK temperatures. On the other hand, for most practical potential uses of a quantum annealer, the qubits will at times operate at frequencies corresponding to thermal temperatures much lower than those achievable with a dilution refrigerator, which make it nearly certain that thermal noise will affect the annealing protocol and drive the system out of its ground state.

Modern dilution refrigerators leverage electromechanical pulse-tube coolers to achieve cooling in two stages, one at 50 K and one at 3 K. These are called "dry" refrigerators, as they do not require consumable liquid helium coolant to reach these temperatures. Then, at 3 K, a closed-cycle mixture of helium isotopes—^{3}He and ^{4}He—is condensed and circulated to achieve cooling through a series of stages at temperatures of 700 mK, 50 mK, and the base temperature of approximately 10 mK. Cooling from room temperature to base temperature generally takes about 36 to 48 hours, and the refrigerator can remain cold indefinitely.

In contemporary commercial dilution refrigerators, the experimental volume at base temperature is about $(0.5 \text{ m})^3$ and the cooling power at base temperature / 20 mK / 100 mK is approximately 0 (by definition) / 30 μW / 1000 μW, respectively. These are not fundamental limits. Large objects in excess of 1 ton have been cooled to less than 10 mK using a dry dilution refrigerator for the CUORE neutrino detection experiment [13]. Each temperature stage comprises a copper plate of approximately 0.5 m diameter, and they are used to thermalize control wiring from room temperature to base temperature both to cool the wires and to reduce thermal radiation from reaching the qubits [14]. Coaxial cables, attenuators, filters, isolators/circulators, and microwave switches work at cryogenic temperatures and are all used in state-of-art measurement systems.

C.4 CONTROL AND MEASUREMENT PLANE

The control and measurement plane for a superconducting quantum computer needs to generate the bias voltages/currents used to tune the qubits, create the microwave control signals, and reliably detect qubit measurements, while dealing with the large temperature differences that exist between the circuits that generate the control signals and the quantum plane that consumes them.

C.4.1 Control Wiring and Packaging

The delivery of electromagnetic control signals from the room-temperature region where they are generated to the qubits inside the refrigerator at mK temperatures requires careful thermal and electrical engineering. Wiring—whether low-frequency twisted pairs or high-frequency coax—must be thermalized at each temperature stage of the refrigerator to avoid excessive heating of the mixing chamber. Perhaps counterintuitively, the thermal heating of the refrigerator through direct contact (phonons) is not the critical challenge. The largest heat loads occur across the 300 to 3 K transition, and today's refrigerators can readily handle the heat loads of hundreds and even thousands of wires. And, as larger wire counts are needed, larger dilution refrigerators with additional cooling at all stages—in particular, at the 3 K stage—can be built as a straightforward extension of existing technology at proportional cost. For the 3 K to milli-K wires, superconducting NbTi can deliver the electrical signals faithfully, with minimal heating due to the direct thermal connection (phonons).

A more important challenge is mitigating the effects of room-temperature thermal noise on the operation of the qubits. There is a trade-off between efficiently guiding a desired signal to a qubit and preventing noise from impacting its operation. A two-pronged approach is used.

Filtering (attenuating signals that are not in the range of desired frequencies) is used to remove out-of-band radiation—noise that is outside the frequency range of the signals intended to be delivered to the device—but attenuation must be used to reduce the in-band radiation. This means that the amplitude of the control signal is decreased at each stage in the refrigerator, since the size of the thermal noise decreases with temperature. The attenuating cannot all be done at one point, since signal attenuation generates heat and thermal noise that must also decrease as the signal moves to lower temperatures. For similar reasons, the measurement of the qubit must also be done in stages, with the first stages of amplification performed at cryogenic temperatures, to minimize the noise of the amplifier.

One critical constraint in chips with a large number of signals is packaging. The package for a supercomputing chip must house, shield, and route signals to/from a qubit chip; it is a critical part of the control plane. While the superconducting chips are relatively small—typically 5×5 mm^2—it is the number of wires that feed the chip and their connectors that dictate the size of the package. For the high isolation needed for quantum circuits, coaxial connectors, coaxial wiring harnesses, miniature multipin connectors, and so on are types of connectors being used to bring signals into the package. The higher isolation that these connectors provide make them larger than the simple pin or ball connection used in packages for conventional silicon devices, and thus the number of signals per unit area is much smaller. Once the signals are on the package, they need to be routed to the correct location and then connected to the quantum circuit. Signals are connected to the qubit via wires, using bump (connections over the area of the chip) or wire (connections around the perimeter of the chip) bonds [15], or through the free-space of the package itself [16]. As the number of control wires increase, these packages will need to move to area bonding methods (bump bonding) like what was done with conventional silicon packaging. The challenge is to maintain a clean microwave environment for the qubits in the presence of these connectors and wiring. Given these constraints, the packaging problem will become very difficult as the number of signals increase to the thousands.

C.4.2 Control and Measurement

Having established a means to transfer signals between room temperature and the quantum data plane, the control and measurement layer needs to provide the hardware and software to (1) bias the qubit at its operating point; (2) perform logic operations; and (3) measure the qubit state. Contemporary superconducting qubits are operated using a combination of DC bias currents, microwave pulses resonant with the qubit transition—typically around 5 GHz—and baseband pulses.

As was mentioned earlier, qubits can be either "fixed frequency" or "tunable frequency." In a fixed-frequency design, the fabrication sets the qubit frequency, and the measurement system must determine that frequency and adjust its signals to it. The base frequency of tunable qubits is also set during fabrication, but it can be adjusted in situ using a bias current from the control plane. This bias current is connected through the qubit package and then coupled into the desired qubit. Tunable qubits require an extra control line but allow the control system to use a single frequency—or a small set of frequencies—for all qubits.

Control signals for single-qubit and two-qubit logic operations are generated using a stable microwave source, a programmable pulse shape, and a mixer, which combines the two signals to produce the needed microwave pulse. These pulses are around 10 ns (10 billionths of a second), generally much faster than those used for trapped ion qubits. Combinations of microwave pulses and frequency offsets are used to achieve two-qubit gate operation—for example, a controlled-phase gate or an iSWAP gate. These gates are slower than single-qubit operations and take between 40 ns and 400 ns. The exact control signals depend on whether the qubits are directly coupled or use an additional qubit or resonator to minimize background coupling. State-of-art two-qubit error rate is generally at the 1 percent level, with individual examples as low as 0.5 percent.

The requisite room-temperature control electronics—microwave oscillators, arbitrary waveform generators (AWGs) to generate the pulse shapes, mixers, and analog-to-digital converters (ADCs)—are all commercially available items with sufficient precision to not limit the qubit operation. For contemporary superconducting qubit applications, the AWGs and ADCs typically operate with 1-2 GS/s and 10-14 bits of resolution. Commercially available precision-grade local oscillators typically have a 1-12 GHz frequency range with a single-sideband phase noise of −120 dB at 10 kHz offset; this level of phase is generally sufficient to achieve gate error rates at the 10^{-8} level [17]. As the number of qubits increases, the support electronics grow as well. Generally, there are bias current generators, waveform generators, and mixers needed for each qubit. Thus, there is a need to better integrate this support electronics to enable the systems to scale to larger number of qubits.

Unlike natural atoms, which are all identical, artificial atoms are built from circuit elements, which have manufacturing variations. Thus, the qubit parameters (e.g., the transition frequency, qubit-qubit coupling, etc.) will differ from qubit to qubit, from one manufactured device to another, and from one temperature cycle to another. The control processor must have extensive calibration routines, to first determine, and then compensate for these variations. The complexity of this calibration grows superlinearly with the number of qubits in the system, and is one of the critical issues in scaling up the number of qubits.

C.5 NOTES

[1] M.W. Johnson, M.H.S. Amin, S. Gildert, T. Lanting, F. Hamze, N. Dickson, R. Harris, et al., 2011, Quantum annealing with manufactured spins, *Nature* 473:194-198.
[2] D Wave, "Technology Information," http://dwavesys.com/resources/publications.
[3] W.D. Oliver, Y. Yu, J.C. Lee, K.K. Berggren, L.S. Levitov, and T.P. Orlando, 2005, Mach-Zehnder interferometry in a strongly driven superconducting qubit, *Science* 310:1653-1657.
[4] J. Koch, T.M. Yu, J. Gambetta, A.A. Houck, D.I. Schuster, J. Majer, A. Blais, M.H. Devoret, S.M. Girvin, and R.J. Schoelkopf, 2007, Charge-insensitive qubit design derived from the Cooper pair box, *Physical Review A* 76:042319.
[5] A.A. Houck, A. Schreier, B.R. Johnson, J.M. Chow, J. Koch, J.M. Gambetta, D.I. Schuster, et al., 2008, Controlling the spontaneous emission of a superconducting transmon qubit, *Physical Review Letters* 101:080502.
[6] H. Paik, D.I. Schuster, L.S. Bishop, G. Kirchmair, G. Catelani, A.P. Sears, B.R. Johnson, et al., 2011, Observation of high coherence in Josephson junction qubits measured in a three-dimensional circuit QED architecture, *Physical Review Letters* 107:240501.
[7] R. Barends, J. Kelly, A. Megrant, D. Sank, E. Jeffrey, Y. Chen, Y. Yin, et al., 2013, Coherent Josephson qubit suitable for scalable quantum integrated circuits, *Physical Review Letters* 111:080502.
[8] J.E. Mooij, T.P. Orlando, L.S. Levitov, L. Tian, C.H. van der Wal, and S. Lloyd, 1999, Josephson persistent-current qubit, *Science* 285:1036-1039.
[9] T.P. Orlando, J.E. Mooij, L. Tian, C.H. van der Wal, L.S. Levitov, S. Lloyd, and J.J. Mazo, 1999, Superconducting persistent-current qubit, *Physical Review B* 60:15398.
[10] M. Steffan, S. Kumar, D.P. DiVincenzo, J.R. Rozen, G.A. Keefe, M.B. Rothwell, and M.B. Ketchen, 2010, High-coherence hybrid superconducting qubit, *Physical Review Letters* 105:100502.
[11] F. Yan, S. Gustavsson, A. Kamal, J. Birenbaum, A.P. Sears, D. Hover, T.J. Gudmundsen, et al., 2016, The flux qubit revisited to enhance coherence and reproducibility, *Nature Communications* 7:12964.
[12] A. Blais, R.-S. Huang, A. Wallraff, S.M. Girvin, and R.J. Schoelkopf, 2004, Cavity quantum electrodynamics for superconducting electrical circuits: An architecture for quantum computation, *Physical Review A* 69:062320.
[13] V. Singh, C Alduino, F. Alessandria, A Bersani, M. Biassoni, C. Bucci, A. Caminata, et al., 2016, The CUORE cryostat: Commissioning and performance, *Journal of Physics: Conference Series* 718:062054.
[14] R. Barends, J. Wenner, M. Lenander, Y. Chen, R.C. Bialczak, J. Kelly, E. Lucero, et al., 2011, Minimizing quasiparticle generation from stray infrared light in superconducting quantum circuits, *Applied Physics Letters* 99, 024501.
[15] D. Rosenberg, D.K. Kim, R. Das, D. Yost, S. Gustavsson, D. Hover, P. Krantz, et al., 2017, 3D integrated superconducting qubits, *npj Quantum Information* 3:42.
[16] H. Paik, D.I. Schuster, L.S. Bishop, G. Kirchmair, G. Catelani, A.P. Sears, B.R. Johnson, et al., 2011, Observation of high coherence in Josephson junction qubits measured in a three-dimensional circuit QED architecture, *Physical Review Letters* 107:240501.
[17] H. Ball, W.D. Oliver, and M.J. Biercuk, 2016, The role of master clock stability in quantum information processing, *npj Quantum Information* 2:16033.

D

Other Approaches to Building Qubits

Since many technical challenges remain in scaling either trapped ion or superconducting quantum computers, a number of research groups are continuing to explore other approaches for creating qubits. These technologies are much less developed and are still focused on creating single-qubit and two-qubit gates. Scale-up issues for these technologies have many similarities to those faced by ion traps and by superconductors. The rest of this appendix will briefly discuss these methods.

D.1 PHOTONIC QUANTUM COMPUTATION

Photons have some properties that make them extremely attractive for use in quantum computers: photons interact relatively weakly with their environment and with each other. This is the reason that photons can travel quite far in many materials without being scattered or absorbed, giving photonic qubits good coherence properties and making them useful for transmitting quantum information over long distances [1]. Thus, research and development in this area is important for enabling long-distance quantum communication channels even if other technologies turn out to be preferable for large-scale computing applications. Development of photonic quantum manipulation capabilities has potentially transformative applications for quantum sensing and quantum communication.

Experiments probing quantum entanglement of photons have a long history, dating back to the earliest experiments looking for violations of

APPENDIX D

Bell's theorem[1] in the 1970s [2]. Over the past several decades, methods have been developed that overcome many of the impediments to creating, manipulating, and measuring many-photon entangled states. This section describes briefly these advances, the remaining challenges that must be overcome to develop error-corrected photonic processors, and the ultimate limits to scale-up.

In many ways, photons are excellent qubits; single-qubit gates can be performed using standard optical devices such as phase shifters and beamsplitters, and as mentioned earlier they interact weakly with matter and with each other, giving them good coherence. But their strength—weak interactions—also causes a major hurdle to the development of photonic quantum computers, since two-qubit gates become difficult to create. Two strategies for overcoming this issue are described in this section. In linear optics quantum computing, an effective strong interaction is created by a combination of single-photon operations and measurements, which can be used to implement a two-qubit gate. A second approach, which uses optically active defects and quantum dots[2] that interact strongly with photons to induce strong effective interactions between photons, is discussed in Section D.3.1 on optically gated semiconducting qubits.

In photonic quantum computing, typically the qubits are individual photons, with the two different photon polarizations (up-down and left-right) serving as the two qubit states. Single qubit gates can be implemented with standard passive optical components used to rotate the polarization, but two-qubit gates require a low-loss nonlinearity, which is difficult to achieve [3]. As described in the trapped ion section of Chapter 5, coincident measurements on two output ports of a beamsplitter create a strong effective nonlinearity and implement a two-qubit gate [4], but the gate is probabilistic. Fortunately, the gate signals when it was successful (photons are detected on both detectors), which means that algorithms can be implemented, but the timing requirements are complex, and a steady source of suitably initialized photons is needed. More recently, measurement-based quantum computing schemes, in which a highly entangled "cluster state" is constructed before the start of the computation

---

[1] Bell's theorem says that "If [a hidden variable theory] is local it will not agree with quantum mechanics, and if it agrees with quantum mechanics it will not be local." In essence, it suggests that a nonquantum physical theory that explains quantum mechanical phenomena such as entanglement would refute the current understanding of quantum physics (J. Bell, 1987, *Speakable and Unspeakable in Quantum Mechanics*, Cambridge University Press, p. 65).

[2] Also referred to as "nanoparticles," quantum dots are small clusters of atoms with a crystalline structure whose physical properties are quite different from the properties of the elements involved in either atomic or bulk form. Quantum dots exhibit unusual properties—for example, the wavelength of light they absorb or emit may be tuned through engineering of their size.

and the computation itself is implemented by performing measurements, have attracted substantial interest [5].

Many of the technical developments needed to implement photonic quantum computing have been achieved over the past several years. Photonic chips continue to improve, and photon loss rates both within photonic elements and at interfaces are approaching the values needed to be able to implement quantum error correction. Very high efficiency photon detectors have been developed [6], which are key to the implementation of error correction. These nanowire-based detectors operate at helium temperatures (about 4 K), so cooling to this temperature will be required, but as described earlier, such cooling is expected to be entirely feasible. Assuming continued progress in reducing photon loss rates, the main hurdle toward the fabrication of devices of moderate size is to develop a source that generates at a high rate triplets of entangled photons [7]. Sources of triplets of entangled photons exist [8], but the rate at which entangled photon triplets are generated would need to be increased substantially for this strategy to enable large scale computations. As of 2018, the largest entangled and fully connected system of qubits was demonstrated using three degrees of freedom on each of six photons [9], although this method faces its own challenges and is unlikely to scale.

Ultimate scalability: Because the photons used in photonic quantum computing typically have wavelengths that are around a micron, and because the photons move at the speed of light and are typically routed along one dimension of the optical chip, the number of photons, and hence the number of qubits, in a photonic device cannot be made as large as in systems with qubits that can be localized in space. However, arrays with many thousands of qubits are expected to be possible [10]. In addition, the technology will be crucial for developing switching networks that will enable quantum communication on large scales.

D.2 NEUTRAL ATOM QUANTUM COMPUTATION

Rather than creating an array of ions and using the charges on the ions to hold them in place, one can use lasers to create an array of optical traps that confine neutral atoms [11,12]. This approach has technological similarities to ion trap quantum computation, and uses optical and microwave pulses for qubit manipulation, with the potential for making individual arrays with up to a million qubits. Neutral atom technology may be extremely useful for providing an interface between photons and other types of qubits, including superconducting qubits [13]. To date, arrays of about 50 atoms have been made, and a 51-atom quantum simulator has been demonstrated [14]. Assuming a typical 5-micron spacing, 10^4 atoms can be trapped in a 0.5 mm two-dimensional (2D) array, and a million atoms can be trapped in a 0.5 mm three-dimensional (3D) array. The qubit states are the energy levels of an alkali atom (often rubidium or cesium), there is one atom per trap, and the qubit manipulation and readout are performed optically.

Like trapped ion systems, lasers are used to cool the atoms to micro-Kelvin temperatures, and then these very cold atoms are loaded into optical traps in a vacuum system. Another laser is used to initialize the state of the qubit, logic gates are carried out via a combination of optical and microwave fields, and the output is detected via resonance fluorescence [15]. In this system there are a number of challenges just to create the starting state of the system:

- *Light-assisted collisions during laser cooling tend to cause atoms to pair and leave the trap.* Vacancies complicate the array's use as a quantum computer. However, recently methods have been developed that take traps with vacancies and reconfigure them to create traps with full occupancy, so this difficulty is not insurmountable.
- *Neutral atoms are vulnerable to being knocked out of their traps by collisions with residual background gas atoms.* In standard systems, these collisions occur about once every 100 seconds per atom. Lifetimes exceeding tens of minutes are possible in cryogenic vacuum systems. Eventually, error correction schemes will need to be employed to deal with this infrequent loss. Atom reloading from an auxiliary reservoir of precooled atoms, which provides a path toward continuous operation, has been demonstrated on a small scale [16].
- *Currently, sideband laser cooling has been used to get about 90 percent of the atoms in a trap in their absolute 3D vibrational ground state.* This is cold enough for most quantum computing schemes, but it is believed that the cooling can be improved significantly; theoretical cooling limits approach 100 percent ground state occupation.

Because single-qubit gate times range from a few to a few hundred microseconds, in principle, on the order of 10^5 operations can be performed within the longest demonstrated decoherence times (these are best-case numbers). Single-qubit gates of low error rates (down to 0.004) have been demonstrated [17]; in experiments the fidelity is limited by inhomogeneities in the microwave field, variability in the trap-induced shifts in qubit transition frequencies, and errors arising from imprecision or imperfections in the laser beam that affect nontargeted sites [18].

The strategies for two-qubit gates are again similar to those for trapped ions. One method requires moving the desired atoms close together; since the atoms are neutral, the spacing must be small, so accurate enough control of moving traps and the motional states of the atoms is challenging. The other method is to temporarily excite the atoms to highly excited Rydberg states (where an electron is very weakly bound to the atom), in which they have strong mutual dipolar interactions. This second approach has been pursued by several groups. Theoretical calculations predict that an entanglement error rate of 0.01 percent should be achievable; as of mid-2018, entanglement error rates of 3 percent have been achieved [19]. Known sources of infidelity such as heating of the atoms and the finite radiative lifetimes of the Rydberg states in current experiments are not sufficient to explain this large value, but it is known that fluctuating background electric fields due to atoms and molecules adsorbed on the container surfaces could yield greater infidelity during two-qubit gates because of the large susceptibility of the Rydberg atoms. This problem could be addressed by the development of appropriate surface coatings. Experimental improvement of the two-qubit gates is critical for this technology to be competitive with superconducting and ion trap qubits.

Ultimate scalability: The trapping mechanism for neutral atoms is different than for trapped ions, but this platform will use similar control and measurement planes. The vision for scaling beyond the number of qubits that can be controlled in a single array is to connect multiple arrays using photonic entanglement, again following the architecture that is being developed for trapped ion systems.

D.3 SEMICONDUCTOR QUBITS

Semiconductor qubits can be divided into two types, depending on whether they are manipulated optically or electrically. Optically gated semiconductor qubits typically use optically active defects or quantum dots that induce strong effective couplings between photons, while electrically gated semiconductor qubits use voltages applied to lithographically defined metal gates to confine and manipulate the electrons that form the qubits, a technology that is very similar to that used for current classical computing electronics. Optically gated semiconducting qubits can be used to implement strong effective interactions with photons, which greatly enhances the capabilities of photonic qubits—for example, by being a mechanism for implementing a quantum memory for optical photons. Electrically gated semiconducting qubits are attractive because the methods used to fabricate and control them are quite similar to those used in classical computing electronics, potentially enabling the large investments that have enabled the tremendous scalability of classical electronics to facilitate the scaling of quantum information processors.

D.3.1 Optically Gated Qubits in Crystals

An optically gated semiconductor qubit is a system in a semiconductor (typically either a defect in a crystal or a quantum dot in a host material) whose optical response depends on the quantum state of that defect/dot. Defect and quantum dot systems have somewhat complementary strengths and weaknesses, but also have many commonalities. Qubits constructed from optically active impurities or quantum dots in semiconductors provide a means of introducing strong nonlinearities into photonic approaches and also have the potential to be transformative for communication and sensing applications.

A defect system that has been the focus of intense interest is the nitrogen-vacancy (NV) center in diamond [20,21]. This defect, which consists of a nitrogen atom substituting for a carbon together with a vacancy, is a paramagnetic center that can be manipulated and measured optically. Initialization, manipulation, and measurements of individual NV centers have been demonstrated [22]. Quantum manipulation has been demonstrated of defect centers in other materials, including vacancies in silicon carbide [23]. Remarkably, quantum coherence in these systems can persist at temperatures as high as room temperature [24]. Because of their quantum coherence at high temperatures and their good biocompatibility, optically active defect centers in semiconductors are expected to have important applications as quantum sensors [25], including for biological applications [26].

Two-qubit gates between these qubits either requires them to be extremely close together [27] (tens of nanometers), which makes optical addressing of the detects extremely hard, or requires them to be coupled using photons [28]. Using photons allows the qubits to be spaced meters apart, but because the interaction between the defects and photons tends to be weak, entanglement-generating gates tend to be slow (typically, many attempts at the entangling operation must be made before one succeeds). While successful gate operation is heralded, the slow entanglement rates complicate attempts to create entanglement between large numbers of qubits.

Optically active quantum dots also have been demonstrated to have promise for applications requiring quantum coherence. Two-qubit gates have been implemented using tunnel couplings between quantum dots [29], and strong coupling between photons and quantum dots has been achieved [30], which is promising for the development of high-fidelity photon-mediated two-qubit gates. Qubit speeds in these systems tend to be very fast, but decoherence rates are also fast. The strong coupling between quantum dots and photons makes them attractive as a mechanism for integration with photonic quantum computing, enabling creation of entangled states of three photons [31] and enabling the implementations of quantum memories for photonic circuits [32].

Materials development will be key to improving optically gated semiconducting qubits. For defect centers in semiconductors, it would be extremely useful to find a defect-material combination in which the couplings between the defect and crystal lattice excitations are very weak, so that essentially all the optical decays do not transfer energy to the crystal lattice. While there has been some important work showing the importance and demonstrating the promise of theoretical techniques for predicting robust qubits in new materials [33], more needs to be done in this area. It is also important to increase the relatively weak coupling between photons and the defects; much recent progress has been enabled by improving control of the optical fields to increase coupling, and further improvements should be possible. This also relates to exploring mechanisms for spin decoherence and strategies to increase quantum coherence times [34]. For quantum dots, a major limitation currently arises from the difficulties in developing well-controlled and reproducible fabrication methods: because the optical properties of a quantum dot depend on its size and shape, uniform and predictable quantum dot sizes are critical.

Ultimate scalability: Because the requirements of ensuring optical access to be able to address each qubit individually places significant constraints on qubit densities, scale-up to very large numbers of qubits in these systems will be challenging. However, they are likely to be very important as interconnects, providing a method to interface material-based qubits with optical photons that can maintain coherence over extremely long distances [35]. In addition, because of sensing applications, systems with moderate numbers of qubits are likely to be important commercially, providing a means of establishing commercial viability of quantum systems as they are scaled up to sizes relevant for information processing applications.

D.3.2 Electrically Gated Semiconductor Qubits

Electrically gated semiconducting quantum computing technologies have the potential to scale up to extremely large number of qubits, because of the qubits' small size and because of the use of fabrication methods very similar to those used in classical electronics. Electrically gated semiconducting qubits are defined and manipulated by applying voltages to lithographically defined metal gates on semiconductor surfaces [36]. The fabrication and lithographic methods are very similar to those used in classical electronics, and the similarity of methods makes it plausible that the large investments that have been made to enable scale-up of classical electronics can be leveraged to facilitate scale-up to very large numbers of qubits.

However, in this platform a significant amount of materials and technique development was required to be able to construct even single qubits, and high-fidelity single-qubit gates have been achieved only relatively recently [37]. Over the past few years, high-fidelity single-qubit gates have been implemented by several groups, and there has been substantial recent progress toward the implementation of high-fidelity two-qubit gates [38], and very recently quantum algorithms have been implemented on a programmable two-qubit quantum processor [39]. A key enabler of these recent advances was the development of new materials systems and lithographic methods that have enabled experimenters to overcome limitations of previous materials platforms and lithography strategies. The first electrically gated semiconducting qubits were fabricated in heterostructures of gallium arsenide and aluminum gallium arsenide [40], but in this materials system the decohering effects of the nuclear spins in the host material greatly complicated the implementation of high-fidelity gate operations. The development of qubits in silicon-based structures [41-43] has greatly reduced decoherence from nuclear spins, because natural silicon has an abundant zero-spin nuclear isotope, and isotopically enriched silicon in which more than 99 percent of the nuclei have spin zero has recently become available, which has led to further substantial increases in the coherence times [44]. Another important development was the development of new device designs that enabled more compact gate patterns and also enabled a transition from doped to accumulation-mode devices. These changes enabled the fabrication of devices with small (~25 nm) dots with reasonable device yields.

The current challenge for the field is the development of reliable and high-fidelity two-qubit gates. Current two-qubit gate error rates [45-48] are about 10 percent, and further improvements are needed to achieve fault-tolerant operation. Currently, charge noise in these devices limits gate coherence, but recent work points to strategies that are expected to enable high-fidelity gating in the near term [49-52]. Recent progress has been rapid, but it is constrained by the mediocre fabrication yields in current university-based fabrication facilities of the complex multilayer gate patterns separated by very thin oxide layers. Fabrication yields are expected to improve rapidly with the recent entry into this area by industry, including HRL Laboratories and Intel, and by participation by Department of Energy (DOE) laboratories such as Sandia National Laboratories.

In principle, electrically gated semiconducting qubits have the potential for scalability to billions of qubits, because the methods used for fabrication are so similar to those used for classical electronics and the qubit footprints are substantially less than a square micron. In practice, in addition to developing two-qubit gates with the requisite fidelities, measurement fidelities need to be improved and the measurement methods need to be made compatible with large-scale qubit arrays. Also, because of similarities in the cooling requirements, the control strategies, and the frequency range of the qubit control voltages with those of superconducting qubits, it will be necessary to overcome crosstalk and fanout issues similar to those faced by the superconducting qubit community. These issues will be especially challenging in this system, since the small spacing between the qubits will exacerbate the coupling between wires, and it will be harder to create scalable control/measurement layers that can interface with the qubits.

D.4 TOPOLOGICAL QUBITS

Development of topological quantum computing architectures is an approach for constructing qubits that could plausibly achieve extremely low intrinsic error rates so that implementation of error correction using logical qubits would not be necessary or would at least enable error correction with substantially less overhead. If successful, this approach would greatly reduce the number physical qubits needed to achieve the computational power to solve problems that are not tractable on classical computers compared to other approaches. Thus, it could be a promising path to scaling for a quantum computer.

Topological quantum computation enables operations on the physical qubits to have extremely high fidelities because the qubit operations are protected by topological symmetry implemented at the microscopic level. Topological protection of quantum information is also the basis underlying the surface code, so one can view topological quantum computation as the implementation of the error-correction mechanism into the microscopic physics instead of by application of an error-correction algorithm on nontopological qubits. The potential to achieve the extremely high fidelities required to solve commercially interesting problems that are intractable on classical computers without the need to incur the large overheads involved in error correction is a strong motivation for the significant investments in this strategy for quantum computation by companies like Microsoft. However, the committee notes that the technology is significantly less developed than the others described in this report: there are nontrivial steps to demonstrating even the capability of single-qubit operations experimentally at the time of the writing of this report (2018) [53].

To implement topological quantum computation, one must construct a system in which there is a large number of degenerate ground states that cannot be obtained from each other from local changes. A simple example relevant to current efforts to implement topological quantum computation experimentally is shown in Figure D.1. This figure illustrates

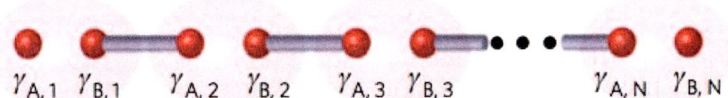

FIGURE D.1 Schematic of a one-dimensional (1D) system supporting Majorana zero modes. Each spinless fermion decomposes into two Majorana fermions, one on each site (denoted by γ's and shown in red). The Majoranas pair in the bulk (denoted by the thick lines connecting them), leaving two zero-energy Majorana modes at the ends of the chain. The large spatial separation between the two ends underlies the resistance to decoherence of quantum computing implemented in this architecture. SOURCE: J. Alicea, Y. Oreg, G. Refael, F. von Oppen, and M.P.A. Fisher, 2011, Non-Abelian statistics and topological quantum information processing in 1D wire networks, *Nature Physics* 7(5):412-417.

that there are systems of spinless fermions whose ground states can be viewed as collections of Majorana fermions paired on neighboring sites, with two "leftover" sites on the ends. The unpaired Majorana fermions can be arbitrarily far apart, and recombining them requires modifying the quantum state of the entire length of the system, which makes the excitations extremely resistant to local perturbations.

The interest in developing materials systems that can support Majorana zero modes was sparked by Kitaev's work (2003) showing that a quantum computer can be constructed if these topological excitations could be constructed and manipulated appropriately [54]. Much work has been done to make the construction of an appropriate system more feasible experimentally, with recent work demonstrating that quantum computation can be implemented if arrays of nanowires of a material with strong spin-orbit coupling that are strongly coupled to superconducting films where the single-particle excitations are highly suppressed can be constructed and measured [55]. While experimental demonstration of non-trivial manipulation of Majorana zero modes has not yet been achieved, the evidence that such nanowires have excitations at the nanowire ends that exhibit interactions that decay exponentially with the wire length is very strong [56]. Given a well-controlled materials system that supports Majorana zero modes, there is expected to be a reasonably straightforward experimental path toward the demonstration of the performance of a nontrivial qubit operation [57]. However, substantial materials and fabrication challenges remain in order to do so. Some of the complexities that must be dealt with are that the excitations on the superconducting nanowires are measured via coupling to nonsuperconducting quantum dots, and the couplings between these dissimilar systems must be well controlled and tunable to implement the necessary operations.

Once successful nontrivial manipulation and measurement of Majorana zero modes has been demonstrated experimentally, it will be possible to determine whether the excellent fidelities that have been predicted theoretically are indeed achieved in experiment. If experimentally measured fidelities do indeed improve exponentially with the length of the nanowires on the expected length scale of microns, then nanowires with modest lengths could yield gates with extremely high fidelities.

It should be noted that, similar to proposed implementations of the surface code, implementation of Clifford gates is expected to be significantly more straightforward than the realization of an additional gate (often called the "T gate") necessary to implement universal quantum computation. Recent theoretical work predicts that high-fidelity T gates are achievable using the same hardware architecture as that used for the Clifford gates [58], but the implementation of these gates is an additional step necessary for the implementation of a universal quantum computer using this technology.

As discussed above, significant materials, fabrication, and measurement challenges must be overcome to demonstrate even single-qubit gates of a topological quantum computer. However, the possibility of being able to implement extremely high fidelity gates that do not require error correction, or require very little error correction, is strong motivation to pursue this approach, partly because of the challenges that arise in the implementation of quantum error correction and partly because the necessary processor sizes would be much smaller than those needed for error-corrected architectures.

D.5 NOTES

[1] J. Yin, Y. Cao, Y.-H. Li, S.-K. Liao, L. Zhang, J.-G. Ren, W.-Q. Cai, et al., 2017, Satellite-based entanglement distribution over 1200 kilometers, *Science* 356:1140-1144.

[2] S.J. Freedman and J.F. Clauser, 1972, Experimental test of local hidden-variable theories, *Physical Review Letters* 28:938-941.

[3] J.W. Silverstone, D. Bonneau, J.L. O'Brien, and M.G. Thompson, 2016, Silicon quantum photonics, *IEEE Journal of Selected Topics in Quantum Electronics* 22: 390-402.

[4] E. Knill, R. Laflamme, and G. J. Milburn, 2001, A scheme for efficient quantum computation with linear optics, *Nature* 409:46-52.

[5] T. Rudolph, 2017, Why I am optimistic about the silicon-photonic route to quantum computing, *APL Photonics* 2:030901.

[6] M.K. Akhlaghi, E. Schelew, and J.F. Young, 2015, Waveguide integrated superconducting single-photon detectors implemented as near-perfect absorbers of coherent radiation, *Nature Communications* 6:8233.

[7] T. Rudolph, 2017, Why I am optimistic about the silicon-photonic route to quantum computing, *APL Photonics* 2:030901.

[8] M. Khoshnegar, T. Huber, A. Predojević, D. Dalacu, M. Prilmüller, J. Lapointe, X. Wu, P. Tamarat, B. Lounis, P. Poole, G. Weihs, and H. Majedi, 2017, A solid state source of photon triplets based on quantum dot molecules, *Nature Communications* 8:15716.

[9] X.-L. Wang, Y-H. Luo, H.-L. Huang, M.-C. Chen, Z.-E. Su, C. Liu, C. Chen, et al., 2018, 18-qubit entanglement with six photons' three degrees of freedom, *Physical Review Letters*, doi:10.1103/PhysRevLett.120.260502.

[10] See, for example, J.W. Silverstone, D. Bonneau, J.L. O'Brien, and M.G. Thompson, 2016, Silicon quantum photonics, *IEEE Journal of Selected Topics in Quantum Electronics* 22:390-402;

T. Rudolph, 2017, Why I am optimistic about the silicon-photonic route to quantum computing," *APL Photonics* 2:030901.

[11] M. Saffman, 2016, Quantum computing with atomic qubits and Rydberg interactions: Progress and challenges, *Journal of Physical B* 49:202001.

[12] D.S. Weiss, and M. Saffman, 2017, Quantum computing with neutral atoms, *Physics Today* 70:44.

[13] J.D. Pritchard, J.A. Isaacs, M.A. Beck, R. McDermott, and M. Saffman 2014, Hybrid atom-photon quantum gate in a superconducting microwave resonator, *Physical Review A* 89:01031.

[14] H. Bernien, S. Schwartz, A. Keesling, H. Levine, A. Omran, H. Pichler, S. Choi, et al., 2017, "Probing Many-Body Dynamics on a 51-Atom Quantum Simulator," preprint arXiv:1707.04344.

[15] M. Saffman, 2016, Quantum computing with atomic qubits and Rydberg interactions: Progress and challenges, *Journal of Physical B* 49:202001.

[16] B.A. Dinardo and D.Z. Anderson, 2016, A technique for individual atom delivery into a crossed vortex bottle beam trap using a dynamic 1D optical lattice, *Review of Scientific Instruments* 87:123108.

[17] T. Xia, M. Lichtman, K. Maller, A.W. Carr, M.J. Piotrowicz, L. Isenhower, and M. Saffman, 2015, Randomized benchmarking of single-qubit gates in a 2D array of neutral-atom qubits, *Physical Review Letters* 114:100503.

[18] M. Saffman, 2016, Quantum computing with atomic qubits and Rydberg interactions: Progress and challenges, *Journal of Physical B* 49:202001.

[19] H. Levine, A. Keesling, A. Omran, H. Bernien, S. Schwartz, A.S. Zibrov, M. Endres, M. Greiner, V. Vuletić, and M.D. Lukin, 2018, "High-Fidelity Control and Entanglement of Rydberg Atom Qubits," preprint arXiv:1806.04682.

[20] M.W. Doherty, N.B. Manson, P. Delaney, F. Jelezko, J. Wrachtrup, and L.C.L. Hollenberg, 2013, The nitrogen-vacancy colour centre in diamond, *Physics Reports* 528:1-45.

[21] V.V. Dobrovitski, G.D. Fuchs, A.L. Falk, C. Santori, and D.D. Awschalom, 2013, Quantum control over single spins in diamond, *Annual Review of Condensed Matter Physics* 4:23-50.

[22] T. Gaebel, M. Domhan, I. Popa, C. Wittmann, P. Neumann, F. Jelezko, J.R. Rabeau, et al., 2006, Room-temperature coherent coupling of single spins in diamond, *Nature Physics* 2:408-413.

[23] W.F. Koehl, B.B. Buckley, F.J. Heremans, G. Calusine, and D.D. Awschalom, 2011, Room temperature coherent control of defect spin qubits in silicon carbide, *Nature* 479:84-88.

[24] See, for example, T. Gaebel, M. Domhan, I. Popa, C. Wittmann, P. Neumann, F. Jelezko, J.R. Rabeau, et al., 2006, Room-temperature coherent coupling of single spins in diamond, *Nature Physics* 2:408-413;

W.F. Koehl, B.B. Buckley, F.J. Heremans, G. Calusine, and D.D. Awschalom, 2011, Room temperature coherent control of defect spin qubits in silicon carbide, *Nature* 479:84-88.

[25] J.M. Taylor, P. Cappellaro, L. Childress, L. Jiang, D. Budker, P.R. Hemmer, A. Yacoby, R. Walsworth, and M.D. Lukin, 2008, High-sensitivity diamond magnetometer with nanoscale resolution, *Nature Physics* 4:810-816.

[26] D. Le Sage, K. Arai, D.R. Glenn, S.J. DeVience, L.M. Pham, L. Rahn-Lee, M.D. Lukin, A. Yacoby, A. Komeili, and R.L. Walsworth, 2013, Optical magnetic imaging of living cells, *Nature* 496:486-489.

[27] F. Dolde, I. Jakobi, B. Naydenov, N. Zhao, S. Pezzagna, C. Trautmann, J. Meijer, P. Neumann, F. Jelezko, and J. Wrachtrup, 2013, Room-temperature entanglement between single defect spins in diamond, *Nature Physics* 9:139-143.

[28] H. Bernien, B. Hensen, W. Pfaff, G. Koolstra, M.S. Blok, L. Robledo, T.H. Taminiau, M. Markham, D.J. Twitchen, L. Childress, and R. Hanson, 2013, Heralded entanglement between solid-state qubits separated by three metres, *Nature* 497:86-90.

[29] D. Kim, S.G. Carter, A. Greilich, A.S. Bracker, and D. Gammon, 2011, Ultrafast optical control of entanglement between two quantum-dot spins, *Nature Physics* 7:223-229.

[30] K. Müller, A. Rundquist, K.A. Fischer, T. Sarmiento, K.G. Lagoudakis, Y.A. Kelaita, C. Sánchez Muñoz, E. del Valle, F.P. Laussy, and J. Vučković, 2015, Coherent generation of nonclassical light on chip via detuned photon blockade, *Physical Review Letters* 114:233601.

[31] M. Khoshnegar, T. Huber, A. Predojević, D. Dalacu, M. Prilmüller, J. Lapointe, X. Wu, P. Tamarat, B. Lounis, P. Poole, G. Weihs, and H. Majedi, 2017, A solid state source of photon triplets based on quantum dot molecules, *Nature Communications* 8:15716.

[32] K. Heshami, D.G. England, P.C. Humphreys, P.J. Bustard, V.M. Acosta, J. Nunn, and B.J. Sussman, 2016, Quantum memories: Emerging applications and recent advances, *Journal of Modern Optics* 63:S42-S65.

[33] J.R. Weber, W.F. Koehl, J.B. Varley, A. Janotti, B.B. Buckley, C.G. Van de Walle, and D.D. Awschalom, 2010, Quantum computing with defects, *Proceedings of the National Academy of Sciences of the U.S.A.* 8513-8518.

[34] H. Seo, A.L. Falk, P.V. Klimov, K.C. Miao, G. Galli, and D.D. Awschalom, 2016, Quantum decoherence dynamics of divacancy spins in silicon carbide, *Nature Communications* 7:12935.

[35] J. Yin, Y. Cao, Y.-H. Li, S.-K. Liao, L. Zhang, J.-G. Ren, W.-Q. Cai, et al., 2017, Satellite-based entanglement distribution over 1200 kilometers, *Science* 356:1140-1144.

[36] D. Loss and D.P. DiVincenzo, 1998, Quantum computation with quantum dots, *Physical Review A* 57:120-126.

[37] J.J. Pla, K.Y. Tan, J.P. Dehollain, W.H. Lim, J.J. Morton, D.N. Jamieson, A.S. Dzurak, and A. Morello, 2012, A single-atom electron spin qubit in silicon, *Nature* 489:541-545.

[38] See, for example, M. Veldhorst, C.H. Yang, J.C.C. Hwang, W. Huang, J.P. Dehollain, J.T. Muhonen, S. Simmons, A. Laucht, F.E. Hudson, K.M. Itoh, A. Morello, and A.S. Dzurak, 2015, A two-qubit logic gate in silicon, *Nature* 526:410-414;

J.M. Nichol, L.A. Orona, S.P. Harvey, S. Fallahi, G.C. Gardner, M.J. Manfra, and A. Yacoby, 2017, High-fidelity entangling gate for double-quantum-dot spin qubits, *npj Quantum Information* 3:3;

D.M. Zajac, A.J. Sigillito, M. Russ, F. Borjans, J.M. Taylor, G. Burkard, and J. R. Petta, 2017, "Quantum CNOT Gate for Spins in Silicon," preprint arXiv:1708.03530.

[39] T.F. Watson, S.G.J. Philips, E. Kawakami, D.R. Ward, P. Scarlino, M. Veldhorst, D.E. Savage, M.G. Lagally, M. Friesen, S.N. Coppersmith, M.A. Eriksson, L.M.K. Vandersypen, 2017, "A Programmable Two-Qubit Quantum Processor in Silicon," preprint arXiv:1708.04214.

[40] See, for example, J.R. Petta, A.C. Johnson, J.M. Taylor, E.A. Laird, A. Yacoby, M.D. Lukin, C.M. Marcus, M.P. Hanson, and A.C. Gossard, 2005, Coherent manipulation of coupled electron spins in semiconductor quantum dots, *Science* 309:2180-2184;

M.D. Shulman, O.E. Dial, S. Pasca Harvey, H. Bluhm, V. Umansky, and A. Yacoby, 2012, Demonstration of entanglement of electrostatically coupled singlet-triplet qubits, *Science* 336:202-205.

[41] J.J. Pla, K.Y. Tan, J.P. Dehollain, W.H. Lim, J.J. Morton, D.N. Jamieson, A.S. Dzurak, and A. Morello, 2012, A single-atom electron spin qubit in silicon, *Nature* 489:541-545.

[42] F.A. Zwanenburg, A.S. Dzurak, A. Morello, M.Y. Simmons, L.C.L. Hollenberg, G. Klimeck, S. Rogge, S.N. Coppersmith, and M.A. Eriksson, 2013, Silicon quantum electronics, *Reviews of Modern Physics* 85:961-1019.

[43] D. Kim, Z. Shi, C.B. Simmons, D.R. Ward, J.R. Prance, T. Seng Koh, J. King Gamble, D.E. Savage, M.G. Lagally, M. Friesen, S.N. Coppersmith, and M.A. Eriksson, 2014, Quantum control and process tomography of a semiconductor quantum dot hybrid qubit, *Nature* 511:70-74.

[44] M. Veldhorst, C.H. Yang, J.C.C. Hwang, W. Huang, J.P. Dehollain, J.T. Muhonen, S. Simmons, A. Laucht, F.E. Hudson, K.M. Itoh, A. Morello, and A.S. Dzurak, 2015, A two-qubit logic gate in silicon, *Nature* 526:410-414.

[45] J.M. Nichol, L.A. Orona, S.P. Harvey, S. Fallahi, G.C. Gardner, M.J. Manfra, and A. Yacoby, 2017, High-fidelity entangling gate for double-quantum-dot spin qubits, *npj Quantum Information* 3:3.

[46] M. Veldhorst, C.H. Yang, J.C.C. Hwang, W. Huang, J.P. Dehollain, J.T. Muhonen, S. Simmons, A. Laucht, F.E. Hudson, K.M. Itoh, A. Morello, and A.S. Dzurak, 2015, A two-qubit logic gate in silicon, *Nature* 526:410-414.

[47] T.F. Watson, S.G.J. Philips, E. Kawakami, D.R. Ward, P. Scarlino, M. Veldhorst, D.E. Savage, M.G. Lagally, M. Friesen, S.N. Coppersmith, M.A. Eriksson, L.M.K. Vandersypen, 2017, "A Programmable Two-Qubit Quantum Processor in Silicon," preprint arXiv:1708.04214.

[48] D.M. Zajac, A.J. Sigillito, M. Russ, F. Borjans, J.M. Taylor, G. Burkard, and J.R. Petta, 2017, "Quantum CNOT Gate for Spins in Silicon," preprint arXiv:1708.03530.

[49] J.M. Nichol, L.A. Orona, S.P. Harvey, S. Fallahi, G.C. Gardner, M.J. Manfra, and A. Yacoby, 2017, High-fidelity entangling gate for double-quantum-dot spin qubits, *npj Quantum Information* 3:3.

[50] M.D. Reed, B.M. Maune, R.W. Andrews, M.G. Borselli, K. Eng, M.P. Jura, A.A. Kiselev, T.D. Ladd, S.T. Merkel, I. Milosavljevic, and E.J. Pritchett, 2016, Reduced sensitivity to charge noise in semiconductor spin qubits via symmetric operation, *Physical Review Letters* 116(11):110402.

[51] F. Martins, F.K. Malinowski, P.D. Nissen, E. Barnes, S. Fallahi, G.C. Gardner, M.J. Manfra, C.M. Marcus, and F. Kuemmeth, 2016, Noise suppression using symmetric exchange gates in spin qubits, *Physical Review Letters* 116:116801.

[52] T. F. Watson, S.G.J. Philips, E. Kawakami, D.R. Ward, P. Scarlino, M. Veldhorst, D.E. Savage, M.G. Lagally, M. Friesen, S.N. Coppersmith, M.A. Eriksson, and L.M.K. Vandersypen, 2017, "A Programmable Two-Qubit Quantum Processor in Silicon," preprint arXiv:1708.04214.

[53] R.M. Lutchyn, E.P.A.M. Bakkers, L.P. Kouwenhoven, P. Krogstrup, C.M. Marcus, and Y. Oreg , 2017, "Realizing Majorana Zero Modes in Superconductor-Semiconductor Heterostructures," preprint arXiv:1707.04899.

[54] A.Y. Kitaev, 2003, Fault-tolerant quantum computation by anyons, *Annals of Physics* 303:2-30.

[55] T. Karzig, C. Knapp, R.M. Lutchyn, P. Bonderson, M.B. Hastings, C. Nayak, J. Alicea, K. Flensberg, S.Plugge, Y. Oreg, C.M. Marcus, and M.H. Freedman, 2017, Scalable designs for quasiparticle-poisoning-protected topological quantum computation with Majorana zero modes, *Physical Review B* 95:235305.

[56] M.T. Deng, S. Vaitiek nas, E.B. Hansen, J. Danon, M. Leijnse, K. Flensberg, J. Nygård, P. Krogstrup, and C.M. Marcus, 2016, Majorana bound state in a coupled quantum-dot hybrid-nanowire system, *Science* 354:1557-1562.

[57] T. Karzig, C. Knapp, R.M. Lutchyn, P. Bonderson, M.B. Hastings, C. Nayak, J. Alicea, K. Flensberg, S. Plugge, Y. Oreg, C.M. Marcus, and M.H. Freedman, 2017, Scalable designs for quasiparticle-poisoning-protected topological quantum computation with Majorana zero modes, *Physical Review B* 95:235305.

[58] J. Haah, M.B. Hastings, D. Poulin, and D. Wecker, 2017, "Magic State Distillation with Low Space Overhead and Optimal Asymptotic Input Count," preprint arXiv:1703.07847.

E

Global R&D Investment

A recent bibliometric analysis conducted by researchers at the Naval Surface Warfare Center's Dahlgren Division provides a time series look at the public-facing research output by nation (Figure E.1). According to this analysis, U.S. institutions have produced more research papers in quantum computing and quantum algorithms than any nation overall, and for every year since 1996. However, efforts from Chinese researchers rose significantly after 2006, with the two countries far outpacing all other countries each year since 2012. When including post-quantum cryptography and quantum key distribution, China's output has surpassed that of the United States in the number of papers produced each year since (although U.S. publications remain more heavily cited).

Several noteworthy non-U.S. national-level programs and initiatives in quantum science and technology have recently been announced, which may reshape the research landscape in years to come. These initiatives, summarized in Table 7.2, illustrate the commitment of the corresponding governments to leadership in quantum science and engineering writ large. In general, they span a range of fields under quantum science and technology and are not focused on quantum computing exclusively.

E.1 THE EU QUANTUM TECHNOLOGIES FLAGSHIP

The European Union (EU) has supported research in quantum science and technology for more than 20 years, with a cumulative budget of around €550 million through its Framework Programmes for Research

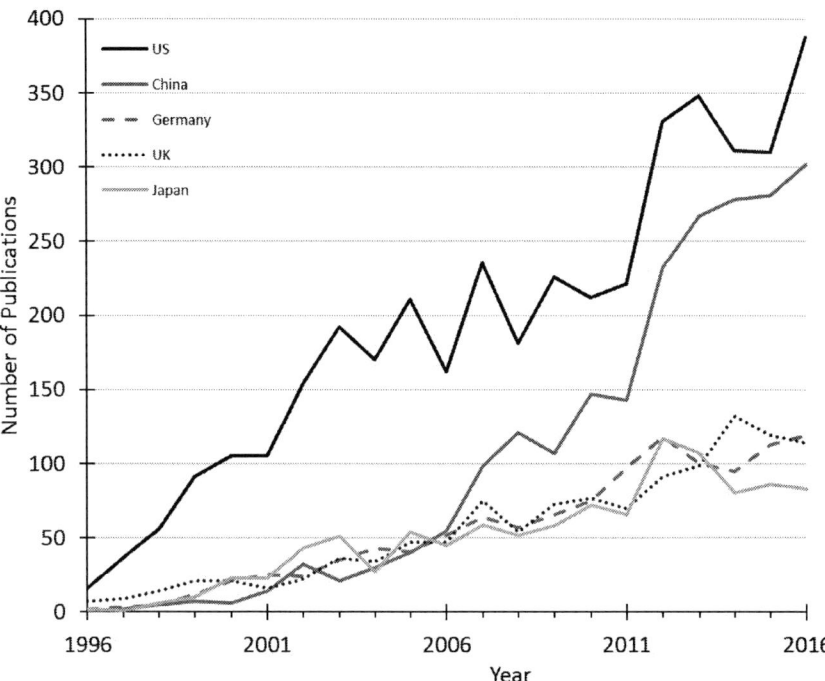

FIGURE E.1 Number of papers published by nation of origin for top five global producers in quantum computing and algorithms. Includes only research publications that are accessible to the public. Data are the result of a bibliometric analysis conducted by a team at the Naval Surface Warfare Center Dahlgren Division. SOURCE: Data courtesy of Jacob Farinholt.

and Development. In 2016, a strategy for research and development in quantum technology (the "Quantum Manifesto") signed by more than 3,000 individuals from academia, industry, and governments was presented to the European Commission (EC). Soon after, in line with this strategy, the EC announced plans for an ambitious €1 billion, 10-year flagship research program on quantum technologies to begin in 2018 as part of the EC's Horizon 2020 research initiative. Funding for this coordinated program will come from Horizon 2020 and other EU and national sources. The manifesto and follow-on planning documents identify four major areas for R&D: quantum communication, computation, simulation, and sensing and metrology. Each area is to be addressed across three dimensions: education/training, software/theory, and engineering/control. The first call for proposals under this initiative was published in October 2017, targeting five areas: collaborative research projects that span at least three different institutions in at least three European countries, each eligible for funding up to €130 million [1,2].

Underneath this flagship, additional, nation-specific programs have emerged. For example, the Swedish Wallenberg Centre for Quantum Technology was announced in 2017 and is sponsored by the Knut and Alice Wallenberg Foundation (SEK600 million) and industrial sources (SEK400 million). Its objectives include those of the EU Flagship program, with a 10-year core goal of developing a 100-qubit superconducting quantum computer. The program spans four universities, includes a dedicated graduate school, and aims to recruit new faculty and research scientists to establish a quantum workforce that will persist after the program expires [3,4].

E.2 THE UK NATIONAL QUANTUM TECHNOLOGIES PROGRAM

In 2014, the United Kingdom's Engineering and Physical Sciences Research Council launched a coordinated national initiative to support and accelerate the development of quantum technologies. The UK National Quantum Technologies Program, funded at a level of £270 million over 5 years, includes an emphasis in quantum sensors and metrology, quantum enhanced imaging, networked quantum information technologies, and quantum communications technologies. While research in quantum science continues under established funding mechanisms, the program is designed specifically to transform scientific output into practical technologies with beneficial applications and establish U.K. leadership in the field. The initiative is governed by a strategic advisory board with international membership, which meets three times annually to oversee and coordinate program activities and engage in roadmapping and visioning for future technologies, and a programme operations group, which meets six times annually to facilitate coordination among government agencies [5].

E.3 THE AUSTRALIAN CENTRE FOR QUANTUM COMPUTING AND COMMUNICATION TECHNOLOGY

In 2017, the Australian Research Council (ARC) funded the Centre for Quantum Computation and Communication Technologies through its Centre of Excellence Program. Funded at a level of $33.7 million over seven years and led by the University of New South Wales, the centre emphasizes research in the areas of quantum communication, optical quantum computing, silicon quantum computing, and quantum resources and integration. The centre includes facilities at six Australian universities, and formal collaborations and partnerships with universities abroad. In addition to development of component technologies, the centre is also focused on frameworks for scaling, integrating, and bringing quantum technologies to market, including a vision for developing a quantum Internet.

E.4 THE CHINESE QUANTUM NATIONAL LABORATORY FOR QUANTUM INFORMATION SCIENCE

Many recent news articles have highlighted progress by researchers in China in the areas of quantum communication and quantum cryptography. Demonstration of quantum communications via satellites and long-path optical fibers have received much attention. An intercity channel to enable quantum key distribution (QKD) has been established between Beijing and Shanghai. QKD has recently been deployed internationally for the first time using satellite as well as ground connections, with what has been billed as the first quantum-encrypted video teleconference between China and Vienna. While the communication route reportedly included several security weaknesses and classical stopovers, it was the first demonstrated use of QKD for intercontinental communications [6].

In addition to reported advances in quantum communications, China announced in 2017 plans to build a centralized National Laboratory for Quantum Information Science in Hefei, Anhui province, with an expected completion time frame of 2.5 years. While the effort is expected to span a range of potential applications of quantum technology, quantum metrology and quantum computing were emphasized. A goal of 2020 for achieving quantum supremacy has been announced [7].

E.5 NOTES

[1] A. Acín, I. Bloch, H. Buhrman, T. Calarco, C. Eichler, J. Eisert, D. Esteve, et al., 2017, "The European Quantum Technologies Roadmap," arXiv:1712.03773.
[2] European Commission, 2016, "European Commission Will Launch €1 Billion Quantum Technologies Flagship," May 17, https://ec.europa.eu/digital-single-market/en/news/european-commission-will-launch-eu1-billion-quantum-technologies-flagship.
[3] Chalmers University of Technology, 2017, "Engineering of a Swedish Quantum Computer Set to Start," *EurekAlert!*, November 15, https://www.eurekalert.org/pub_releases/2017-11/cuot-eoa111417.php.
[4] Chalmers University of Technology, 2017, "Research Programme Description: Wallenberg Centre for Quantum Technology," Chalmers University of Technology, http://www.chalmers.se/en/news/Documents/programme_description_WCQT_171114_eng.pdf.
[5] U.K. National Quantum Technologies Programme, "Overview of Programme," updated 2018, http://uknqt.epsrc.ac.uk/about/overview-of-programme/.
[6] S. Chen, 2018, "Why This Intercontinental Quantum-Encrypted Video Hangout Is a Big Deal," *Wired.com*, January 20, https://www.wired.com/story/why-this-intercontinental-quantum-encrypted-video-hangout-is-a-big-deal/.
[7] S. Chen, 2017, "China Building World's Biggest Quantum Research Facility," *South China Morning Post*, September 11, http://www.scmp.com/news/china/society/article/2110563/china-building-worlds-biggest-quantum-research-facility.

F

Committee and Staff Biographical Information

COMMITTEE

MARK A. HOROWITZ, *Chair*, is the Yahoo! Founders Professor at Stanford University and was chair of the Electrical Engineering Department from 2008 to 2012. He received his B.S. and M.S. in electrical engineering from Massachusetts Institute of Technology in 1978, and his Ph.D. from Stanford University in 1984. Dr. Horowitz is a fellow of the Institute of Electrical and Electronics Engineers (IEEE) and the Association for Computing Machinery (ACM) and is a member of the American Academy of Arts and Science. He has received many awards, including a 1985 Presidential Young Investigator Award, the 1993 ISSCC Best Paper Award, the ISCA 2004 Most Influential Paper of 1989, the 2006 Don Pederson IEEE Technical Field Award, the 2011 SIA Faculty Researcher Award, and the ChipEx Global Leadership Award in 2015. Dr. Horowitz's research interests are quite broad and span using electrical engineering and computer science analysis methods to problems in molecular biology to creating new design methodologies for analog and digital Very Large Scale Integration (VLSI) circuits. He has worked on many processor designs, from early reduced instruction set computer (RISC) chips to creating some of the first distributed shared memory multiprocessors, and is currently working on creating very power efficient systems using specialized accelerators. Recently he has worked on a number of problems in computational photography. In 1990, he took leave from Stanford to help start Rambus, Inc., a company designing high-bandwidth memory interface technology, and his work at both Rambus and Stanford drove high-speed I/O for over a decade.

ALÁN ASPURU-GUZIK is currently a Canada 150 Research Chair in quantum chemistry and a professor of chemistry and computer science at the University of Toronto. He is also a faculty member of the Vector Institute for Artificial Intelligence and a CIFAR senior fellow. Dr. Aspuru-Guzik was a professor of chemistry and chemical biology at Harvard University, where he started his independent career in 2006 and was promoted to associate professor in 2010 and full professor from 2013 to 2018. Dr. Aspuru-Guzik received his undergraduate degree in chemistry from the National Autonomous University of Mexico (UNAM) in 1999. He received the Gabino Barreda Medal from UNAM, which prizes the top achiever in each field of study. After receiving his Ph.D. in physical chemistry from the University of California, Berkeley, in 2004, under Professor William A. Lester Jr., he was a postdoctoral scholar in the group of Martin Head-Gordon at the University of California, Berkeley, from 2005-2006. Professor Aspuru-Guzik carries out research at the interface of computer science, physics, and chemistry. In particular, he has pioneered the interface of quantum information and chemistry, with special focus on early applications of quantum computers such as dedicated quantum simulators for chemical systems. Dr. Aspuru-Guzik carries out research on materials acceleration platforms, which integrate artificial intelligence, high-throughput quantum chemical screening, and robotics to accelerate materials discovery. Applications include organic semiconductors, photovoltaics, organic batteries, and organic light-emitting diodes. In 2009, Professor Aspuru-Guzik received the DARPA Young Faculty Award, the Camille and Henry Dreyfus Teacher-Scholar Award and the Sloan Research Fellowship. In 2010, he received the Everett-Mendelsohn Graduate Mentoring Award and received the HP Outstanding Junior Faculty Award from the Computers in Chemistry Division of the American Chemical Society (ACS). In the same year, he was selected as a Top Innovator under 35 by the *Massachusetts Institute of Technology Review* magazine. In 2012, he was elected as a fellow of the American Physical Society (APS), and in 2013, he received the ACS Early Career Award in Theoretical Chemistry. He is associate editor of the journal *Chemical Science*.

DAVID D. AWSCHALOM is Liew Family Professor in Spintronics and Quantum Information and deputy director at the Institute for Molecular Engineering (IME) at the University of Chicago. He was a research staff member and manager of the Nonequilibrium Physics Department at the IBM Watson Research Center in Yorktown Heights, New York. In 1991, Dr, Awschalom joined the University of California, Santa Barbara, as a professor of physics, and in 2001 was additionally appointed as a professor of electrical and computer engineering. Prior to joining IME, he served as the Peter J. Clarke Professor and director of the California NanoSystems Institute and as director of the Center for Spintronics and Quantum Computation. Professor Awschalom received the APS Oliver E. Buckley Prize and Julius Edgar Lilienfeld Prize, the European Physical Society Europhysics Prize, the Materials Research Society David Turnbull Award and Outstanding Investigator Prize, the American Association for the Advancement of Science (AAAS) Newcomb Cleveland Prize, the International Magnetism Prize and the Néel Medal from the International Union of Pure and Applied Physics, and an IBM Outstanding Innovation Award. He is a member of the American Academy of Arts and Sciences, the National Academy of Sciences (NAS), the National Academy of Engineering, and the European Academy of Sciences. Dr. Awschalom received his B.Sc. in physics from the University of Illinois, Urbana-Champaign, and his Ph.D. in experimental physics from Cornell University.

BOB BLAKLEY is the global director of information security innovation at Citigroup. He recently served as plenary chair of the National Strategy for Trusted Identities in Cyberspace Identity Ecosystem Steering Group and as research and development co-chair of the Financial Services Sector Coordinating Council for Critical Infrastructure Protection and Homeland Security. He is currently a member of the Forum on Cyber Resilience— a National Academies of Sciences, Engineering, and Medicine roundtable. Prior to joining Citigroup, Dr. Blakley was distinguished analyst and agenda manager for identity and privacy at Gartner and Burton Group. Before that, he was chief scientist for security and privacy at IBM. He is past general chair of the IEEE Security and Privacy Symposium and the Annual Computer Security Applications (ACSA) New Security Paradigms workshop. He was awarded the ACSAC Distinguished Security Practitioner Award in 2002, and is a frequent speaker at information security and computer industry events. Dr. Blakley was general editor of the Open Management Group CORBASecurity specification and the OASIS SAML specification, and is the author of *CORBASecurity: An Introduction to Safe Computing with Objects*. He was the first chair of the OATH Joint Coordinating Committee. He also participated in the National Academies studies on "Authentication Technologies and Their Privacy Implications" and "Whither Biometrics." Dr. Blakley holds 20 patents in cryptography and information security, and he publishes regularly in the academic literature on information security and privacy. He received an A.B. in classics from Princeton University, and a M.S. and Ph.D. in computer and communications science from the University of Michigan.

DAN BONEH is a professor of computer science and heads the applied cryptography group at Stanford University, where he has been on the faculty since 1997. Dr. Boneh's research focuses on applications of cryptography to computer security. His work includes cryptosystems with novel properties, Web security, security for mobile devices, digital copyright protection, and cryptanalysis. He is the author of over a hundred publications in the field and a recipient of the Packard Award, the Alfred P. Sloan Award, and the RSA award in mathematics. In 2011, Dr. Boneh received the Ishii Award for industry education innovation. Professor Boneh received his Ph.D. in computer science from Princeton University.

SUSAN COPPERSMITH is the Robert E. Fassnacht and a Vilas Research Professor of Physics at the University of Wisconsin, Madison. She is a theoretical condensed matter physicist who has worked on a broad range of problems in the area of complex systems and has made substantial contributions to the understanding of subjects including glasses, granular materials, the nonlinear dynamics of magnetic flux lattices in type-II superconductors, and quantum computing. Dr. Coppersmith has served as chair of the University of Wisconsin, Madison, Physics Department, as a member of the NORDITA advisory board, as a member of the Mathematical and Physical Science Advisory Committee of the National Science Foundation, and as a trustee at the Aspen Center for Physics. She has served as chair of the Division of Condensed Matter Physics of the APS, chair of the Section on Physics of the AAAS, chair of the board of trustees of the Gordon Research Conferences, and chair of the External Advisory Board of the Kavli Institute for Theoretical Physics at the University of California, Santa Barbara. Dr. Coppersmith is a fellow of the APS, the AAAS, and the American Academy of Arts and Sciences, and is a member of the NAS. Dr. Coppersmith received her Ph.D. in physics from Cornell University.

JUNGSANG KIM is a professor in the departments of Electrical and Computer Engineering, Physics, and Computer Science at Duke University. Dr. Kim leads the Multifunctional Integrated Systems Technology group at Duke University, where his group uses trapped atomic ions and a range of photonics technologies in an effort to construct scalable quantum information processors and quantum communication networks. After his thesis work on semiconductor-based single-photon sources and detectors, he joined Bell Laboratories, Lucent Technologies, in 1999, where he served as a member of technical staff and a technical manager. His work at Bell Labs included development of novel optical and wireless communication gear. Since joining Duke University in 2004, he shifted his research focus to quantum information processing and high-resolution optical sensors.

He pioneered introduction of new technologies, such as microfabricated ion traps, optical micro-electromechanical systems, advanced single-photon detectors, compact cryogenics, and vacuum technologies, toward a functional integration of quantum computers using trapped ions. In 2015, he co-founded IonQ, Inc., with Professor Christopher Monroe at the University of Maryland, leading the commercialization effort of trapped ion quantum computers. He is a fellow of the OSA, and a senior member of IEEE. Dr. Kim received his bachelor's degree from Seoul National University, and his Ph.D degree from Stanford University, both in physics.

JOHN M. MARTINIS is a professor of physics at the University of California, Santa Barbara (UCSB), and works with Google to build quantum computers. Dr. Martinis's thesis was a pioneering demonstration of quantum-bit states in superconductors. After completing a post-doctoral position at the Commisiariat Energie Atomic in Saclay, France, he joined the Electromagnetic Technology Division at National Institute of Standards and Technology (NIST) in Boulder, Colorado. At NIST, he developed a new fundamental electrical standard based on counting electrons, and invented microcalorimeters based on superconducting sensors for x-ray microanalysis and astrophysics measurements. In 2004, he moved to UCSB, where he currently holds the Worster Chair in experimental physics. At UCSB, he has continued work on quantum computation, demonstrating a variety of new quantum devices and capabilities. Along with Andrew Cleland, he was awarded in 2010 the AAAS science breakthrough of the year for an experiment showing the first quantum behavior of a mechanical oscillator. In 2014, he was awarded the London Prize for low-temperature physics research. In 2014, he joined the Google Quantum-AI team, and he now heads an effort to build the first practical quantum computer. Dr. Martinis attended the University of California, Berkeley, from 1976 to 1987, where he received two degrees in physics: B.S. (1980) and Ph.D. (1987).

MARGARET MARTONOSI is the Hugh Trumbull Adams '35 Professor of Computer Science at Princeton University, where she has been on the faculty since 1994. She is also director of the Princeton Keller Center for Innovation in Engineering Education, and an A.D. White Visiting Professor-at-Large at Cornell University. From August 2015 through March 2017, Dr. Martonosi served as a Jefferson Science Fellow within the U.S. Department of State. Dr. Martonosi's research interests are in computer architecture and mobile computing. Her work has included the development of the Wattch power modeling tool and the Princeton ZebraNet mobile sensor network project for the design and real-world deployment of zebra tracking collars in Kenya. Her current research focuses on hardware-software interface approaches in both classical and quantum computing systems. Dr. Martonosi is a fellow of both IEEE and ACM. Her papers have received numerous long-term impact awards including the 2015 ISCA Long-Term Influential Paper Award, 2017 ACM SIGMOBILE Test-of-Time Award, 2017 ACM SenSys Test-of-Time Paper Award, 2018 (Inaugural) HPCA Test-of-Time Paper Award, and inclusion on the 2013 list of 25 most significant papers from the first 20 years of FCCM. Other notable awards include the 2018 IEEE Computer Society Technical Achievement Award, 2010 Princeton University Graduate Mentoring Award, the 2013 National Center for Women and Information Technology (NCWIT) Undergraduate Research Mentoring Award, the 2013 Anita Borg Institute Technical Leadership Award, and the 2015 Marie Pistilli Women in EDA Achievement Award. In addition to many archival publications, Martonosi is an inventor on seven granted U.S. patents, and has co-authored two technical reference books on power-aware computer architecture. Dr. Martonosi completed her Ph.D. at Stanford University, and also holds a master's degree from Stanford and a bachelor's degree from Cornell University, all in electrical engineering.

MICHELE MOSCA is co-founder of the Institute for Quantum Computing at the University of Waterloo, a professor in the Department of Combinatorics and Optimization of the Faculty of Mathematics, and a founding member of the Waterloo Perimeter Institute for Theoretical Physics. Dr. Mosca was the founding director of CryptoWorks21, a training program in quantum-safe cryptography. He co-founded the ETSI-IQC workshop series in quantum-safe cryptography, which brings together a broad range of stakeholders working toward globally standardized quantum-safe cryptography. He co-founded evolutionQ, Inc., in order to support organizations as they evolve their quantum-vulnerable systems and practices to quantum-safe ones and softwareQ, Inc., to provide quantum software tools and services. Dr. Mosca obtained his doctorate in mathematics in 1999 from the University of Oxford on the topic of quantum computer algorithms. His research interests include quantum computation and cryptographic tools that will be safe against quantum technologies. He is globally recognized for his drive to help academia, industry, and government prepare our cyber systems to be safe in an era with quantum computers. Dr. Mosca's work is published widely in top journals, and he co-authored the respected textbook *An Introduction to Quantum Computing*. Dr. Mosca has won numerous awards and honors, including 2010 Canada's Top 40 under 40, the Premier's Research Excellence Award (2000-2005), fellow of the Canadian Institute for Advanced Research (CIFAR) since 2010, Canada Research Chair in Quantum Computation (2002-2012), University Research Chair at the University of Waterloo (2012-present), Queen Elizabeth II Diamond Jubilee Medal (2013), SJU Fr. Norm Choate Lifetime Achievement Award (2017), and a knighthood (Cavaliere) in the Order of Merit of the Italian Republic (2018).

WILLIAM D. OLIVER is a laboratory fellow at the Massachusetts Institute of Technology (MIT) Lincoln Laboratory, professor of the practice in the MIT Physics Department, and associate director of the MIT Research Laboratory of Electronics. Dr. Oliver is a principal investigator in the Quantum Information and Integrated Nanosystems Group (MIT Lincoln Laboratory) and the Engineering Quantum Systems Group (MIT campus), where he provides programmatic and technical leadership for programs related to the development of quantum and classical high-performance computing technologies for quantum information science applications. His interests include the materials growth, fabrication, design, and measurement of superconducting qubits, as well as the development of cryogenic packaging and control electronics involving cryogenic CMOS and single-flux quantum digital logic. Dr. Oliver received his Ph.D in electrical engineering from Stanford University.

KRYSTA SVORE is a principal research manager at Microsoft Research in Redmond, Washington, where she leads the Quantum Architectures and Computation group. Dr. Svore's research includes the development and implementation of quantum algorithms, including the design of a software architecture for translating a high-level quantum program into a low-level, device-specific quantum implementation, and the study of quantum error correction codes to enable fault tolerance and scalability. She has also developed machine-learning methods for Web applications, including ranking, classification, and summarization algorithms. Dr. Svore received an ACM Best of 2013 Notable Article award. In 2010, she was a member of the winning team of the Yahoo! Learning to Rank Challenge. She is a senior member of the ACM, serves as a representative for the Academic Alliance of the NCWIT, and is an active member of the APS. She currently serves as chair of the steering committee for the Quantum Information Processing Conference. Dr. Svore received her Ph.D. in computer science with highest distinction from Columbia University in 2006 and her B.A. from Princeton University in mathematics and French in 2001.

UMESH V. VAZIRANI is the Roger A. Strauch Professor of Electrical Engineering and Computer Science at the University of California, Berkeley, and the director of the Berkeley Quantum Computation Center. His research interests lie primarily in quantum computing. He is also the author of a textbook on algorithms. Dr. Vazirani is one of the founders of the field of quantum computing. His 1993 paper with his student Ethan Bernstein on quantum complexity theory defined a model of quantum Turing machines that was amenable to complexity-based analysis. This paper also gave an algorithm for the quantum Fourier transform, which was then used by Peter Shor within a year in his celebrated quantum algorithm for factoring integers. Dr. Vazirani received his Ph.D. in computer science from the University of California, Berkeley.

STAFF

EMILY GRUMBLING is a program officer at the Computer Science and Telecommunications Board (CSTB) of the National Academies. Dr. Grumbling previously served as an AAAS Science and Technology Policy Fellow in the Directorate for Computer and Information Science and Engineering at the National Science Foundation (2012-2014), and an ACS Congressional Fellow in the U.S. House of Representatives (2011-2012). She received her Ph.D. in physical chemistry from the University of Arizona in 2010, and her B.A. with a double major in chemistry and film/electronic media arts from Bard College in 2004.

JON EISENBERG is the senior board director of the CSTB. Dr. Eisenberg has also been study director for a diverse body of work, including a series of studies exploring Internet and broadband policy and networking and communications technologies. In 1995-1997, he was an AAAS Science, Engineering, and Diplomacy fellow at the U.S. Agency for International Development, where he worked on technology transfer and information and telecommunications policy issues. Dr. Eisenberg received his Ph.D. in physics from the University of Washington in 1996 and B.S. in physics with honors from the University of Massachusetts, Amherst, in 1988.

KATIRIA ORTIZ is an associate program officer for the CSTB. Ms. Ortiz previously served as an intern under the U.S. Department of Justice and as an undergraduate research assistant at the Cybersecurity Quantification Laboratory at the University of Maryland, College Park. She received her M.A. in international science and technology policy from George Washington University and her B.S. in cell biology and molecular genetics and B.A. in criminology and criminal justice from the University of Maryland, College Park.

JANKI PATEL is a senior program assistant at the CSTB. Ms. Patel has also formerly worked as a program assistant with the Board on Energy and Environmental Systems at the National Academies and as a geotechnical engineering lab assistant for AB Consultants, Inc., in Lanham, Maryland. She received a B.S. in physical sciences with a primary concentration in atmospheric and oceanic sciences, geology, and environmental science and technology from the University of Maryland, College Park. She is currently in the process of receiving her M.S. in environmental management and technology from the University of Maryland, University College.

SHENAE BRADLEY is an administrative assistant at the CSTB. Prior to this, she served as a senior project assistant with the board. Before coming to the National Academies, Ms. Bradley managed a number of apartment rental communities for Edgewood Management Corporation in the Maryland/DC/Delaware metropolitan areas. Ms. Bradley is in the process of earning her B.S. in family studies from the University of Maryland, College Park.

G

Briefers to the Committee

MARCH 23-24, 2017

Brad Blakestad, Intelligence Advanced Research Projects Activity
Alex Cronin, National Science Foundation
Jake Farinholt, Naval Surface Warfare Center, Dahlgren Division
David Honey, Office of the Director of National Intelligence
Michael Mandelberg, Laboratory for Physical Sciences
Dmitry Maslov, National Science Foundation
Dustin Moody, National Institute of Standards and Technology
Ceren Susut-Bennett, Department of Energy
Carl Williams, National Institute of Standards and Technology

JUNE 15-16, 2017

Bela Bauer, Microsoft Research
Ken Brown, Georgia Institute of Technology
Eric Dauler, MIT Lincoln Labatory
Austin Fowler, Google
Jay Gambetta, IBM Research
Andrew Landahl, Sandia National Laboratories
Chris Monroe, University of Maryland
Markus Reiher, ETH Zurich
John Sarrao, Los Alamos National Laboratory

Rob Schoelkopf, Yale University
Nathan Wiebe, Microsoft Research
Will Zeng, Rigetti Computing

JULY 20-21, 2017

Dan Bernstein, University of Illinois
Gary Bronner, Rambus
Bob Colwell, Independent Consultant
Norbert Holtkamp, SLAC National Accelerator Laboratory
Mark Johnson, D-Wave Systems
Mark Kasevich, Stanford University
Helmut Katzgraber, Texas A&M University
Adam Langley, Google
Chris Peikert, University of Michigan
Alejandro Perdomo-Ortiz, NASA Ames Research Center
John Shalf, Lawrence Berkeley National Laboratory

H

Acronyms and Abbreviations

1D	one-dimensional
2D	two-dimensional
3D	three-dimensional
ACM	Association for Computing Machinery
ADC	analog-to-digital converter
AES	Advanced Encryption Standard
API	application programming interface
AQC	adiabatic quantum computing
ARC	Australian Research Council
AWG	arbitrary waveform generator
BOG	binned output generation
BQP	bounded-error quantum polynomial time
CA	certificate authority
CAM	content addressable memory
CMOS	
CNOT	controlled-NOT
CSTB	Computer Science and Telecommunications Board
CW	continuous wave
DC	direct current
DES	data encryption standard

DOD	Department of Defense
DOE	Department of Energy
DSL	domain-specific language
EC	European Commission
ECC	error correction code
ECDSA	elliptic curve digital signature algorithm
EM	electromagnetic
FFT	fast Fourier transform
FPGA	field programmable gate array
GaAs	gallium arsenide
GCM	Galois Counter Mode
GDP	Gross Domestic Product
HOG	heavy output generation
IC	integrated circuit
IEEE	Institute of Electrical and Electronics Engineers
ISA	instruction set architecture
iSWAP	
JJ	Josephson junction
LDPC	low-density parity-check
LMSS	Leighton-Micali signature scheme
LWE	learning with errors
NCWIT	National Center for Women and Information Technology
NISQ	noisy intermediate-scale quantum
NIST	National Institute of Standards and Technology
NP	nondeterministic polynomial time
NSF	National Science Foundation
NV	nitrogen-vacancy
P	polynomial time
PQC	post-quantum cryptography
QA	quantum algorithms
QA	quantum annealing
QAOA	quantum approximate optimization algorithm

QC	quantum computer/quantum computing
QEC	quantum error correction
QECC	quantum error correction code
QEM	quantum error mitigation
QFS	quantum Fourier sampling
QFT	quantum Fourier transform
QIR	quantum intermediate representation
QIST	quantum information science and technology
QKD	quantum key distribution
QRAM	quantum random access memory
qubit	quantum bit
R&D	research and development
RAM	random access memory
RBM	randomized benchmark testing
RCS	random circuit sampling
RF	radio frequency
RISC	reduced instruction set computer
RQL	reciprocal quantum logic
RSA	Rivest-Shamir-Adleman cryptosystem
SFQ	single-flux quantum
SVP	shortest vector problem
TLS	Transport Layer Security
UV	ultraviolet
VLSI	very large scale integration
VQE	variational quantum eigensolver

I

Glossary

Abstraction—A different model (a representation or way of thinking) about a computer system design that allows the user to focus on the critical aspects of the system components to be designed.

Adiabatic quantum computer—An idealized analog universal quantum computer that operates at 0 K (absolute zero). It is known to have the same computational power as a gate-based quantum computer.

Algorithm—A specific approach, often described in mathematical terms, used by a computer to solve a certain problem or carry out a certain task.

Analog computer—A computer whose operation is based on analog signals and that does not use Boolean logic operations and does not reject noise.

Analog quantum computer—A quantum computer that carries out a computation without breaking the operations down to a small set of primitive operations (gates) on qubits; there is currently no model of full fault tolerance for such machines.

Analog signal—A signal whose value varies smoothly within a range of real or complex numbers.

Asymmetric cryptography (also **public key cryptography**)—A category of cryptography where the system uses public keys that are widely known and private keys that are secret to the owner; such systems are commonly used for key exchange protocols in the encryption of most of today's electronic communications.

Basis—Any set of linearly independent vectors that span their vector space. The wave function of a qubit or system of qubits is commonly written as a linear combination of basis functions or states. For a single qubit, the most common basis is $\{|0\rangle, |1\rangle\}$, corresponding to the states of a classical bit.

Binary representation—A series of binary digits where each digit has only two possible values, 0 or 1, used to encode data and upon which machine-level computations are performed.

Certificate authority—An entity that issues a digital certificate to certify the ownership of a public key used in online transactions.

Cipher—An approach to concealing the meaning of information by encoding it.

Ciphertext—The encrypted form of a message, which appears scrambled or nonsensical.

Classical attack—An attempt by a classical computer to break or subvert encryption.

Classical computer—A computer—for example, one of the many deployed commercially today—whose processing of information is not based upon quantum information theory.

Coding theory—The science of designing encoding schemes for specific applications—for example, to enable two parties to communicate over a noisy channel.

Coherence—The quality of a quantum system that enables quantum phenomena such as interference, superposition, and entanglement. Mathematically speaking, a quantum system is coherent when the complex coefficients of the contributing quantum states are clearly defined in relation to each other, and the system can be expressed in terms of a single wave function.

Collapse—The phenomenon that occurs upon measurement of a quantum system where the system reverts to a single observable state, resulting in the loss of contributions from all other states to the system's wave function.

Collision—In hashing, the circumstance where two different inputs are mapped to the same output, or hash value.

Complexity class—A category that is used to define and group computational tasks according to their complexity.

Computational complexity—The difficulty of carrying out a specific computational task, typically expressed as a mathematical expression that reflects how the number of steps required to complete the task varies with the size of the input to the problem.

Compute depth—The number of sequential operations required to carry out a given task.

Concatenation—The ordered combination of two sequences in order. In the context of quantum error correction (QEC), this refers to carrying out two or more QEC protocols sequentially.

Control and measurement plane—An abstraction used to describe components of a quantum computer, which refers to the elements required to carry out operations on qubits and to measure their states.

Control processor plane—An abstraction used to describe components of a quantum computer, which includes the classical processor responsible for determining what signals and measurements are required to implement a quantum program.

Cryostat—A device that regulates the temperature of a physical system at very low temperatures, generally in an experimental laboratory.

Cryptanalysis—The use of a computer to defeat encryption.

Cryptography—The study and practice of encoding information in order to obfuscate its content that relies upon the difficulty of solving certain mathematical problems.

Cryptosystem—A method of deploying a specific cryptographic algorithm to protect data and communications from being read by an unintended recipient.

APPENDIX I   247

Decoherence—A process where a quantum system will ultimately exchange some energy and information with the broader environment over time, which cannot be recovered once lost. This process is one source of error in qubit systems. Mathematically speaking, decoherence occurs when the relationship between the coefficients of a quantum system's contributing states become ill-defined.

Decryption algorithm—A set of instructions for returning an encrypted message to its unencrypted form. Such an algorithm takes as input a cipher text and its encryption key, and returns a cleartext, or readable, version of the message.

Digital gate—A transistor circuit that performs a binary operation using a number of binary single bit inputs to create a single-bit binary output.

Digital quantum computer—A quantum system where the computation is done by using a small set of primitive operations, or gates, on qubits.

Digital signature—An important cryptographic mechanism used to verify data integrity.

Dilution refrigerator—A specialized cooling device capable of maintaining an apparatus at temperatures near absolute zero.

Discrete-log problem on elliptic curves—A specific algebraic problem used as the basis of a specific cryptographic protocol where, given the output, it is computationally hard to compute the inputs.

Distance—In an error-correcting code, the number of bit errors that would be required to convert one valid state of a computer to another. When the number of errors is less than $(D-1)/2$, one can still extract the error-free state.

Encryption—The application of cryptography to protect information, currently widely used in computer systems and Internet communications.

Encryption algorithm—A set of instructions for converting understandable data to an incomprehensible cipher, or ciphertext. In practice, the algorithm takes as input the message to be encrypted along with an encryption key and scrambles the message according to a mathematical procedure.

Entanglement—The property where two or more quantum objects in a system are correlated, or intrinsically linked, such that measurement of one changes the possible measurement outcomes for another, regardless of how far apart the two objects are.

Error-corrected quantum computer—An instance of a quantum computer that emulates an ideal, fault-tolerant quantum computer by running a quantum error correction algorithm.

Fault tolerant—Resilient against errors.

Fidelity—The quality of a hardware operation, sometimes quantified in terms of the probability that a particular operation will be carried out correctly.

Fundamental noise—Noise resulting from energy fluctuations arising spontaneously within any object that is above absolute zero in temperature.

Gate—A computational operation that takes in and puts out one or more bits (in the case of a classical computer) or qubits (in the case of a quantum computer).

Gate synthesis—Construction of a gate out of a series of simpler gates.

Hamiltonian—A mathematical representation of the energy environment of a physical system. In the mathematics of quantum mechanics, a Hamiltonian takes the form of a linear algebraic operator. Sometimes, the term is used to denote the physical environment itself, rather than its mathematical representation.

Host processor—An abstraction used to describe the components of a quantum computing system, referring to the classical computer components driving the part of the system that is user controlled.

Key exchange—A step in cryptographic algorithms and protocols where keys are shared among intended recipients to enable their use in encrypting and decrypting information.

Logical qubit—An abstraction that describes a collection of physical qubits implementing quantum error correction in order to carry out a fault-tolerant qubit operation.

Logic gate—In classical computing, a collection of transistors that input and output digital signals, and that can be represented and modeled using Boolean logic (rules that combine signals that can be either false, 0, or true, 1).

APPENDIX I	249

Lossless—No energy is dissipated.

Measurement—Observation of a quantum system, which yields only a single classical output and collapses the system's wave function onto the corresponding state.

Microprocessor—An integrated circuit that contains the elements of a central processing unit on a single chip.

Noise—Unwanted variations in a physical system that can lead to error and unwanted results.

Noise immunity—The ability to remove noise (unwanted variations) in a signal to minimize error.

Noisy intermediate-scale quantum (NISQ) computer—A quantum computer that is not error-corrected, but is stable enough to effectively carry out a computation before the system loses coherence. A NISQ can be digital or analog.

Nondeterministic polynomial time (NP)—A specific computational complexity class.

One-way functions—Functions that are easy to compute in one direction while being for all intents and purposes impossible to compute in the other direction.

Overhead—The amount of work (for example, number of operations) or quantity of resources (for example, number of qubits or bits) required to carry out a computational task; "cost" is sometimes used synonymously.

Post-quantum cryptography—The set of methods for cryptography that are expected to be resistant to cryptanalysis by a quantum computer.

Primitive—A fundamental computational operation.

Program—An abstraction that refers to the sequence of instructions and rules that a computer must perform in order to complete one or more tasks (or solve one or more tasks) using a specific approach, or algorithm.

Quantum annealer—An analog quantum computer that operates through coherent manipulation of qubits by changing the analog values of the system's Hamiltonian, rather than by using quantum gates. In particular, a quantum annealer performs computations by preparing a set of qubits in some initial state and changing their energy environment until it defines the parameters of a given problem, such that the final state of the qubits corresponds, with a high probability, to the answer of the problem. In general, a quantum annealer is not necessarily universal—there are some problems that it cannot solve.

Quantum communication—The transport or exchange of information as encoded into a quantum system.

Quantum computation—The use of quantum mechanical phenomena such as interference, superposition, and entanglement to perform computations that are roughly analogous to (although operate quite differently from) those performed on a classical computer.

Quantum computer—The general term for a device (whether theoretical or practically realized) that carries out quantum computation. A quantum computer may be analog or gate-based, universal or not, and noisy or fault tolerant.

Quantum cryptography—A subfield of quantum communication where quantum properties are used to design communication systems that may not be eavesdropped upon by an observer.

Quantum information science—The study of how information is or can be encoded in a quantum system, including the associated statistics, limitations, and unique affordances of quantum mechanics.

Quantum interference—When states contributing to coherent superpositions combine constructively or destructively, like waves, with coefficients adding or subtracting.

Quantum sensing and metrology—The study and development of quantum systems whose extreme sensitivity to environmental disturbances can be exploited in order to measure important physical properties with more precision than is possible with classical technologies.

Quantum system—A collection of (typically very small) physical objects whose behavior cannot be adequately approximated by equations of classical physics.

Qubit—A quantum bit, the fundamental hardware component of a quantum computer, embodied by a quantum object. Analogous to a classical bit (or binary digit), a qubit can represent a state corresponding to either zero or one; unlike a classical bit, a qubit can also exist in a superposition of both states at once, with any possible relative contribution of each. In a quantum computer, qubits are generally entangled, meaning that any qubit's state is inextricably linked to the state of the other qubits, and thus cannot be defined independently.

Run time—The amount of time required to carry out a computational task. In practice, the actual time required for a task depends heavily on the design of a device and of its particular physical embodiment, so run time may be described in terms of the number of computational steps.

Scalable, fault-tolerant, universal gate-based quantum computer—A system that operates through gate-based operations on qubits, analogous to circuit-based classical computers, and uses quantum error correction to correct any system noise (including errors introduced by imperfect control signals, or unintended coupling of qubits to each other or to the environment) that occurs during the time frame of the calculation.

SHA256—A specific hash function that outputs a 256-bit hash value regardless of the input size.

Shor's algorithm— A quantum algorithm developed by Peter Shor in the 1990s that, if implemented on a real quantum computer of sufficient scale, would be capable of breaking the encryption used to protect Internet communications and data.

Signal—An electromagnetic field used to convey information in an electronic circuit.

Software tool—A computer program that helps a user design and compose a new computer program.

Standard cell library—A set of predesigned and tested logic gates.

Superposition—A quantum phenomenon where a system is in more than one state at a time. Mathematically speaking, the wave function of a quantum system in a superposition state is expressed as the sum of the contributing states, each weighted by a complex coefficient.

Surface code—A quantum error correction code (QECC) that is less sensitive to noise than other established QECCs, but has higher overheads.

Symmetric encryption—A type of encryption where a secret key, shared by both the sender and the receiver, is used to encrypt and decrypt communications.

Systematic noise—Noise resulting from signal interactions that is always present under certain conditions and could in principle be modeled and corrected.

Transport Layer Security (TLS) handshake—The most common key exchange protocol, used to protect Internet traffic.

Unitary operation—An algebraic operation on a vector that preserves the vector length.

Universal computer—A computer that can perform any computation that could be performed by a Turing machine.

Wave function—A mathematical description of the state of a quantum system, so named to reflect their wave-like characteristics.

Wave-particle duality—The phenomenon where a quantum object is sometimes best described in terms of wave-like properties and sometimes in terms of particle-like properties.